CLASSIC photoshop EFFECTS

Scott Kelby
BEST-SELLING AUTHOR
OF PHOTOSHOP CS DOWN & DIRTY TRICKS

PHOTOSHOP® CLASSIC EFFECTS

The Essential Effects Every User Needs to Know

The Photoshop®
Classic Effects Team

TECHNICAL EDITORS
Chris Main
Polly Reincheld

COPY EDITOR
Polly Reincheld

PRODUCTION EDITOR
Kim Gabriel

PRODUCTION
Dave Damstra

COVER DESIGN AND
CREATIVE CONCEPTS
Felix Nelson

SITE DESIGN
Stacy Behan

STOCK IMAGES
The royalty-free stock images
used in this book are courtesy of

Published by
Peachpit Press

www.peachpit.com
www.scottkelbybooks.com

*For my good friends and business partners
Jim Workman and Jean A. Kendra for all your support,
help, guidance, and friendship over the years.*

ACKNOWLEDGMENTS

Although only one person's name winds up on the spine of a book, it takes a small army of dedicated, hard-working, highly motivated, and uniquely talented people to create it. There's no way I could adequately thank them for everything they've done, but one of the benefits of writing a book is that at least you get to try.

To my wonderful wife Kalebra: Your spirit, warmth, beauty, patience, humor, compassion, and unconditional love continue to prove what everybody always says—I'm the luckiest guy in the world.

To my son Jordan: I'm so thrilled to be your dad, and so proud of the little man you've become. You have such a wonderful heart, and you've already touched so many people that I can't imagine all the wonders, adventures, and happiness life has in store for you.

Jeff: I can't imagine what a brother would have to do to equal what you've done for me over the years, and I can't tell you what a blessing it's been having you as my brother, and as a part of our team. You continue to set the standard for what a great brother should be, and you came across it honestly, from the greatest guy we both have ever known—our dad.

Dave Moser: There are few people with your passion, guts, integrity, vision, and unflinching dedication to quality. Getting to work with you each day is a blast, and having you as such a good friend—even more so. Carry on, soldier.

Jim Workman and Jean A. Kendra: I dedicated this book to you, because I realize how very fortunate I am to have business partners and friends like you who understand what it takes to do what we do, and why we do it all in the first place.

Felix Nelson: If you weren't the most talented and most creative guy I know, you'd only be one of the greatest, most hilarious, most inspiring, and most fun guys on the planet. You're legion of fans continues to grow, and count me at the top of the list.

Chris Main: You've worked on nearly every book I've written, and I'm certain you know by now how highly I regard your skills as an editor, but beyond that you're just one hell of great guy, and I consider myself very lucky to work with someone of your personal and professional caliber.

Polly Reincheld: Welcome to the wild world of tech editing my books. You knew you had big shoes to fill when taking the baton from Chris Main (arguably the world's finest Photoshop tech editor), but you took the challenge and kicked some major butt. As my Executive Editor Steve Weiss would say, "Good on ya!"

Dave Damstra: Having you lay out my books is definitely a strategic advantage, and you set the standard—not only in your work—but in your amazing attitude in life as well. It's an honor to have you on our team.

Kathy Siler: You are just a pleasure to be around, and you make my job and my life so much easier and more enjoyable. I really think you're the greatest, so please keep that in mind when you look up at the scoreboard and my Bucs have once again beaten your Redskins, and I stand up right there in FedEx Field and yell, "In your face! In your face!" (Kidding. Kinda.)

Kim Gabriel: You've become something of a hero within our office because of the amazing job you do keeping a train yard full of locomotives all moving on the same track. Nice job, Kim. Now go and get us John Lynch back, will ya?

Steve Weiss: Once again, my heartfelt thanks to you and to Nancy Ruenzel, Scott Cowlin, Rachel Tiley, and everyone at Peachpit Press who continue to show the industry "This is how it's done!"

Adobe: Thanks to all my friends at the "mother ship," including Julieanne Kost, Rye Livingston, Russell Brown, Terry White, Kevin Connor, John Nack, Karen Gauthier, Gwyn Weisberg, Russell Brady, and Addy Roff. Gone but never forgotten: Barbara Rice and Jill Nakashima.

My personal thanks go to Jeffery Burke at Brand X Pictures for enabling me to use some of their wonderful images in this book.

Kudos and continued thanks to my creative team at KW Media Group: Barbara Thompson, Stacy Behan, Ronni O'Neil, Margie Rosenstein, Dave Gales, Christine Edwards, Daphne Durkee, Dave Cross, Dave "Kid Rock" Korman, and Sarah Hughes.

Thanks to my Photoshop friends Jack Davis and Deke McClelland who have taught me so much over the years, and have inspired, influenced, and even invented many of the effects in this book.

Most importantly, I want to thank God, and His son Jesus Christ, for leading me to the woman of my dreams; for blessing us with such a special little boy; for allowing me to make a living doing something I truly love; for always being there when I need Him; and for blessing me with a wonderful, fulfilling, happy life, and a warm, loving family to share it with.

ABOUT THE AUTHOR

Scott Kelby

Scott is Editor-in-Chief and co-founder of *Photoshop User* magazine, Editor-in-Chief of Nikon's *Capture User* magazine, and Editor-in-Chief of *Mac Design Magazine*. He is President of the National Association of Photoshop Professionals (NAPP), the trade association for Adobe® Photoshop® users, and he's President of KW Media Group, Inc., a Florida-based software education and publishing firm.

Scott is author of the best-selling books *The Photoshop CS Book for Digital Photographers, Photoshop CS Down & Dirty Tricks, Photoshop Photo-Retouching Secrets,* and co-author of *Photoshop CS Killer Tips;* and he's creator and Series Editor for the *Killer Tips* series from New Riders Publishing. Scott has also authored three best-selling Macintosh books: *Mac OS X Panther Killer Tips, The Mac OS X Conversion Kit,* and the award-winning *Macintosh: The Naked Truth.* His latest titles are *The iTunes Book for Windows* and *Adobe InDesign CS Killer Tips,* which was co-authored with Terry White.

Scott introduced his first software title back in 2003 called *Kelby's Notes for Adobe Photoshop,* which adds the answers to the 100 most-asked Photoshop questions, accessed from directly within Photoshop.

Scott is Training Director for the Adobe Photoshop Seminar Tour, Conference Technical Chair for the PhotoshopWorld Conference and Expo, and he is a speaker at graphics trade shows and events around the world. He is also featured in a series of Adobe Photoshop training videos and DVDs and has been training Adobe Photoshop users since 1993.

For more background info on Scott, visit www.scottkelby.com.

TABLE OF CONTENTS

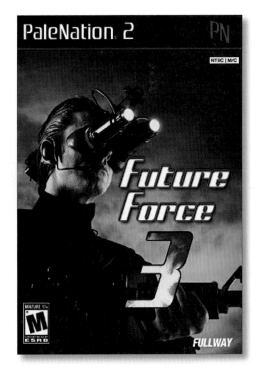

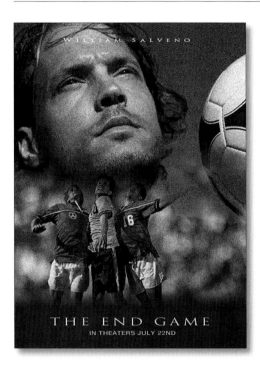

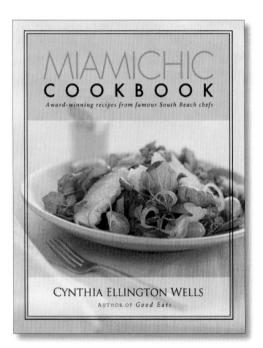

The Tutorial to End All Tutorials

On these next six pages, I will reveal the single most-asked-for, most-talked-about, most-highly-sought-after Photoshop classic effect in the history of all Photoshop effects. Once you learn this technique, you can basically "name your price" and write your own ticket to fame and fortune. Ready? Let's begin.

Step One:

Look, I've got to be straight with you right off the bat. This isn't a tutorial. Okay, I know it looks like a tutorial (that's the whole idea), but I just made it look like a tutorial because I know that if I did, you'd read it. But the sad truth is—this is actually the book's introduction. Whoa! Wait—don't turn the page. I know, I know—you want to skip the introduction and get to the tutorials (don't feel bad, statistics show that virtually no one reads a book's introduction. Okay, there's this one guy in Bozeman, Montana, who does, but outside of him, it's just about nil).

Step Two:

So why did I pull this "fake tutorial" stunt on you? I had to. Of all the introductions I've ever written, this one is the most important. If you skip this brief introduction (meaning the introduction has something to do with underwear), you may wind up getting frustrated and disoriented (meaning, you'll be removed from Asia. Get it? Dis-oriented? Man, I hope these jokes get better). In all serious-ness, there are some things you'll want to know to make this book work for you, to understand why I did certain things the way I did. You'll also learn about some-thing new that I've done to make things faster and easier for you, so go on to Step Three, and I'll fill you in as we go along.

Step Three:

First, you're probably wondering what those screen captures are over to the left. Those are part of my "fake tutorial," so you can just ignore them, but if you want to learn how to blend two images and add noise like that, check out the real tutorial in Chapter 8. Now here's what this book is about. In the world of Photoshop special effects, there are really two categories of effects: classic effects and new effects.

Step Four:

The "classics" are those tried-and-true effects that you see every day—every time you pick up a newspaper, a magazine, turn on the TV, or visit a website. You see these effects at work. They're everywhere—and a lot of people literally make a living using them. They're so popular, and so effective (no pun intended), that these effects have literally become classics, much in the same way certain songs have become classics, or certain food recipes have become classics. For example, if you bought a book titled *Classic Recipes*, you'd expect that it would include some kick-butt recipes for spaghetti sauce, apple pie, buttermilk pancakes, meatloaf, tomato soup, and a wide range of classic dishes, right? Right.

Step Five:

So, would you expect to find some wild new culinary explorations from Wolfgang Puck in a classic recipes book? Not a chance. Instead, you'd find the "meat-and-potatoes" recipes that are used every day by great cooks all over the world. Well, my friends, that's what you're holding—a book of the "meat-and-potatoes" special effects; the same ones used by great Photoshop artists, photographers, and designers all over the world. It's not the wild stuff, it's not the weird stuff—it's the stuff you can really use, the stuff clients ask for and expect that you'll know. But there's more.

Continued

Step Six:

I didn't just want to say, "Here's the effect—have a nice day." I really wanted to teach you these effects by using them in the context they're used in today, by the industry's leading professionals. For example, torn-edge effects have been around for years, but they're used differently today than they were just three or four years ago. I wanted to create a book that has you create not just the simple effect but an entire real-world project that incorporates the effect. That way, not only will you *see* it in the context of today's effects, you'll *use* it in the right context, too!

Step Seven:

So, are these effects just for beginners? Some are, some clearly aren't, but even the very simplest effects are still used every day by the biggest ad agencies, the leading Web developers, and the hottest video houses. It doesn't have to be hard or overly complicated to be good. These are the classics—they've been around a while because they're that good.

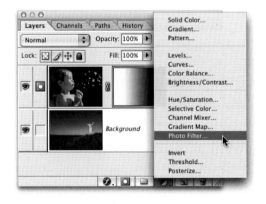

Step Eight:

Here's the thing: If your client is MTV, you can go out and do all the latest, wildest, weirdest effects and they'll love it (like the cutting-edge effects that are in my *Photoshop CS Down & Dirty Tricks* book). But what if your client is CBS or CNN? Try that stuff and they'll show you the door. They need a professional, clean look, and they'll expect you to know the classics and how they're used today. That's what this book is all about—teaching you the handy bag of tricks that you can use again and again to make your clients sing and your cash register ring.

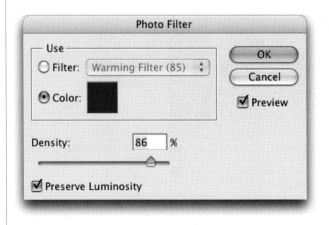

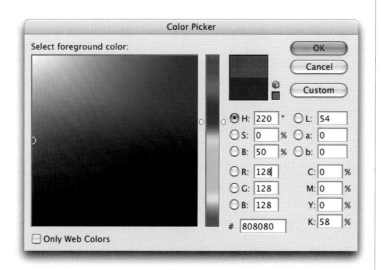

Step Nine:
So that's how you'll learn—by building complete projects that go from blank page to final image—all within just a few pages—and within that project will be the classic effect. The bonus is, of course, that you'll learn much, much more than just the effect. You'll learn to lay out pages, create your own designs, and do things in Photoshop you never thought you could do by replicating what today's pros are doing. I think it's the best, and certainly the most fun way to learn Photoshop special effects.

Step Ten:
By the way, for every classic effect in the book, you'll see a "Cut to the Chase" logo followed by a page number. This is that new idea I mentioned earlier. Here's what it's based on: I figure that when you get this book, you'll try all the projects that interest you, and really spend some time getting your hands dirty learning all these classic special effects. That's great while you have the time, but let's say that four months down the road you're working on tight deadline and you need to add, say...a scan lines effect to your project.

Step Eleven:
Do you have to go back and rebuild the entire Army TV ad project just to get the scan lines effect? Nope. You can "Cut to the Chase" and jump to the page number that appears within the logo. On that page is a simple three-step instruction on how to add the TV scan lines effect in a hurry. It's short, sweet, and to the point. No extra stuff—just the scan lines effect. Think of this as an appendix, a bonus chapter, whatever—just use it when you really need to "Cut to the Chase."

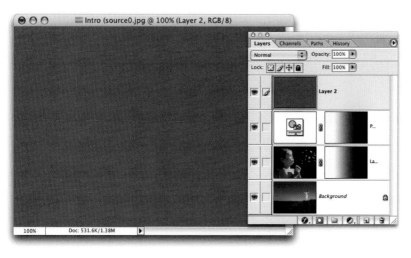

Continued

Step Twelve:

If you want to try these projects using the same photos as I used in the book, you're in luck. The wonderful people at Brand X Pictures have graciously enabled us to make low-res images available for you to download free so you can follow along. You can download these only from www.scottkelbybooks.com/classicphotos/. By the way, I chose Brand X Pictures royalty-free images for a reason—I think they offer the best, and most complete royalty-free stock images out there, bar none. Check out thousands of their images at www.brandx.com and you'll see what I mean.

Step Thirteen:

A few final things: I have no way of knowing whether you're a beginner, or an intermediate, or advanced Photoshop user, so I pretty much lay everything out from soup to nuts. For example, in each tutorial the first time I tell you to do something, I tell you the entire technique, so the first time it appears in a tutorial…

Step Fourteen:

…instead of just saying "create a new layer," I'll say: "Create a new layer by clicking on the Create a New Layer icon at the bottom of the Layers palette." If I need you to create another layer in that same tutorial, as I just laid it all out, I might then just say "create another new layer," assuming all the while that you don't have a serious short-term memory problem. So if you're a more advanced user, don't let it throw you that I spell everything out—I have to do this because I want this book to be accessible to as many users as possible. Also, Photoshop is identical on both the Mac and Windows platforms, but the keyboards on a PC and Mac are different, so I give both keyboard shortcuts every time.

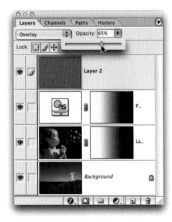

Step Fifteen:

Another thing is this—you can jump in anywhere you want and start trying the effects. There's no "Photoshop Basics" chapter or anything like that that you have to start with first. And since I spell everything out for you, you can start anywhere you like, so don't feel like you have to start with Chapter 1 and work your way through. Find a classic effect that interests you and have at it.

Step Sixteen:

Also, because we're doing complete projects, I used a lot of type and different typefaces (fonts) along the way. Most of the fonts I use either come with Photoshop CS, or they're so common (like Helvetica) that there's a 99% chance you already have them loaded on your system. Occasionally, I used a specialty font, but I always give you the name, and often where to buy it if you so desire, but feel free to substitute your own fonts—if you see I'm using a tall, thick font, choose one of your tall, thick fonts as well.

Step Seventeen:

Okay, now you've learned how to use the book, where to download the photos, how to deal with fonts, and how to "Cut to the Chase." You can see why I had to pull the whole "tutorial scam." These are important aspects of learning from this book, and even if I had to trick you into reading what is ostensively the introduction, now that you've read it, don't you feel an overwhelming sense of self-accomplishment and pride? No? Rats! Oh well, it was only a few short pages, right? Now get on with it. Go have some fun and cook up some yummy effects (and huge invoices).

Chapter ONE

HOOKED ON CLASSICS

THE ABSOLUTELY ESSENTIAL CLASSIC EFFECTS

If you've read any of my previous books *(War and Peace, Moby Dick, Tale of Two Cities, The South Beach Diet)*, you already know two things: (1) I name each chapter after a song title, a TV show, or a movie title, and the subhead below it explains what the chapter is really about. For example, this chapter, "Hooked on Classics," is named after a 1987 rock remake of a classical piece by Mason Williams and Mannheim Steamroller. My 7-year-old son Jordan lobbied pretty hard for me to name this chapter "Classical Gas" instead, which, for some reason, he thinks is just  about the funniest name possible for a chapter. However, I spared you from the shame of aiding and abetting my son in the proliferation of yet another lightly veiled potty joke. And (2) these chapter introductions usually don't have much to do with what's actually in the chapter. However, it does offer a chance for me to write something other than: "Step One: Go under the Filter menu, under Blur, and choose Gaussian Blur" (which is apparently what I do the rest of the time). So think of these intros as some quality "you and me" time…without the quality.

Using One Photo as the Background and the Focal Point

The great thing about this popular technique is that we use the same photo for the ad to create both the focal point and the background by blending and backscreening a version of the photo. You see this technique used in everything from fine jewelry ads to ads for high-tech electronics. This particular layout was inspired by a beautiful print ad for Pierre Kunz USA watches.

Step One:

Create a new document (File>New) in RGB mode. Set your Foreground color to black by pressing "d" and fill the Background layer with black by pressing Option-Delete (PC: Alt-Backspace).

Step Two:

Now open the photo of the product. In this case, it's a sports watch, and we're going to use this same photo to create both the background and the product shot. Select just the watch (you can use the Magic Wand tool and click on the white background area, then go under the Select menu and choose Inverse to select the watch itself).

Brand X Pictures

Step Three:
Once the watch is selected, press the letter "v" to switch to the Move tool, click on the watch, and drag it over on top of your black background (as shown here). (Just leave the selected watch image off to the side of your workspace for now. You'll need it later.)

Step Four:
Press Command-T (PC: Control-T) to bring up the Free Transform command. Then press Command-Zero (PC: Control-Zero) and your document window will resize so you can reach the Free Transform handles. Move your cursor outside the bounding box to the right, and click-and-drag downward to rotate the watch to an approximate 45° angle. Then, hold the Command key (PC: Control key), grab the top-left corner, and drag downward to tip the watch back, giving it a bit of a 3D perspective.

Continued

Step Five:

Now release the Command key (PC: Control key) and grab the top-right corner, then drag outward to increase the size of your watch until the face nearly fills the image area (as shown here). *Note*: We can only get away with scaling the size "up" because it's going to be a background, so a little loss in quality won't hurt us too much.

Step Six:

Press Return (PC: Enter) to lock in your transformation (as shown here).

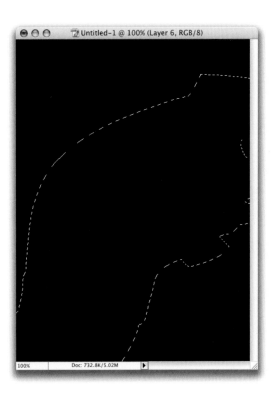

Step Seven:
Go to the Layers palette, hold the Command key (PC: Control key), and click on the skewed watch layer to put a selection around it. Then, while this selection is in place, add a new layer by clicking on the Create a New Layer icon in the Layers palette, and fill this selection with black by pressing Option-Delete (PC: Alt-Backspace), as shown here.

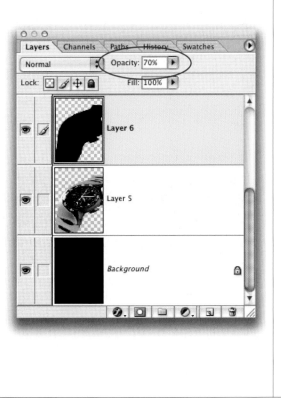

Step Eight:
Lower the Opacity of this black layer in the Layers palette to around 70% (as shown here) to create a kind of gray, screened-back version of the watch. Deselect the watch by pressing Command-D (PC: Control-D).

Continued

Step Nine:

As you can see in the capture here, the watch is now in the background, but before we add some foreground elements, we're going to "burn in" the edges around the watch so they appear to fade out into the black background.

Step Ten:

Go to the Layers palette and click on the Create a New Layer icon. Fill this new layer with black by pressing Option-Delete (PC: Alt-Backspace). Press the letter "m" to switch to the Rectangular Marquee tool and draw a rectangular selection in the center of your image area, but stay an inch or so inside the edges of your image area (as shown here).

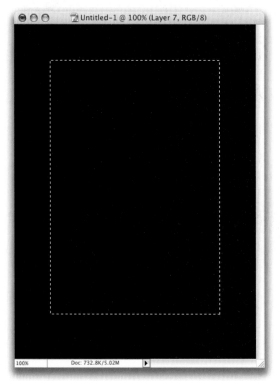

Step Eleven:
Go under the Select menu and choose Feather. When the Feather Selection dialog appears, enter 50 pixels (for high-res, 300-ppi images use 170 pixels). Then click OK. This greatly softens the edges of your rectangular selection, which is necessary to create our "burned-in edges" effect.

Step Twelve:
Press Delete (PC: Backspace) and it knocks out a soft-edged hole, revealing the skewed watch on the layer directly beneath it. The way the feathering works in this case is that the center of the rectangle you deleted is completely transparent, but toward the edges it's slowly less opaque as it fades to black—so it gives the effect of the watch fading away at the edges.

Continued

Step Thirteen:

Now go back to the original watch document (it should still be open, and the watch still selected) and drag that watch onto your black backscreened watch document with the Move tool. Scale this new watch down in size by pressing Command-T (PC: Control-T) to bring up Free Transform. Then hold the Shift key, grab a corner point, and drag inward to scale the watch down (as shown here). Position the watch within the image area and press Return (PC: Enter).

Step Fourteen:

If the background watch seems too intense (it's just supposed to be a very faint version of the watch), you can reduce its intensity by going to the Layers palette, clicking on the skewed watch layer (which should be above your black Background layer), and lowering its Opacity setting (as shown here) until it looks screened back enough.

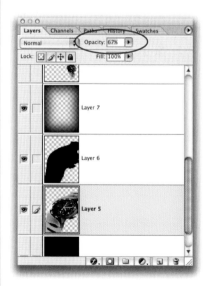

PHILLIPPE RENOIR

CHÊNE-BOURG

The 2600L
Chronograph
Day, Date, and
Time

Step Fifteen:

The final step is to add some type using the Type tool. The fictitious name at the top of the ad was created using the font Minion Regular (from Adobe) selected from the Character palette in the Window menu. The first letter of each word is two points larger than the rest of the letters. The Swiss city "Chéne-Bourg" is set in the same font. The type at the bottom to the left of the watch is set in Helvetica, and the type is aligned right (which you can choose from the Options Bar—while you have the text selected with the Type tool—by clicking on the third justification icon), which completes the effect.

Moving a Background Object in Front of Type

You see this technique used a lot on the cover of major magazines. It's where an object (most often a person's head) appears in front of type. That doesn't sound like that big of a challenge, but once you realize that person is on a flattened background image, with no layers, it becomes a little trickier. Not hard, just a little trickier.

Step One:
Open the background photo that has an object you want to appear in front of some type.

Step Two:
With the Type tool selected, create the type you want to appear behind the object. In this example, we're going to put the nameplate of a magazine behind the person's head. (The font we used is Trebuchet MS, which we selected from the Character palette under the Window menu.) You create the type now to let you know how much (or how little) you need to select in the next step.

Step Three:

Click on your Background layer in the Layers palette and put a selection around the object you want in front of your type. (You can temporarily hide your Type layer by clicking on the Eye icon to the left of the layer in the Layers palette.) I used the Magnetic Lasso tool found under the Lasso tool in the Toolbox and clicked once on the left side of his head, released the mouse button, then traced around the top of his head (as shown here).

Step Four:

Once your object is selected, press Command-J (PC: Control-J) to move that selected area up onto its own layer. Then, in the Layers palette, drag this layer above your Type layer (as shown here). Moving that "top-of-the-head" layer in front of the Type layer makes it appear as though the person is in front of the type. (If you hid your Type layer, make it visible again by clicking on the layer's Eye icon box to the left of the layer.)

Step Five:

Finally, to finish this project, add in any other type you want on your cover using the Type tool and select fonts in the Character palette. The orange type at the top is Helvetica Bold. The word "Stalker" is in the font Trebuchet MS. The main headline "Our annual list…" is set in Adobe Garamond Pro. The rest of the subheads are set in Helvetica.

Putting One Image Inside Another Image

This is a particularly popular effect in catalogs, sales brochures, and ads. It's where you put your own photo (your product, your image, your logo, etc.) into an existing product. One reason this is so popular is that images on TVs, monitors, cell phones, etc. don't photograph well. In our case, we're putting an image into a cell phone, then creating a typical cellular print ad, just so we can learn some other techniques along the way.

Step One:
Open the image you want to place another photo into (in this case, we're going to place a photo inside a cellular phone's screen [with the cell phone image courtesy of Felix Nelson]).

Step Two:
Open the photo you want to place inside the other photo's screen (here I am using a picture of two children).

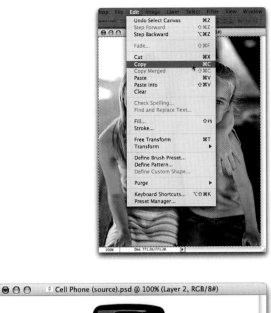

Step Three:
You'll need to select this entire photo, so go under the Select menu and choose All (this puts a selection border around your entire image, as shown here). Then go under the Edit menu and choose Copy.

Step Four:
Go back to your original image. Get the Rectangular Marquee tool from the Toolbox and draw a selection around the area where you want your photo to appear (in this case, I put a rectangular selection around the cell phone's screen, as shown here).

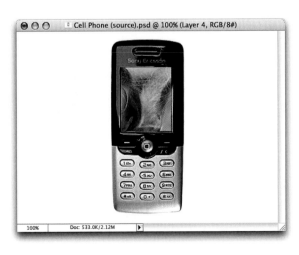

Step Five:
Go under the Edit menu and choose Paste Into, which pastes the copied photo into your rectangular selection. Chances are the photo will appear much larger than the area you're pasting it into, so in the next step you'll adjust its size.

Continued

Step Six:

Press Command-T (PC: Control-T) to bring up the Free Transform command. You probably won't be able to reach (or perhaps even see) the Free Transform handles, so press Command-Zero (PC: Control-Zero) and your image area will resize so you can see all four handles (as shown here).

Step Seven:

While holding the Shift key, grab the bottom-right corner point and drag inward. The photo will be scaled down in size. Keep scaling inward using the corner points and holding the Shift key until the photo fills the screen area of your target image. If you have to reposition the photo, just click within the bounding box and drag the photo into position. Then press Return (PC: Enter).

Step Eight:

Now you'll add a tiny shadow inside the photo's screen so it appears as though the placed photo is inside the screen, rather than on top of it. Choose Inner Shadow from the Add a Layer Style pop-up menu at the bottom of the Layers palette. When the dialog appears (shown here), lower the Distance to 1 and the Size to 1 (that's for low-res, 72-ppi images—for high-res, 300-ppi images, set your amounts higher).

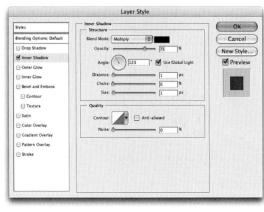

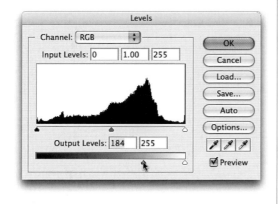

Step Nine:

When you click OK, the placed photo appears embedded into the photo, rather than sitting on top, and the "putting-one-image-into-another-image" effect is complete. However, we're going to take it a step further by creating a typical cellular phone ad (besides being fun, it just gives me an opportunity to include a couple more classic techniques).

Step Ten:

Choose New from the File menu to create a new blank document for your ad (the one shown here is in RGB mode at 6x8" set at 72 ppi). Press the letter "v" to switch to the Move tool and drag your original full-size photo onto the blank document and position it at the top of the image area (as shown here). If you need to make it larger or smaller, use the Free Transform command again.

Step Eleven:

You'll need to put text over this photo, so you'll need to: (1) remove the color by going under the Image menu, under Adjustments, and choosing Desaturate; and (2) backscreen the photo by pressing Command-L (PC: Control-L) to bring up the Levels dialog. Grab the bottom-left Output Levels slider and drag to the right to lighten the entire image.

Continued

Step Twelve:

Now that the photo is screened back, press Shift-M until you have the Elliptical Marquee tool and drag out a huge oval selection (one that extends right off the image area by quite a bit, like the one shown here) until it creates a curved selection that slopes down (it's going to take a really big oval selection, so don't let that freak you out). If you need to re-do your selection, just press Command-D (PC: Control-D) to deselect. Next, create a new layer by clicking on the Create a New Layer icon on the bottom right of the Layers palette.

Step Thirteen:

Click on the Foreground color swatch in the Toolbox and choose an orange color (I used R=228, G=151, B=41) from the Color Picker. Fill your oval selection with this orange color by pressing Option-Delete (PC: Alt-Backspace). Then deselect by pressing Command-D (PC: Control-D). Now, go to your cell phone image (the one you put the photo into), hide the Background layer by clicking on its Eye icon, and select Merge Visible from the Layers palette's flyout menu. Now, with the Move tool, drag the image right on top of the ad's screened area and position it.

Step Fourteen:

Choose Drop Shadow from the Add a Layer Style pop-up menu at the bottom of the Layers palette. When the dialog appears, lower the Opacity to 51, set the Distance at 12, Angle at 124°, and the Size to 9 (that's for low-res, 72-ppi images—for high-res, 300-ppi images, set the Size amount higher).

Step Fifteen:

Click OK and the drop shadow is added to your phone, which helps give some depth to the ad (as shown). To complete the ad, create some text using the Type tool and format it with the Character palette. All the headline and body copy text is Helvetica. The little globe for the logo of the fictitious company is one of Photoshop's built-in shapes, which you can add using the Custom Shape tool. The words "Global Net" are set in the font Minion, and the word "Wireless" is set in Futura Condensed Extra Bold. You can also add a line that separates the phone description from the sales info by using the Line tool (it's one of the Shape tools).

Blending a Photo into a Solid-Color Background

This is a very popular effect in print advertising because it lets you use a photo at the top of the ad and blend it down into a solid color at the bottom, where you can add advertising copy. In this case, I'll show you two different examples of this easy yet effective technique.

Step One:

Create a new blank document (File>New) in RGB mode (in the example shown here, the image is 6x8" set at 72 ppi). Set your Foreground color to black by pressing "d", then fill the Background layer with black by pressing Option-Delete (PC: Alt-Backspace). We're doing this so the photo can blend into black, and we'll add our body copy over this solid black area.

Step Two:

Open the photo you want to use in your ad (in this case, we're using a photo of a very serious-looking security guard).

Step Three:
Press the letter "v" to switch to the Move tool, and click-and-drag this photo of the guard onto your black background document. If the image is too large (like the example here) you'll have to scale it down, so press Command-T (PC: Control-T) to bring up the Free Transform command. You probably won't be able to reach the Free Transform handles, so press Command-Zero (PC: Control-Zero) and the image window will resize so you can reach all the handles (as shown here).

Step Four:
Hold the Shift key, grab a corner point, and drag inward to scale your photo until it fills the image area as much as possible (as shown here). Press Return (PC: Enter). Then go to the bottom of the Layers palette and click the Add a Layer Mask icon (it's the second icon from the left) to add a layer mask. We'll use this layer mask to create our blend.

Continued

Step Five:
Press "g" to get the Gradient tool, and in the Options Bar, click on the down-facing arrow next to the gradient thumbnail to open the Gradient Picker. Choose the Black to White gradient (it's the third gradient in the default set of gradients).

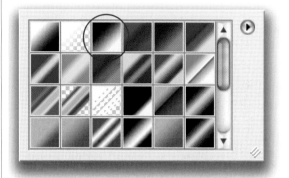

Step Six:
With the Gradient tool, click on the man's pants (it sounds weird, I know) and drag upward. The area where you first clicked will become black, and it will now gradually fade into the security guard photo. If you don't like your first attempt, just click-and-drag again until your blend looks like the one shown here.

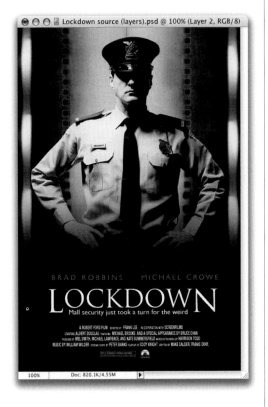

Step Seven:

The blend—from photo to solid color (black)—is complete (see, I told you it was easy). To finish this image off, we're going to make it into a movie poster for a fictitious film using the Type tool and Character palette. The fictitious actors' names are set in the font Gill Sans Regular (from Adobe); the movie title is set in Trajan Pro (which comes with Photoshop CS); and the tag line beneath it is set in Gill Sans Regular. The tiny movie credit type at the bottom is set in Helvetica Neue Condensed. Now, let's use the same blending technique with a different image.

Brand X Pictures

Step Eight:

Here's another take on the same technique: Create a new document (File>New) in RGB mode, drag a photo into this document with the Move tool, size it using Command-T (PC: Control-T), and position it at the top of the window (as shown), then press Return (PC: Enter). Press the letter "i" to switch to the Eyedropper tool and click on the sky to steal that blue color. Go to the Layers palette, click on the Background layer, then press Option-Delete (PC: Alt-Backspace) to fill the Background layer with that blue from the sky.

Continued

Step Nine:

Now use the blending technique: Click on the photo's layer, click on the Add a Layer Mask icon at the bottom of the Layers palette, get the Gradient tool (with the Black to White gradient), and click-and-drag from the bottom of the photo upward to blend the bottom of the photo into the solid blue background (as shown here).

Step Ten:

All that's left is to add some text with the Type tool. The headline is set in Caflisch Script Pro (which comes with Photoshop CS). "The Retreat" is set in the font Papyrus, and "at hideaway harbor village" is set in Copperplate Gothic Regular, all lowercase. The type at the bottom of the ad is set in Adobe Garamond Pro Regular (which comes with Photoshop CS).

Double Glows

You see this multicolor glow effect used a lot in print advertising, billboards, and on the Web for product shots. The effect has one glow hugging your object, and then a glow of a different color peeking outside from that. In our project, you're going to create a poster for a gym, using this two-color outer glow technique.

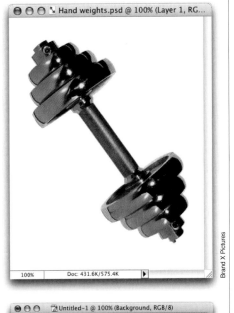

Step One:

Open the photo that has an object that you want to apply a double outer glow to. Make sure the object is on its own layer. In the example here, I clicked on the white background with the Magic Wand tool to select it, and then chose Inverse under the Select menu to select the weights instead of the background. I then pressed Shift-Command-J (PC: Shift-Control-J) to cut the weights from the Background layer and copy them onto their own layer.

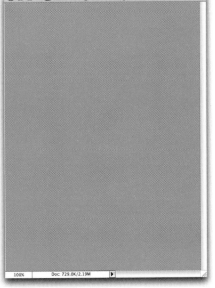

Step Two:

Open a new document (File>New) that you want to serve as the background for your double glow. Click on the Foreground color swatch and set your Foreground color to an orange shade (like the one shown here) in the Color Picker and click OK. Then fill your Background layer with this orange color by pressing Option-Delete (PC: Alt-Backspace).

Continued

Step Three:

Go back to the weights document, select the weights layer in the Layers palette, and with the Move tool, click-and-drag the weights layer onto your orange background and position it as shown here. Next, you'll add your first glow.

Step Four:

Choose Outer Glow from the Add a Layer Style pop-up menu at the bottom of the Layers palette. When the dialog appears, change the Blend Mode pop-up menu from Screen to Normal, then click on the color swatch and change the glow color to white in the Color Picker. After clicking OK in the Color Picker, increase the Spread to 7 and the Size to 16 in the Outer Glow dialog.

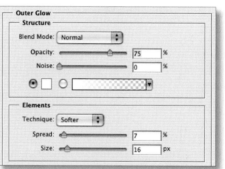

Step Five:

When you click OK, the first of the glows (a white one) will appear around the weights.

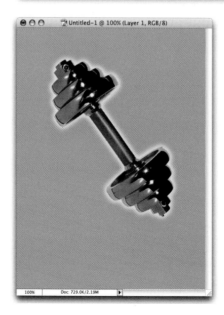

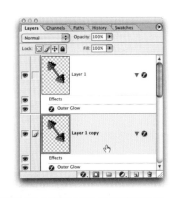

Step Six:

Duplicate this weights layer by pressing Command-J (PC: Control-J). In the Layers palette, drag this copy (Layer 1 copy) beneath your original layer (Layer 1) as shown here.

Step Seven:

In the Layers palette, double-click on the words "Outer Glow" in the duplicate layer to bring up the Outer Glow dialog (shown here). Click on the white color swatch and change the color to yellow in the Color Picker and click OK. Then increase the Size to 24 in the Outer Glow dialog. By making this glow larger, it extends beyond the borders of the white glow, giving you the two-glow effect.

Step Eight:

To complete the project you'll need to add some text. Go to the Layers palette and click on the Background layer. Add a new blank layer, press the letter "m" to switch to the Rectangular Marquee tool, and drag out a horizontal selection at the bottom of the image area. Press the letter "d" to set your Foreground color to black, then fill this selection with black by pressing Option-Delete (PC: Alt-Backspace). Lastly, add some white text over the black bar you just created. The headline shown here is set in the font Stencil Std. The subhead and Web address are set in the font Copperplate Gothic.

Fade-Away Reflection

This is a popular technique for products that are displayed on a white background. It makes the product look as if it were shot on a reflective surface, and the reflection just fades away underneath it. Here we're going to create a poster for a fictitious Apple® reseller, and we'll apply the fade-away reflection to the computer.

Step One:

Open the image you want to add a fade-away reflection to. (In this example, we're going to use an illustration of an iMac drawn from scratch in Photoshop by our Creative Director Felix Nelson. You have to hate anyone who can draw like that, don'tcha?) The iMac needs to be on its own layer above the Background layer, so press the letter "w" to switch to the Magic Wand tool. In the Options Bar, set the Tolerance to 0 and make sure the Contiguous checkbox is on. Click once on the white background in the image and then choose Inverse from the Select menu to select the iMac. Press Shift-Command-J (PC: Shift-Control-J) to cut the iMac from the Background layer and copy it onto its own layer.

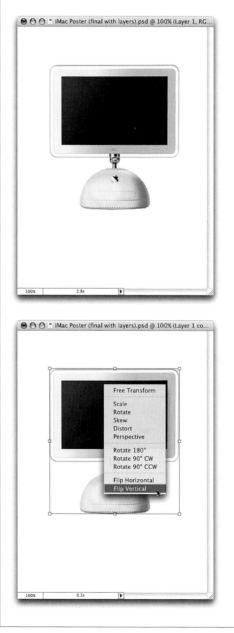

Step Two:

With the new iMac layer still active in the Layers palette, press Command-J (PC: Control-J) to duplicate the layer. Then, press Command-T (PC: Control-T) to bring up the Free Transform command. Control-click (PC: Right-click) within the bounding box and choose Flip Vertical from the pop-up menu that appears.

Step Three:
Press Return (PC: Enter) to complete the vertical flip of your duplicate layer. Press the letter "v" to switch to the Move tool, hold the Shift key, then click on the flipped iMac and drag it straight down until the bottoms of the two iMacs meet (as shown here), creating a mirror reflection.

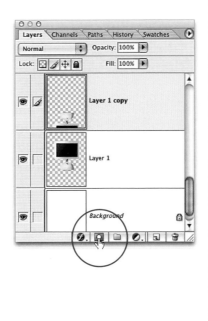

Step Four:
Now that the reflection is in place, it's time to fade it away. Click on the Add a Layer Mask icon at the bottom of the Layers palette (as shown here).

Continued

Step Five:

Press the letter "g" to switch to the Gradient tool, then press Return (PC: Enter), and the Gradient Picker will appear at the current location of your cursor. Choose the Black to White gradient (it's the third gradient in the default set of gradients), and then click within the reflected image, right about where the upside-down Apple logo is, and drag upward until you reach the base of the reflected iMac (as shown here). The reflected iMac will now fade away. If you go too far, or not far enough, just try dragging the gradient again.

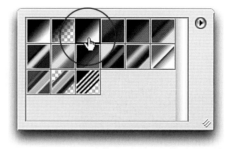

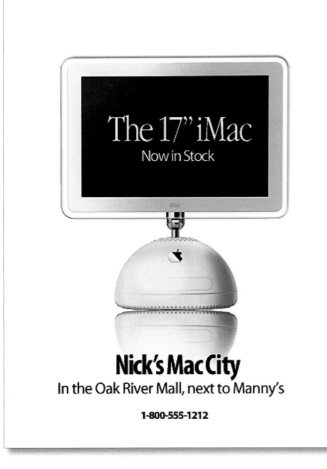

Step Six:
To finish off the poster project, just add some type using the Type tool and Character palette. The white headline within the monitor is Garamond Light Condensed, and the "Now in Stock" is Myriad Pro (which comes with Photoshop CS). The name of the fictitious Apple dealer and the phone number are set in Myriad Bold, and the direction line under the dealer name is in Myriad Regular.

Chapter TWO

SHADOWS OF THE NIGHT
SOFT SHADOW EFFECTS

Okay, this isn't an entire chapter on just shadow effects but is it just a coincidence that nearly every effect in this chapter has a drop shadow somewhere in the project? I think not. Okay, what about the title? Come on, that's an easy one—Pat Benatar. Of course, if you're under the age of 40 you probably have no idea who Pat Benatar is, but as I remember it, she was either a state assemblywoman from Ohio's 16th district or a hugely popular rock singer whose name still resounds with people who today drive Buick LeSabres and listen to oldies stations. I can't remember which. Anyway, creating shadows (inner shadows, drop shadows, cast shadows, etc.) is so important for creating depth in our projects that we'll be using them all throughout the book. Why? Because we can. Do they deserve an entire chapter of their own? Absolutely. If not them, who? If not now, when? Am I babbling? Perhaps. But just think of this—what if it were revealed that I get paid by the word, like a writer for magazines? You know what that would mean? That would mean this introduction would be a lot longer. So if I don't get paid by the word, how do I get paid? By the number of drop shadows used. Hey, it's part of my contract.

Cast Shadows

Cast shadows make it appear as though your object is standing vertically on the background with light coming from the side, casting a shadow that fades off into the distance. These are critical for shots of people, products, and other objects that you want to appear as if they're "standing." In our project here, the cast shadow part appears near the end, but you get to learn a pretty cool product background technique in the meantime.

Step One:

Create a new RGB document (6x8" at 72 ppi). Click the Foreground color swatch in the Toolbox to select a medium green in the Color Picker (I used R=41, G=119, B=37), and fill the Background layer with this green by pressing Option-Delete (PC: Alt-Backspace). Go to the Layers palette and create a new layer by clicking on the Create a New Layer icon at the bottom of the palette. Press Shift-M until you have the Elliptical Marquee tool selected in the Toolbox, and draw a large oval selection in the center of your image, with the ends of your oval extending off the sides of the document (as shown here). You can press the Spacebar after you start drawing your oval to reposition it off the edge of the document. Release the Spacebar to finish drawing the oval.

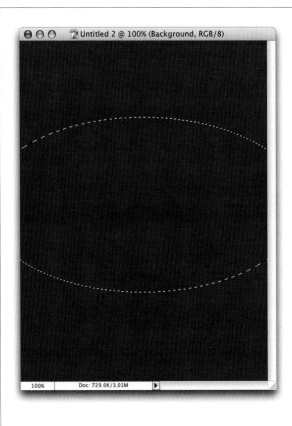

Step Two:

To soften the edges of the oval, go under the Select menu and choose Feather. Enter 50 pixels and click OK.

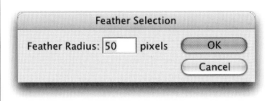

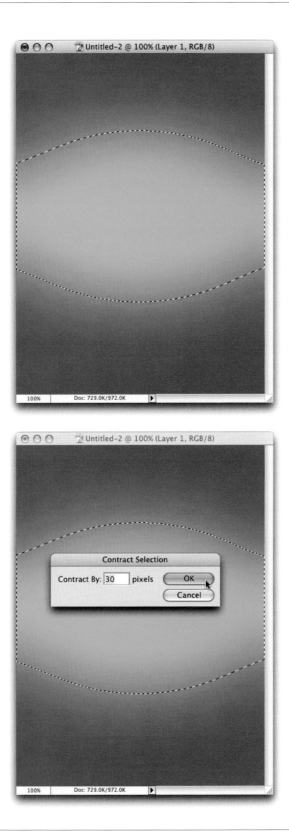

Step Three:
Now click your Foreground color swatch in the Toolbox to select a lighter shade of green from the Color Picker (I chose R=70, G=152, B=66). Fill your soft-edged oval with this green by pressing Option-Delete (PC: Alt-Backspace).

Step Four:
To create a double soft-spot effect, go under the Select menu, under Modify, and choose Contract. When the dialog appears, enter 30 pixels (as shown here) and click OK to shrink the size of your soft-edged oval selection.

Continued

Step Five:

Now click your Foreground color swatch in the Toolbox to select an even lighter shade of green (I chose R=152, G=225, B=149), and fill this smaller oval with this lighter green by pressing Option-Delete (PC: Alt-Backspace). Now you can deselect by pressing Command-D (PC: Control-D).

Step Six:

You'll need to merge this soft-oval layer with the Background layer by pressing Command-E (PC: Control-E). Now press the letter "m" to switch to the Rectangular Marquee tool and make a selection from the bottom of the image area, leaving a third of the top unselected (as shown here).

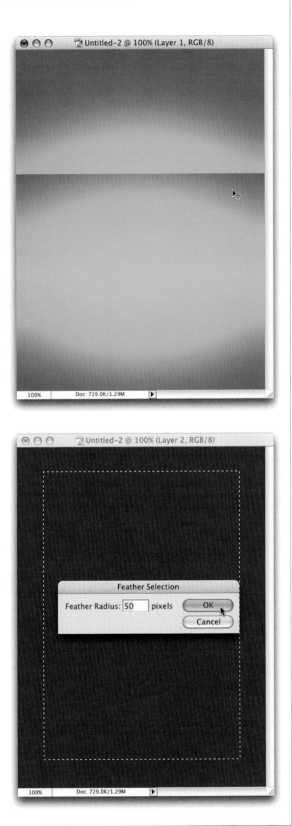

Step Seven:
Press Command-J (PC: Control-J) to copy this area up onto its own separate layer. Now press the letter "v" to switch to the Move tool, hold the Shift key, click inside the image area, and drag this duplicated layer straight down to reveal the top of the soft oval on the Background layer beneath (as shown here). Next, we'll use the burned-in portrait technique I have covered elsewhere in this book.

Step Eight:
Go to the Layers palette and create a new layer by clicking on the Create a New Layer icon. Click your Foreground color swatch in the Toolbox to select a dark green (I used R=28, G=82, B=26), and fill this layer with this green by pressing Option-Delete (PC: Alt-Backspace). Press the letter "m" to switch to the Rectangular Marquee tool and draw a rectangular selection that is about a half-inch from the sides of the image (as shown). To soften this selection, go under the Select menu and choose Feather. Enter 50 pixels and click OK.

Continued

Step Nine:

Now just press Delete (PC: Backspace) to create the burned-in portrait effect (as shown here). Go to the Layers palette and turn the visibility of this layer on and off by clicking its Eye icon a few times to really get an idea of how powerful a burned-in portrait effect is. Press Command-D (PC: Control-D) to deselect. Now, open the object you want to apply a cast shadow to (in this case, it's a steering wheel).

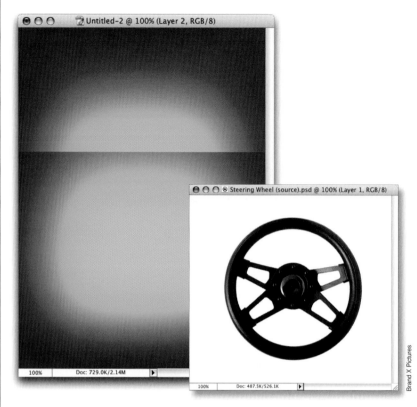

Step Ten:

Select the wheel by pressing the letter "w" to switch to the Magic Wand tool, and while holding down the Shift key, click on all the white background areas. Then go to the Select menu and choose Inverse. When just the image is selected, press the letter "v" for the Move tool and drag the image over onto your green background. Position it as shown here.

Step Eleven:
Duplicate the wheel layer by pressing Command-J (PC: Control-J). Then fill this duplicate wheel with dark green by pressing Shift-Option-Delete (PC: Shift-Alt-Backspace). Press Command-T (PC: Control-T) to bring up the Free Transform bounding box around your wheel.

Step Twelve:
Hold the Command key (PC: Control key), grab the top-center point, and drag to the left and down to skew the shadow onto the background (as if you're laying it down). When it's positioned where you'd like the cast shadow to appear, press Return (PC: Enter) to lock in your transformation.

Continued

Step Thirteen:

Now we need to soften the cast shadow. Go under the Filter menu, under Blur, and choose Gaussian Blur. When the dialog appears, enter 5 pixels in the Radius field (as shown here) and click OK to soften your shadow (as seen in the capture in the next step).

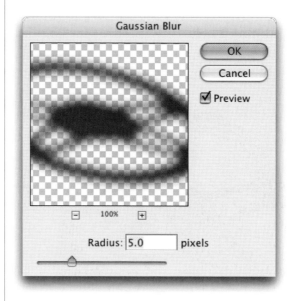

Step Fourteen:

Go to the Layers palette and lower the Opacity of the shadow layer to around 55%. While in the Layers palette, drag this layer below your black wheel layer to complete the cast shadow effect. (*Note*: Although you applied the Gaussian Blur to the entire shadow at once, if you wanted to go the extra step for realism, you could've done this instead: Put a rectangular selection around the bottom half of the shadow using the Rectangular Marquee tool, apply a 10-pixel Feather from the Select menu, and then blur that part just 2 pixels by choosing Filter>Blur>Gaussian Blur. Then, choose Inverse from the Select menu and blur the back half of the shadow 5 pixels by choosing Filter>Blur>Gaussian Blur, so the shadow is more realistic—less blurry nearest the wheel, and more blurry as it moves away. Hey, it's just a thought.)

Step Fifteen:

You can finish up the project by simply adding some type with the Type tool. We used Helvetica Regular and Helvetica Bold as the type, which we selected in the Character palette.

Post-it® Notes

This is an incredibly popular effect in print advertising, and just before I wrote this, I saw it used numerous times just within the magazines that I receive at home. What's nice about this technique is that once you've created your Post-it-like note, you can drag-and-drop it onto any photo to add a quick note effect.

Step One:

Open a new document (File>New) that's 7x5" at 72 ppi in RGB mode. Click the Create a New Layer icon at the bottom of the Layers palette to create a new layer, then press the letter "m" to switch to the Rectangular Marquee tool. Hold the Shift key and click-and-drag out a square selection (like the one shown here). Click on the Foreground color swatch, set your Foreground color to a Post-it note–like yellow in the Color Picker, and click OK. Then fill your square selection with this yellow by pressing Option-Delete (PC: Alt-Backspace). Deselect by pressing Command-D (PC: Control-D).

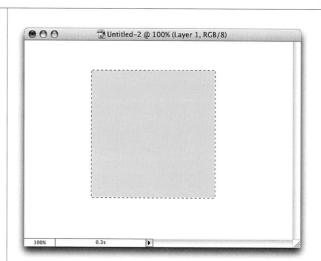

Step Two:

Take the Rectangular Marquee tool and draw a selection around your entire square that's a little larger than the square (as shown), then go under the Filter menu, under Distort, and choose Shear. In the Shear dialog, click on the middle of the line in the center of the grid and drag it just a little to the left (as shown right) to bend the note a little to the left. Click OK.

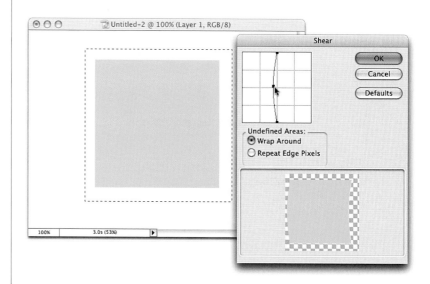

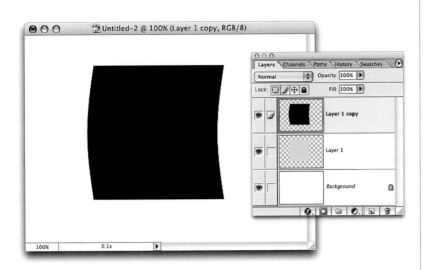

Step Three:

Deselect by pressing Command-D (PC: Control-D). Now duplicate this bended yellow layer by pressing Command-J (PC: Control-J). Press the letter "d" to set your Foreground color to black, then press Shift-Option-Delete (PC: Shift-Alt-Backspace) to fill your duplicate layer with black (as shown here). Now go to the Layers palette and drag this black note layer below the yellow note layer, as it will become its shadow.

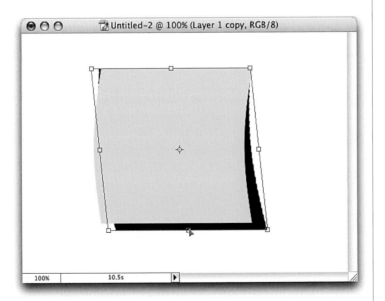

Step Four:

Press the letter "v" to switch to the Move tool, click in the image area, and drag this black shadow layer down and to the right a little. Press Command-T (PC: Control-T) to bring up the Free Transform command. Hold the Command key (PC: Control key), grab the top-center point, and drag to the left to skew the top of the shadow so the top-right corner of the shadow is hidden behind the yellow Post-it note. Then grab the bottom-center point and drag to the right, skewing it out a bit (as shown here), and press Return (PC: Enter) to lock in your transformation.

Continued

Step Five:

Now to soften the shadow, go under the Filter menu, under Blur, and choose Gaussian Blur. When the filter dialog appears, enter 3.5 pixels and click OK (as shown).

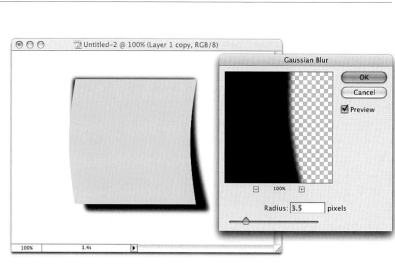

Step Six:

If any of your shadow extends outside the left side of your Post-it note, go back to Free Transform, hold the Command key (PC: Control key) again, but this time grab the top-left corner point and drag it down behind the yellow note layer (as shown here). When it looks good to you, press Return (PC: Enter) to lock in your changes. The shadow looks a bit dark, so go to the Layers palette and lower the Opacity setting for the shadow to around 60% (you'll see the lower setting for the shadow reflected in the next step).

Step Seven:

Now you'll add a little highlighting. First, press "x" to set white as your Foreground color. Hold the Command key (PC: Control key), go to the Layers palette, and click on your yellow Post-it note layer to put a selection around it. Click on the top layer (the yellow note layer) in the Layers palette, then click on the Create a New Layer icon. Press the letter "g" to switch to the Gradient tool, and press Return (PC: Enter) to bring up the Gradient Picker. Choose the second gradient in the Picker, which is the Foreground to Transparent gradient (as shown here).

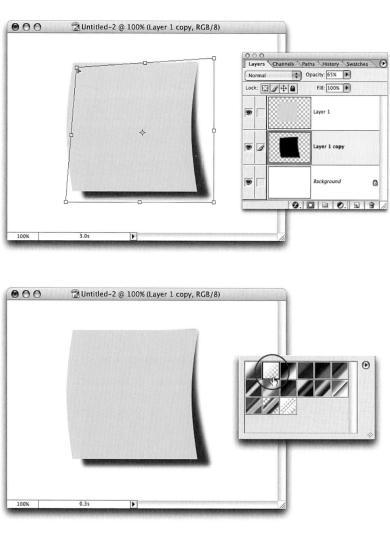

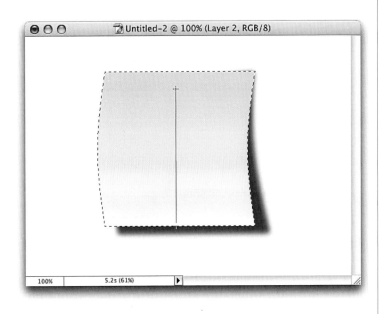

Step Eight:

Take the Gradient tool and click-and-drag from the bottom of the selection to the top, so that white is at the bottom of the selection, and it fades away to transparency at the top, revealing the yellow Post-it note below. Deselect by pressing Command-D (PC: Control-D). Next, in the Layers palette, lower the Opacity setting for this gradient layer to around 30% to give the note a highlighting effect (you can see this effect in the capture in Step Nine).

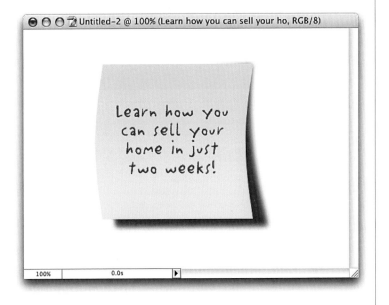

Step Nine:

Now it's time to add some text with the Type tool. I chose a font that looks like it's handwritten (the font is Litterbox ICG, which you can find at www.fonts.com). Okay, that takes care of the Post-it note itself; now let's put it to use. (But before merging the layers, you may want to choose File>Save As and save a copy of your note so you can apply it to other images later.) First, in the Layers palette, hide the Background layer by clicking on its Eye icon in the first column, then choose Merge Visible from the palette's flyout menu. This combines all your Post-it note parts into one single layer, with a transparent background, so you can drag-and-drop this note onto another image (as you'll see in the next step).

Continued

Step Ten:

Open a new document (File>New) that's 6x8" set at 72 ppi in RGB mode. Click on the Foreground color swatch, choose a tan color in the Color Picker (I used R=223, G=214, B=178), and click OK. Fill the Background layer with this tan color by pressing Option-Delete (PC: Alt-Backspace). Open the photo of a house that you want to use, and press the letter "v" to switch to the Move tool. Then click-and-drag the house onto your tan background and position it as shown here. (You can download this same house photo from this book's companion website at www.scottkelbybooks.com/ classicphotos.)

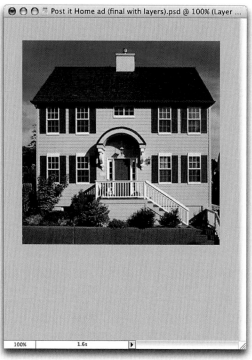

Step Eleven:

Go back to your Post-it note document and use the Move tool to drag the note over onto your house photo. Press Command-T (PC: Control-T) to bring up the Free Transform command. Hold the Shift key, grab a corner point, and drag inward to scale your note down to size. Then release the Shift key, move your cursor outside the bounding box to the right, and click-and-drag upward to rotate your note (as shown).

Are you considering selling your home?

If you're thinking of selling your home, keep this in mind: the average bay area home takes more than 16 weeks to sell. But it doesn't have to be that way now. We have a proven method for selling homes that lets us guarantee that we'll sell your home within two weeks, and if it doesn't sell, we'll buy it ourselves. That's our promise and you can ask any of our clients. It's how we do business.

Rogers Realty
Your partner in homes

Step Twelve:
Press Return (PC: Enter) to lock in your transformation. Now all that's left to do is add some type with the Type tool. The headline shown here is set in Helvetica Black, as is the fictitious realty company's name. The body copy and the realty company's tag line are set in Helvetica Regular. The key icon above "Rogers Realty" is a built-in custom shape found in the Custom Shape Picker library. You can find that shape by getting the Custom Shape tool from the Toolbox, then go up to the Options Bar, click on the icon next to the word "Shape" to bring up the Custom Shape Picker, and from the Picker's flyout menu choose Objects to load this library of shapes. Click Append, and that's where you'll find the key shape. If you want to return to the default set of shapes, just choose Reset Shapes from the flyout menu. That's it!

Polaroid® Effect

This classic effect of creating a "Polaroid look" has been around for years, but I'm not sure if it's ever been more popular than it is right now. In fact, an Applebee's Neighborhood Grill and Bar® recently opened near our headquarters, and son-of-a-gun, right there on the cover of their menu was a great example of the Polaroid effect. Here's how to create the look. We'll finish off this project by re-creating the look of the Applebee's menu cover.

Step One:

Open the photo you want to apply the Polaroid effect to. Press Command-A (PC: Control-A) to put a selection around the entire photo, then press Shift-Command-J (PC: Shift-Control-J) to cut the photo off the Background layer and copy it onto its own layer (as shown here).

Step Two:

To add the Polaroid effect, you'll need to add some space around your photo. First, set your Foreground and Background colors to their defaults of black and white by pressing the letter "d". Then go under the Image menu and choose Canvas Size. When the dialog appears, turn on the Relative checkbox, enter 2 inches in both the Width and Height fields, and choose White in the Canvas Extension Color pop-up menu (as shown).

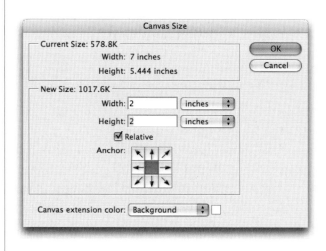

Step Four:
Now to add the border: Choose Stroke from the Add a Layer Style pop-up menu at the bottom of the Layers palette. When the dialog appears, increase the Size to 15 pixels, change the Position pop-up menu to Inside (so the corners of the stroke don't appear rounded), click on the Color swatch, and choose a very light gray in the Color Picker (I choose R=225, G=225, B=225). This light gray will be the color for your Polaroid border. Click OK in the Color Picker, but don't click OK in the Layer Style dialog yet. Even though you haven't clicked OK, you'll still see a preview of your border within your image area (as shown here).

Step Five:
Click directly on the words "Drop Shadow" in the Styles list on the left-hand side of the Layer Style dialog to bring up the Drop Shadow options. Change the Angle to 89°, the Distance to 6, and the Size to 16. Now you can click OK in the Layer Style dialog.

Continued

Step Six:

When you click OK, the stroke and the drop shadow are both applied to your photo, creating the Polaroid effect (as shown here). Now that you know how to create the effect, you can put it to use by re-creating the cover like the one from Applebee's menu. (*Tip*: Try their Chicken Fajita Rollup.)

Step Seven:

Open a new document (File>New) that's 6x8". Click on the Foreground color swatch and choose a red in the Color Picker and click OK. Then fill the Background layer with this red by pressing Option-Delete (PC: Alt-Backspace). Press the letter "m" to switch to the Rectangular Marquee tool, and draw a horizontal rectangular selection around the bottom quarter of the image window. Click the Foreground color swatch, choose green in the Color Picker, and fill your selection with green. Deselect by pressing Command-D (PC: Control-D). Now go back to your Polaroid document, press the letter "v" to switch to the Move tool, and drag your Polaroid image onto the red background. Press Command-T (PC: Control-T) to bring up Free Transform. Hold the Shift key, grab one of the corner points of the bounding box, and drag inward to shrink the image down to size (as shown here). Click Return (PC: Enter) to lock in your transformation.

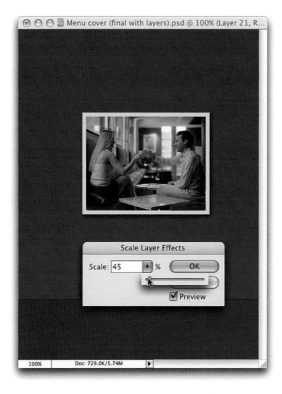

Step Eight:
When you scale the photo down to size, you'll notice that the Polaroid border remains the same width (as shown in Step Seven). To scale the Polaroid border and shadow down in size to match the new smaller size of the photo, go under the Layer menu, under Layer Style, and choose Scale Effects. When the dialog appears, decrease the Scale amount until the border looks right (as shown here), then click OK.

Step Nine:
Open another photo, use the Move tool to drag it into the menu document, and use the Free Transform command to scale the new photo down to match the size of your first image. While the Free Transform border is still in place, move your cursor outside the bounding box to the right, and click-and-drag upward to rotate the photo. Press Return (PC: Enter) to lock in your scaling and rotation (as shown here). In the Layers palette, drag the layer with the new image (Layer 2) below the layer with the original image (Layer 1). Now there's only one problem—this rotated photo has no Polaroid border. But you'll fix that with one click in the next step.

Continued

Step Ten:

Take a look in the Layers palette and you'll see the word "Effects" below your Polaroid layer. Below that you'll see the name of the two effects that you applied—Drop Shadow and Stroke (as shown here). To copy these effects to your newly rotated photo layer, just click directly on the word "Effects," and drag-and-drop it just below Layer 2 (your rotated layer).

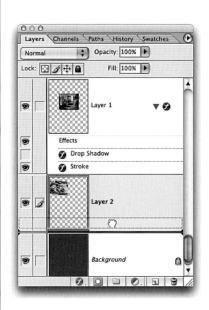

Step Eleven:

When you drag-and-drop the layer style, the stroke and drop shadow are applied to your rotated photo (as shown here). To finish the project, add more photos of food (I put a few on the book's website for you to download if you like) and scale and rotate them—don't forget to drag the word "Effects" to these other photos.

Step Twelve:
Here's the menu cover with a number of different photos of food added. Each photo has the Polaroid border added to it, which completes the effect.

Soft Lighting Effect

Okay, I have to admit, this technique really belongs in my *Photoshop CS Down & Dirty Tricks* book because it shows you how to fake a studio product shot. Although setting this up in a studio is a classic, doing it digitally in Photoshop is something that is just catching on, but I didn't figure you'd mind if I added this cool trick to the book.

Step One:

Open the photo that you want to give a soft spotlight background. This effect was inspired by a graphic on Sony's website. Unfortunately, I didn't have a photo of a Sony camcorder, but I was able to find a Fuji digital camera (courtesy of Jim DiVitale), so that's what we'll be using here.

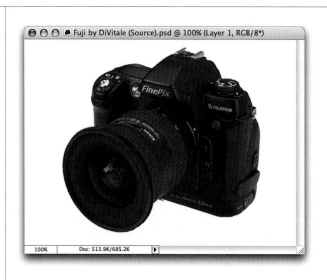

Step Two:

Open a new, large, blank document (I've created an 8x5" RGB document at 72 ppi). Click your Foreground color swatch to select a blue shade (I used R=83, G=104, B=122), and fill the background of your new document with this color by pressing Option-Delete (PC: Alt-Backspace). Put a selection around the camera with the Magic Wand tool by clicking on the white background and going to the Select menu and choosing Inverse. Then press the letter "v" to switch to the Move tool and drag the selected camera onto your blue background and position it (as shown here).

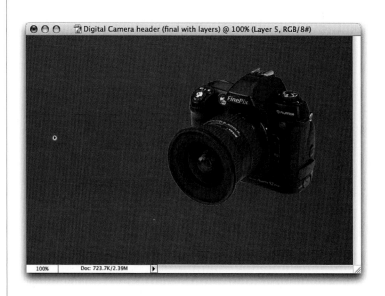

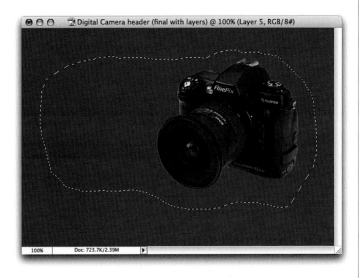

Step Three:

Go to the Layers palette, hold the Command key (PC: Control key), and click on the Create a New Layer icon at the bottom of the Layers palette to create a new layer beneath the camera. Press the letter "L" to switch to the Lasso tool and draw a large, very loose selection around the camera (like the one shown here).

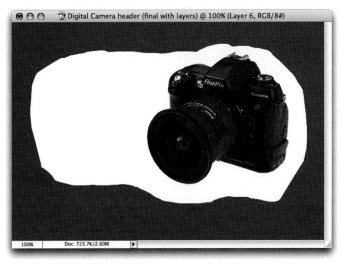

Step Four:

Set your Foreground color to white by pressing "x" and fill your selection with white by pressing Option-Delete (PC: Alt-Backspace). Now you can deselect by pressing Command-D (PC: Control-D), leaving the large white area you see here. In the next step, we'll start transforming that into a soft spotlight.

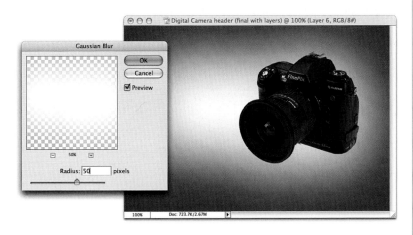

Step Five:

Go under the Filter menu, under Blur, and choose Gaussian Blur. When the Gaussian Blur dialog appears, set the Radius to 50 pixels (for high-res, 300-ppi images, try 170 pixels) and click OK to soften the white area (as shown here).

Continued

Soft Shadow Effects   Chapter 2   53

Step Six:

Okay, you've got a spotlight shining on your background now, but it's not soft enough. Go to the Layers palette and lower the Opacity of this white blurry layer to 70% to get the softer effect (as shown here).

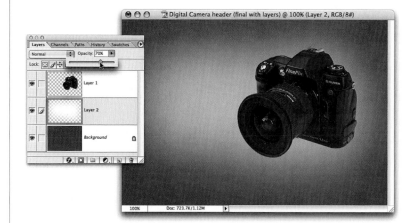

Step Seven:

Now you'll paint a shadow under the camera. Click on the Create a New Layer icon at the bottom of the Layers palette. Press "d" to set your Foreground color to black. Then press the letter "b" to switch to the Brush tool, click on the icon next to the word "Brush" in the Options Bar to bring up the Brush Picker, and choose a medium soft-edge brush. Trace along the bottom of the camera (as shown here) with part of the brush tip extending into the camera (don't worry, this layer is beneath the camera layer so you can't paint on the camera itself).

Step Eight:

Once your shadow is painted, go to the Layers palette and lower the Opacity of this layer to 40% so it's not so dark, making it look more natural.

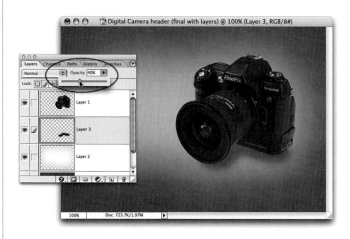

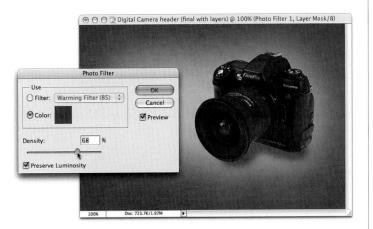

Step Nine:

The camera looks too red to have really been shot on a background this blue, so we'll need to tone down that red by adding in some blue. Click on the camera layer in the Layers palette and choose Photo Filter from the Create New Adjustment Layer pop-up menu at the bottom of the palette. When the Photo Filter dialog appears, click on the color swatch, and when the Color Picker appears, move your cursor outside the dialog and click on the blue background color to use that color. Click OK in the Color Picker. Now increase the Density to 68% in the Photo Filter dialog and click OK to make the camera appear bluer, like it was shot on that background.

Step Ten:

To complete the effect, just add some type with the Type tool. The type shown here is (once again) Helvetica Regular (however the "8 megapixel SLR" is in Helvetica Condensed Bold).

Example:

This soft-light background is very versatile. Here's the exact same background, with a different product (an iron) and updated text. Each time you visited Sony's website (or even just refreshed the homepage), a new product would appear, with essentially the same background. This shows you how easy it is to do just that, once you have the background in place.

True Confessions
tried-and-true special effects

PHOTOSHOP
CLASSIC
EFFECTS

CHAPTER
3

SIDE ONE
SK-355-A
STEREO

PRODUCED BY BIG ELECTRIC CAT RECORDING STUDIOS • MFG. BY KW MEDIA GROUP, INC

Chapter THREE

TRUE CONFESSIONS
TRIED-AND-TRUE SPECIAL EFFECTS

There are certain special effects that have been used over and over again through the years and have become staples of the Photoshop effects industry. These are those "tried-and-true" special effects you see every day, which left me with two possible words to use in my chapter title: tried or true. I went with "true" because I could then use the title *True Confessions* from the 1981 movie starring Robert De Niro. Why *True Confessions*? I thought it kinda had a little bit of a naughty sound to it—true confessions—and naughty stuff sells books,

right? In fact, the original working title for this book was *Photoshop Naked Nudie Effects* (now admit it—is that a title that would move some books off the shelves or what?). But my publisher thought it was a bit too racy and suggested I change the name to *Photoshop Scantily Clad Effects*, which frankly just doesn't have the same punch to it, so I went with the more conservative title of *Photoshop Classic Effects*. But if you want to think of it under its original working title, I won't tell anyone. It'll be your own true confession.

Adding a Different Reflection to Sunglasses

Unfortunately, with studio photos all you get reflected in the subject's sunglasses is generally the studio lighting, so it's fairly common to add something else, especially for effect. You see this technique in everything from movie posters (like the reflection added in the movie poster for *Natural Born Killers*) to print ads to the Web, where you can put anything you want as a reflection in those shades.

Step One:
Open a photo where the subject is wearing sunglasses (as shown here). In our project, we're going to make it look like the subject is looking at a poker hand.

Step Two:
Press the letter "L" to switch to the Lasso tool (or any selection tool you're comfortable with) and make a selection around the inside of the sunglasses (as shown here).

Brand X Pictures

Step Three:
Open the photo you want to appear reflected inside the sunglasses (in this case, a poker hand). Press Command-A (PC: Control-A) to select the entire photo, then press Command-C (PC: Control-C) to copy it into memory.

Step Four:
Return to the sunglasses photo where your selection should still be in place. Go under the Edit menu and choose Paste Into to paste the poker hand photo into your lens selection. It will probably be much too big, so press Command-T (Control-T) to bring up the Free Transform command. Hold the Shift key, grab a corner point (as shown here), and drag inward to scale the photo so it fits inside the lens selection. Press Return (PC: Enter) to lock in the transformation.

Continued

Step Five:

To make the reflection look like it's in the glasses (rather than stuck on top), choose Inner Shadow from the Add a Layer Style pop-up menu at the bottom of the Layers palette. When the dialog appears, lower the Distance to 1, the Size to 3, change the Angle to 120° and click OK to add a thin shadow inside the poker hand photo (as shown here).

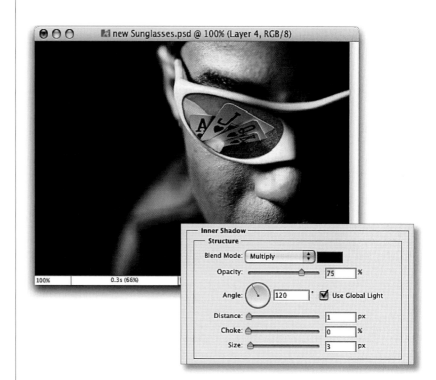

Step Six:

To help the pasted-in card photo blend in with the sunglasses, go to the Layers palette and change the layer blend mode of the card layer from Normal to Screen (as shown here).

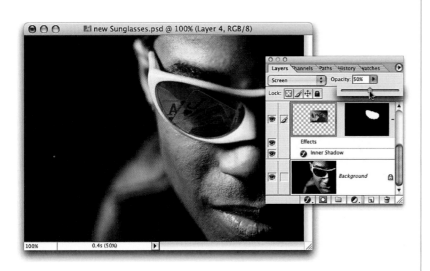

Step Seven:
To help the reflection look less intense (and more reflected) lower the Opacity of this layer to 50% in the Layers palette (as shown).

Step Eight:
The final step is to add some text to finish off the project. The type shown here is set in the font Helvetica Regular.

Brushed Metal

I recently saw this classic brushed-metal effect used in *FORTUNE* magazine in an ad for Garmin, a company that makes a GPS-based PDA navigation system. They did a great job of subtly integrating it without making it look overly techie, and in their example, it was a perfect "bed" for their headline and product shot. Here's how to re-create a similar effect and layout.

Step One:

Our project starts with a photo, so open the source image (you can download this same image at the book's companion website at www.scottkelbybooks.com/ classicphotos). Press the letter "d" to set your Foreground color to black and your Background color to white. You're going to add some text below the photo, so go to the Image menu and choose Canvas Size. Turn on the Relative checkbox, and in the Height field enter 3 inches. In the Anchor grid, click the top-center square, and in the Canvas Extension Color pop-up menu choose White (as shown). Click OK to add 3 inches of white space below your photo.

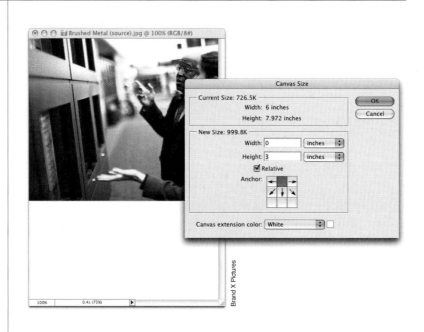

Step Two:
Press the letter "m" to switch to the Rectangular Marquee tool and draw a rectangular selection just inside your entire document's borders (as shown here). In the next step you'll put a stroke around this selection, which will serve as the boundary for your ad, so go ahead and create a new blank layer for the stroke by clicking on the Create a New Layer icon at the bottom of the Layers palette.

Step Three:
Now you're going to add a stroke around your selection. Go under the Edit menu and choose Stroke. When the dialog appears, enter 1 pixel for Width, choose Center for Location, and click OK to put a thin, black stroke around your selection. Don't deselect yet.

Step Four:
Go under the Select menu and choose Inverse. This selects all the area outside your thin black stroke. In the Layers palette, click on the Background layer to make it active, then press Delete (PC: Backspace) to erase the areas of the photo that extend beyond that stroke (as shown here). Now you can deselect by pressing Command-D (PC: Control-D).

Continued

Step Five:

Click the Create a New Layer icon in the Layers palette. Take the Rectangular Marquee tool and draw a horizontal selection just under your photo, like the one shown here. This is where you'll build a brushed metal "bar" and your headline text will go over that brushed metal.

Step Six:

Press the letter "g" to switch to the Gradient tool, then press Return (PC: Enter) to bring up the Gradient Picker. Click on the Copper gradient, as shown here (it's in the second row in the default set of gradients). Now take the Gradient tool, click in the top-left corner of your selection, and drag diagonally across to the bottom-right corner of your selection (as shown here) to apply a copper gradient to your selection. Don't deselect yet.

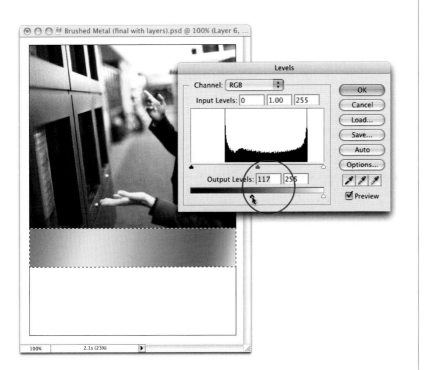

Step Seven:

Now you'll need to remove the copper color from the gradient, so press Shift-Command-U (PC: Shift-Control-U), which desaturates all the color, leaving you with a metallic-looking gradient. Next, to lighten the gradient up a bit, go under the Image menu, under Adjustments, and choose Levels. In the Levels dialog, drag the bottom-left Output Levels slider to the right (as shown) to lighten the overall tone of your metallic bar, then click OK.

Step Eight:

Okay, so you've got the metal—now it's time for the "brushed" part. Go under the Filter menu, under Noise, and choose Add Noise. When the dialog appears (shown here), set the Amount to 20%, the Distribution to Gaussian, and turn on the Monochromatic checkbox (if you don't turn on Monochromatic, the noise you create will have little red, green, and blue dots). Click OK to apply a noise pattern over your metallic gradient (as shown here).

Continued

Step Nine:

To turn that noise into brushed metal, go under the Filter menu, under Blur, and choose Motion Blur. Set the Angle to 0˚ (for a horizontal blur), the Distance to 200, and click OK. Press Command-D (PC: Control-D) to deselect. That creates the brushed-metal effect. Now, you'll just finish things off by adding a bevel, a shadow, and some text, so continue on to the next step.

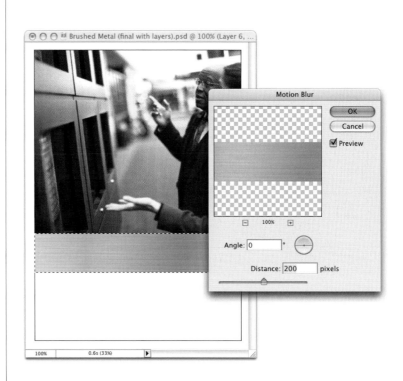

Step Ten:

To add a sharp beveled edge to your brushed metal bar, choose Bevel and Emboss from the Add a Layer Style pop-up menu at the bottom of the Layers palette. You're only going to make two changes: (1) Increase the Depth to 200%, and (2) decrease the Size to 1 pixel. This gives you a sharp, slightly beveled edge on the top and bottom of your brushed metal bar (as shown here). Don't click OK yet.

Step Eleven:
Next you'll add a very soft, light drop shadow under your brushed metal bar, so click directly on the words "Drop Shadow" in the list of Styles on the left-hand side of the Layer Style dialog. Lower the Opacity to 40% (to make it lighter), set the Angle to 85° (so the shadow appears directly below the bar, rather than offset to the left or right), and increase the Size to 10 to make the shadow softer (as shown). Now click OK.

Step Twelve:
In the real ad, they had a PDA extending up into the photo from the metallic bar, but since I didn't have a PDA photo, I used this image of a flat-panel display (you can download this flat panel from the book's website). Open the image of the flat-panel display. First, we need to select the display, so press the letter "w" to switch to the Magic Wand tool, hold the Shift key, and click on all the white background areas in the image. Choose Inverse in the Select menu to select just the display. Press the letter "v" to switch to the Move tool, click inside the selection, and drag the flat-panel display onto your ad and position it on the bar (as shown here). Use the Free Transform command (Command-T; PC: Control-T) to size the image if needed.

Continued

Step Thirteen:

Now press the letter "t" to switch to the Type tool and add a headline. The headline here is set in the font Cronos (from Adobe) in all caps, but if you don't have Cronos, try the next best thing—Myriad Pro (which comes with Photoshop CS). In the real ad they used an effective little trick that made the type look embossed into the metal. Start by duplicating your Type layer by pressing Command-J (PC: Control-J). Press the letter "d" then "x" to set white as your Foreground color, then fill this duplicate headline layer with white by pressing Option-Delete (PC: Alt-Backspace). In the Layers palette, drag this white Type layer below your black Type layer, then switch to the Move tool. Now, press the Left Arrow key on your keyboard once to offset the white type, which creates the effect.

Step Fourteen:

To finish off the project, just add some body copy with the Type tool (in this case, it's set in the font Cronos as well), including the fictitious company's name and tag line.

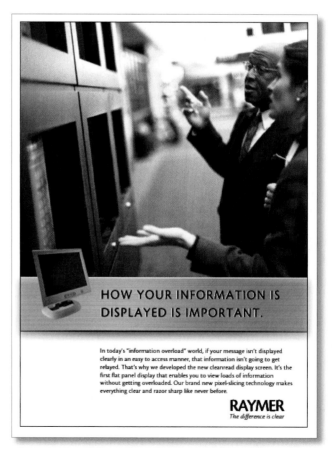

Photo Tinting

Tinting a color photo with a solid color is very popular and fairly easy—once you know how. That's why in this tutorial, I not only show you how to tint a photo but also how to take that tinted print and add some simple elements to create a full-size poster. What I really like about this technique is that it lets you take a fairly boring photo and turn it into something artistic quickly and easily.

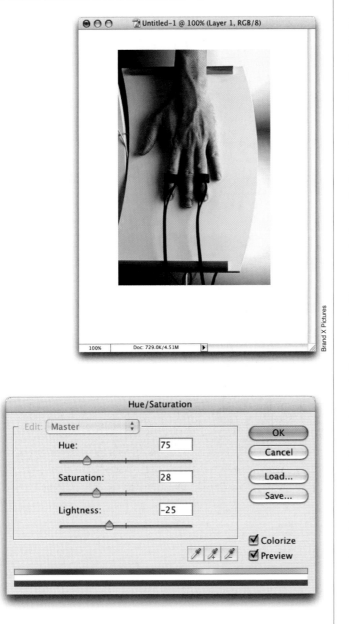

Step One:

Open the photo you want to apply a tint effect to. Create a new blank document (File>New) that's larger than the photo, then press the letter "v" to switch to the Move tool and drag-and-drop your photo onto this larger document (as shown here). We're doing this because we're not only going to tint the photo, but create a poster with the tinted photo (of course, the tinting is the technique—the poster part is to expand the technique by creating a real-world project using the tinted image).

Step Two:

Command-click (PC: Control-click) on the photo's thumbnail in the Layers palette to put a selection around the image. Choose Hue/Saturation from the Create New Adjustment Layer pop-up menu (it's the fourth icon from the left) at the bottom of the Layers palette. When the dialog appears, click on the Colorize checkbox. Then move the Hue slider to choose your tint (in this case, move the Hue slider to 75). Then, because this photo has large areas of lighter tones, you'll need to darken the image a bit by lowering the Lightness slider to -25. Click OK and a greenish tint is applied to the image. Easy enough, eh? Now on to the rest of the poster project.

Continued

Step Three:

Let's add a stroke—choose Stroke from the Create a Layer Style pop-up menu at the bottom of the Layers palette. When the dialog appears, click on the Color swatch and change the stroke color to black. Increase the Size to 8 and change the Position pop-up menu to Inside so the stroke doesn't have rounded corners. Click OK to apply the stroke.

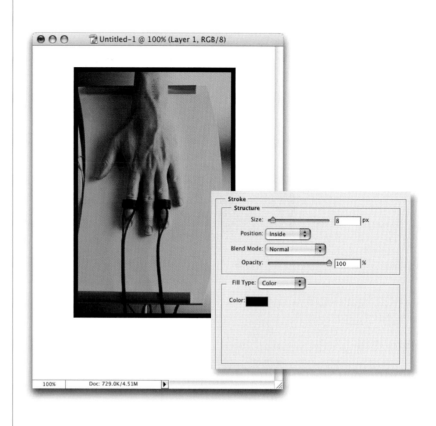

Step Four:

Now, we'll add two of the three "high-tech" elements we learned in the "high-tech" tutorial earlier in this chapter. Add two small paragraphs using the Type tool set to white, setting the font as Helvetica at 3 points in the Character palette, and drop in a couple of larger plus signs (+). And maybe a deep thoughtful line of text, like "Where does one find the truth?" set in Helvetica in all caps. Lower the Opacity of the Type layers in the Layers palette.

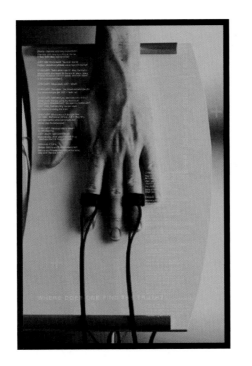

truth in advertising
AN EXHIBITION BY AUTHUR M. WONG

5TH STREET GALLERY · SAN DIEGO

Step Five:
To finish the poster, you can add some text below the image (as shown here). The words "truth in advertising" are set in Helvetica Regular. The type directly below that is set in Copperplate Gothic Regular. The fictitious gallery name is set in Trajan Pro (which comes with Photoshop CS), and that completes the project.

Adding a Pattern to an Object

This classic effect adds a pattern to any selected object within your image. Before layer styles came along (back in Photoshop 6), we had to do all this manually, and it was really kind of a pain. But layer styles changed all that, and now it's pretty painless.

Step One:
Open the photo that has an area you want to apply a pattern to. In this example, we're going to apply a pattern to the fabric of this umbrella.

Step Two:
The first step to making this happen is to select the fabric. Start by pressing the letter "w" to switch to the Magic Wand tool. Click once on the left side of the fabric to select that area (as shown here). (*Note:* If the Magic Wand doesn't select a very large area, try raising the Tolerance in the Options Bar and clicking again.)

Step Three:
Hold the Shift key, and then click the Magic Wand tool on the center panel of the umbrella to select the rest of the fabric. Chances are it won't select every last bit of fabric, so press the letter "L" to switch to the Lasso tool, hold the Shift key again, and click-and-drag to "lasso" over any areas that still aren't selected until you have the entire fabric area selected (as shown here).

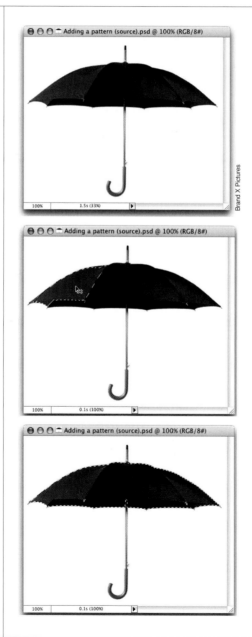

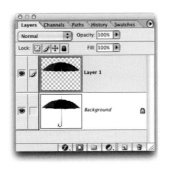

Step Four:
To be able to use the Pattern Overlay layer style, your object has to be on its own layer, so press Command-J (PC: Control-J) to copy the fabric up onto its own separate layer (as shown here).

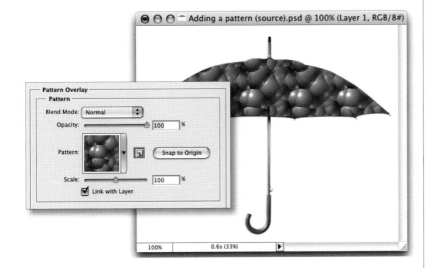

Step Five:
Now choose Pattern Overlay from the Add a Layer Style pop-up menu at the bottom of the Layers palette (it's the first icon from the left). When the dialog appears, it will put the default pattern (some weird blue blobs) over your fabric. It won't blend in, mind you; it will completely cover it (as shown here), which looks mighty bad.

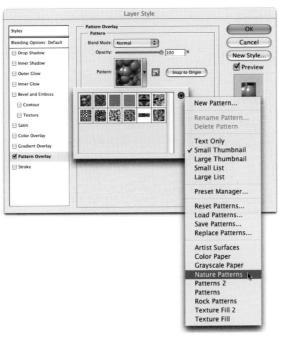

Step Six:
First, let's find a decent-looking pattern, then we'll work on making it blend in. In the Pattern dialog, click on the Pattern thumbnail to bring up the Pattern Picker. Click on the little right-facing arrow at the top right and a flyout menu will appear. At the bottom of the menu will be a list of pattern sets you can load. Choose Nature Patterns (as shown here). When the dialog appears, click the Append button to add these nature patterns to your Pattern Picker.

Continued

Step Seven:

In the Pattern Picker, you'll see that this set of patterns has been added to the end of your current set. Click on the Blue Daisies pattern (as shown here), to switch to a nice flower pattern. Don't click OK just yet.

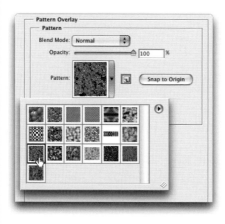

Step Eight:

When you look back at your image, you'll see that the weird blue blobs have been replaced by the purplish daisies (as shown here). So the pattern looks better, but it's still covering the fabric, not blending in with it.

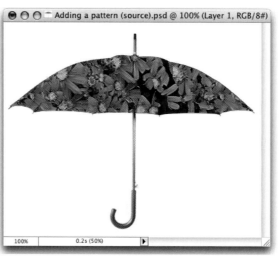

Step Nine:

To make the pattern blend in with your umbrella, change the Blend Mode pop-up menu in the Pattern category of the dialog. Normally, the Overlay mode works well; but in this case, it made the pattern too dark, so instead try Color Dodge (which brightens the flowers). Lower the Opacity to 65% to keep the effect from being too intense (as shown here). Now you can click OK to apply your pattern. In the next two steps, we'll turn the photo into an ad for anti-depressant medication.

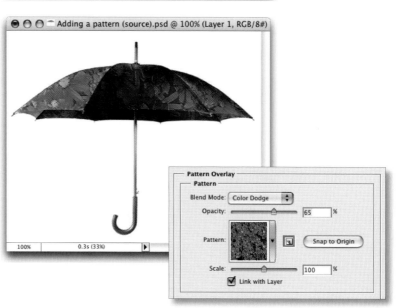

Step Ten:
To create some white space under your image so you can add a headline and some body copy, go under the Image menu and choose Canvas Size. Turn on the Relative checkbox; enter 3 inches for Height; and in the Anchor Grid, click on the top-center square. For Canvas Extension Color, choose White in the pop-up menu.

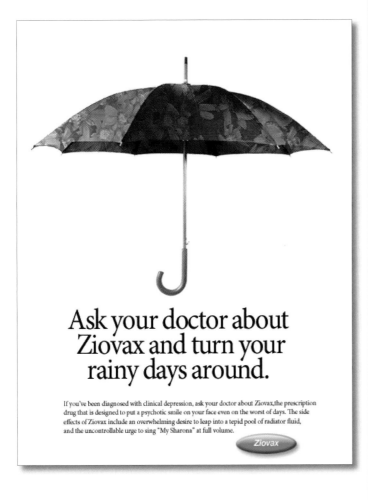

Step Eleven:
When you click OK, it adds 3 inches of white space beneath your umbrella. Now you can add your text with the Type tool. The font used in the headline and the body copy is Minion Pro (which comes with Photoshop CS). The type in the light blue oval logo is Helvetica Bold Italic. To make the oval, I created a new layer, drew an ellipse with the Elliptical Marquee tool, and filled it with a light blue. From the Add a Layer Style pop-up menu in the Layers palette, I chose Bevel and Emboss, and then chose Drop Shadow from the left side of the dialog. This completes the effect.

Creating DVD Menus

Okay, technically, although we're building a DVD menu in this project, this is not really a DVD menu technique—and it's not really one technique, it's four (like an all-in-one project). The first and most important technique lets you create a popular tinted grain effect that's used in backgrounds. After that, you'll learn three more along the way.

Step One:

Open the photo that you want to use as the background for your DVD menu (in this case, we're building a DVD menu for a fictitious military rescue mission movie). Press Command-A (PC: Control-A) to Select All, then press Command-Shift-J (PC: Control-Shift-J) to cut the image from the background and copy it onto its own layer.

Step Two:

Go under the Image menu, under Adjustments, and choose Desaturate. This removes all the color from the photo. Then go under the Filter menu, under Noise, and choose Add Noise. When the Add Noise dialog appears, set the Amount to 7, for Distribution choose Gaussian, and make sure you check the Monochromatic checkbox (so the noise you create doesn't have little red, green, and blue dots). Click OK.

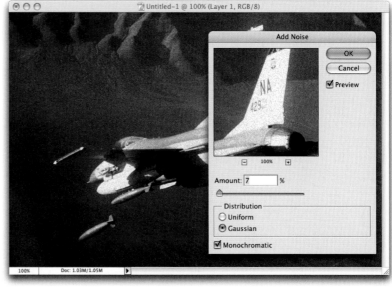

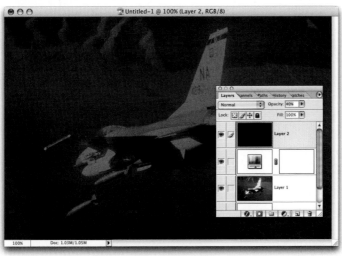

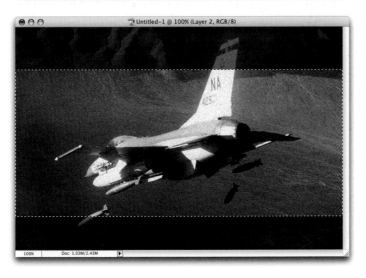

Step Three:

Choose Hue/Saturation from the Create New Adjustment Layer pop-up menu at the bottom of the Layers palette. When the dialog appears, click on the Colorize checkbox, then drag the Hue slider to 200 to put a blue tint over your noisy photo (as shown here). Then click OK. At this point, the first technique—the very popular noisy tinted background—is complete, but since we're working on a DVD menu, we might as well keep learning other cool stuff, right? Right.

Step Four:

The next technique is a popular way to add backscreening, so you can put type over one or more parts of a photo so it can easily be seen. To do this, click on the Create a New Layer icon at the bottom of the Layers palette. Set black as your Foreground color by pressing "d" and fill this new layer with black by pressing Option-Delete (PC: Alt-Backspace). Then, in the Layers palette lower the Opacity setting of this layer to 40% so you can still see the jet.

Step Five:

Press the letter "m" to switch to the Rectangular Marquee tool and make a large rectangular selection around the area where you want your DVD chapter sections to appear. Then press Delete (PC: Backspace) to knock a large rectangular hole out of the black layer (as shown). This leaves a 40% backscreened horizontal bar at the top and bottom of your DVD menu so you can add navigation text. Deselect by pressing Command-D (PC: Control-D). That completes the second technique—creating backscreened bars so you can put text over your photo.

Continued

Step Six:

Now, the third part...To create some depth, we're going to add a stroke and a glow around these 40% black bars. Choose Stroke from the Add a Layer Style pop-up menu at the bottom of the Layers palette. When the dialog appears, click on the small color swatch, and change the color to white in the Color Picker. Then, in the Styles list on the left side of the dialog, click directly on the words "Outer Glow." Change the Blend Mode pop-up menu to Linear Dodge, click on the small color swatch and change it to white, then increase the Spread to 18 and the Size to 18. Click OK.

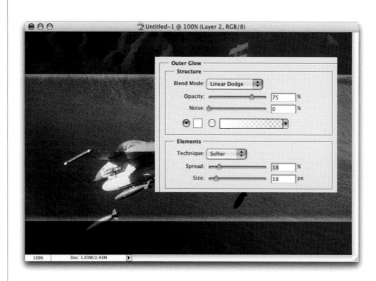

Step Seven:

Here's the fourth technique: putting a photo inside a circle. Press Shift-M until you get the Elliptical Marquee tool, hold the Shift key, and draw a circular selection where you want your first chapter section photo to appear (as shown here).

Step Eight:

Open the first photo you want to appear in this circle. Press Command-A (PC: Control-A) to put a selection around the entire photo, then press Command-C (PC: Control-C) to copy this photo into memory. Now, return to your DVD menu (your selection will still be in place) and choose Paste Into from the Edit menu. Your photo will be pasted into your circular selection on a new layer. Press Command-T (PC: Control-T) to bring up the Free Transform command. Hold the Shift key, grab a corner point, and drag inward to scale your photo down to size (as shown here). Press Return (PC: Enter) to lock in your transformation.

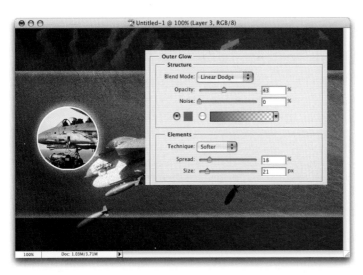

Step Nine:

Now you'll add a glow and a white stroke around your circular photo. Choose Outer Glow from the Add a Layer Style pop-up menu at the bottom of the Layers palette. Change the Blend Mode pop-up menu to Linear Dodge, lower the Opacity setting to 43%, and set the Glow Color to a light blue by clicking on the small color swatch. Increase the Spread to 18 and Size to 21. Then, in the Styles list on the left side of the dialog, click on the word "Stroke." Just change the Stroke color to white and click OK.

Step Ten:

For the other chapter photos, repeat the same process of making a circular selection, opening the photo you want to use, selecting all, copying it into memory, then returning to the DVD menu and pasting the photo into that circle. Use the Free Transform command to size the image. Then, in the Layers palette, click on the word "Effects" underneath your first circle photo, and drag-and-drop it under your second circle photo layer in the Layers palette. The glow and stroke effects will be copied to that layer. Repeat these steps until all four circular photos are in place (as shown).

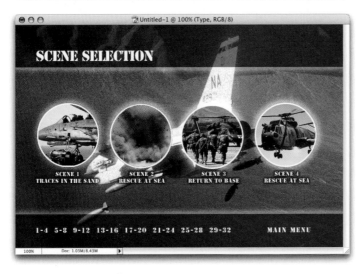

Step Eleven:

Lastly, just add some text with the Type tool. The text shown here is set in the font Stencil Std Bold in all caps. To make the scene text headers easier to read, you might want to go to the Add a Layer Style pop-up menu in the Layers palette and add a black Outer Glow to the text underneath each circle (as shown here) with the Blend Mode set to Normal, which completes the DVD menu.

High-Teching a Photo

This is a very simple yet incredibly popular technique for taking a regular photo and giving it a high-tech, futuristic feel by adding a grid, some very small text, and a few plus signs. I know, it sounds pretty lame, and that's why Photoshop's not an audio program—it looks better than it sounds.

Step One:

Open the image you want to "high-tech up" a bit.

Step Two:

First we'll create the grid. Go under the File menu and choose New. In the New dialog, create a new document that is .25 inches by .25 inches at whatever resolution you like (I chose 72 ppi just for speed's sake) set in RGB mode.

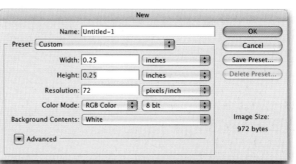

Step Three:

Click OK and you've got one very tiny document. Press Command-A (PC: Control-A) to select the entire image area, then go to the Layers palette and click the Create a New Layer icon. Now go under the Edit menu and choose Stroke. In the Stroke dialog, for Width enter 1 pixel, for Location choose Center, and click OK to put a 1-pixel black stroke around the tiny square area.

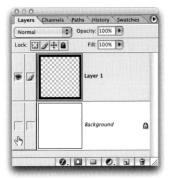

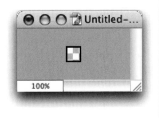

Step Four:

Go to the Layers palette and hide the Background layer from view by clicking on the Eye icon in the first column (as shown here). The reason we're hiding the Background layer is so that when we create a pattern, the area inside the square is transparent. If we didn't hide the Background layer, the area inside would be white.

Step Five:

Go under the Edit menu and choose Define Pattern. Give your pattern a name and click OK to save this pattern into Photoshop's Pattern Library.

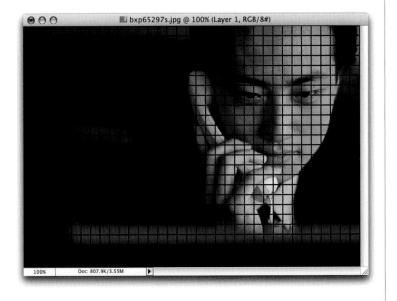

Step Six:

Return to your photo image and create a new layer by clicking on the Create a New Layer icon at the bottom of the Layers palette. Then go under the Edit menu and choose Fill. When the Fill dialog appears, choose Pattern under the Contents pop-up menu. Then click on the Custom Pattern swatch and in the Pattern Library that appears, choose the last pattern (that's the one you just created in the other document), as shown above. Click OK and a repeating grid pattern will appear over your image (as shown here).

Continued

Step Seven:
Press Command-I (PC: Control-I) to Invert your grid, changing the black lines to white lines (as shown here).

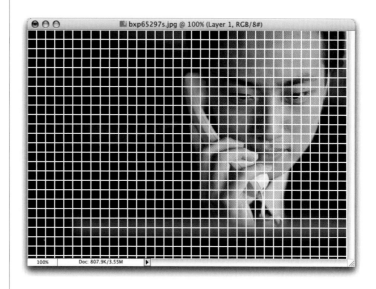

Step Eight:
Click on the Add a Layer Mask icon at the bottom of the Layers palette (shown circled here) to add a layer mask to your white grid layer. Press the letter "g" to switch to the Gradient tool, press the Return key (PC: Enter key), and the Gradient Picker will appear onscreen at the location of your cursor. Click on the Black to White gradient (it's the third gradient in the default set of gradients). Also, make sure you have the Linear Gradient selected in the Options Bar. It's the first icon in the group of five icons near the left.

Step Nine:
Click the Gradient tool in the center of your grid and drag upward to the top of the image. The area below where you clicked will become transparent and it will gradually fade up to your full white grid (as shown here).

Step Ten:

Go to the Layers palette and lower the Opacity of your grid layer to around 15% (you can make it slightly higher or lower, depending on how dark the background is). That completes the grid portion of this effect, but now we'll add text elements to make the image look more futuristic.

Step Eleven:

Press the letter "t" to switch to the Type tool, set your font in the Character palette (under the Window menu) to a san serif font, such as Helvetica or Arial, and begin typing a few short paragraphs of text. It really doesn't matter what you write (song lyrics, a poem, random words, etc.) because once you've created your type, you're going to lower the size to 3 points in the Character palette, so the type won't be readable (and that's the point). Then, click somewhere else within the image with the Type tool. Type a plus sign (+) at a large size setting, such as 30 points. Position it with the Move tool, and lower this layer's Opacity setting to 24% in the Layers palette. Duplicate this layer by pressing Command-J (PC: Control-J) and reposition your new layer, too.

Example:

Remember the DVD menu we did in the previous project? Here's the exact same grid, 3-point type blocks, and plus signs copied over into that document. I just dragged-and-dropped the "high-tech" layers from the Layers palette onto the opened DVD menu image. I raised the Opacity setting of the grid layer a bit because it was getting lost in the sky. It's amazing what a difference adding little bits of high-tech shenanigans did to the DVD menu to give it a more high-tech look.

Chapter FOUR

CLASSIC ROCK
ROCKIN' SPECIAL EFFECTS

This was just too good a chapter title to pass up. Now I know what you're thinking: "Scott, classic rock is a genre, not the name of song." Oh, if that were only true, but it's so much more—it's a genre and the title of about a dozen or so CDs (including *Classic Rock, Vol. 1*). So what makes a classic effect rock? I have no idea. In fact, I was hoping you'd know because I got so caught up with "Classic Rock" as the perfect chapter title that I honestly didn't think much beyond that. You know what, let's change the subject.

Hey, do you ever watch that TV show *Blind Date*? It's on TV right now as I'm writing this and I have to say, I think it might be rigged because some things just don't add up. For example, here's all these great-looking people out on their dates, but not once, not even once does anybody ever take their laptop computer on their date with them. How realistic is that? I mean, hello—how can they use Photoshop if they don't even have a laptop? Just how gullible do they think we are?

Clipping Mask Effect

If you've ever wanted to know how to fit (or clip) a photo inside a specific shape so that none of the photo extends beyond that shape—this is how. The project we're building here was inspired by an AMC Entertainment Card that was in my wallet (got it as a stocking stuffer). The AMC card makes great use of this technique.

Step One:

Our clipping project will be a gift card for a fictitious record store, so start by creating a new document (File>New) that's 7x5" set at 72 ppi, then add a new layer by clicking on the Create a New Layer icon at the bottom of the Layers palette. Press "d" to set your Foreground color to black, then get the Rounded Rectangle tool from the Toolbox (as shown). Go up to the Options Bar and in the group of three icons on the left, click on the third icon from the left (as shown) so the tool will create pixels, rather than a path or a shape layer. While you're in the Options Bar, set the Radius (the roundness of the corners) to 10 pixels. Now use the tool to drag out a rounded rectangle in the shape of a credit card (as shown here).

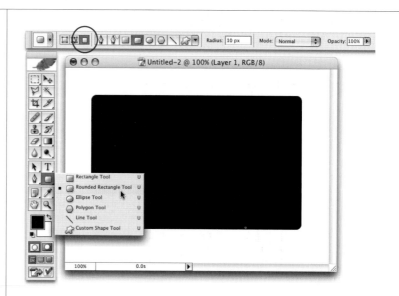

Step Two:

You're going to need to mark the horizontal center of this credit card shape. This is an easy three-step process: (1) Press Command-T (PC: Control-T) to bring up the Free Transform bounding box around your shape. (2) Press Command-R (PC: Control-R) to make your rulers visible. (3) Click directly on the top ruler and drag down a guide until it reaches the Free Transform's center point. (*Note:* If you have Snap turned on in the View menu, the guide will "snap" to the center point.) Now that Free Transform has helped you find the center, you don't need it anymore, so press the Escape key.

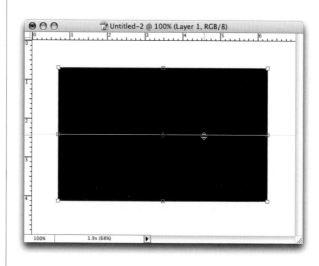

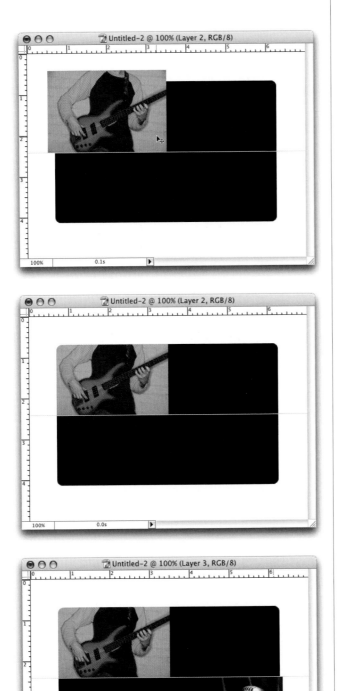

Step Three:

Open the first photo you want to "clip" into your credit card shape. Press the letter "v" to switch to the Move tool and drag the image over onto your credit card shape, and position it where you want it to appear (as shown here). If you need to resize your image, press Command-T (PC: Control-T) to bring up the Free Transform command. Use the guide to line up the bottom of the photo to the center half of the card.

Step Four:

To clip your photo inside the black credit card shape, just press Command-G (PC: Control-G) and the photo will fit neatly inside the shape (as shown here). Once it's clipped inside, if you need to reposition it, just use the Move tool. (The image will stay within the boundaries of the shape, which is one of the coolest things about clipping groups.) So that's how it's done. Now, on to the rest of the project.

Step Five:

Open another image that you want clipped and use the Move tool to drag it over onto your credit card shape and position it approximately where you want it to appear within the card (as shown here). Use the guide to line up the top of the photo to the center half of the card. Again, if you need to resize your image, use the Free Transform command.

Continued

Step Six:

Press Command-G (PC: Control-G) and the photo will now be clipped inside the shape. Later, we'll want to add a tint to this one image, but for now let's just remove the color by going under the Image menu, under Adjustments, and choosing Desaturate so the image appears in black and white (as shown here).

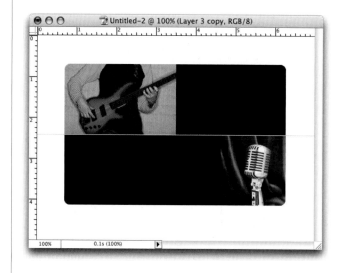

Step Seven:

Now we'll add a strip of color to the bottom of the card to the left of the microphone image. Go to the Layers palette and click the Create a New Layer icon. Press the letter "i" to switch to the Eyedropper tool, and click one of the tiny blue areas in the bass guitar strap to make that blue your Foreground color (you may need to use the Zoom tool from the Toolbox for a better view). Now press the letter "m" to switch to the Rectangular Marquee tool and drag a rectangular selection over the open area to the left of the microphone and below the bass player (as shown here). Fill that area with blue by pressing Option-Delete (PC: Alt-Backspace). Now you can deselect by pressing Command-D (PC: Control-D). Press Command-G (PC: Control-G), and the blue rectangle will now be clipped inside the shape (as shown here).

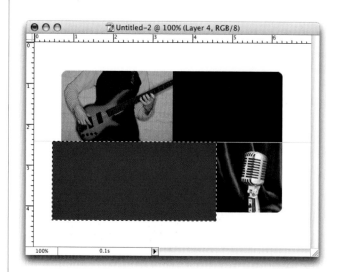

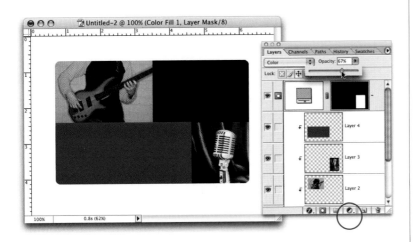

Step Eight:
Now we'll add the tint that I mentioned earlier to the microphone image. Go to the Layers palette and click on the microphone layer to make it active. Hold the Command key (PC: Control key) and click on the microphone layer to put a selection around it. Then choose Solid Color from the Create New Adjustment Layer pop-up menu at the bottom of the Layers palette (it's the fourth icon from the left). When the Color Picker appears, move your cursor outside the dialog and click on the yellow in the bass player's sleeves to make that your Foreground color. Click OK, then in the Layers palette change the blend mode of this Solid Color layer from Normal to Color. Lastly, lower the Opacity to 65% so it doesn't look so saturated.

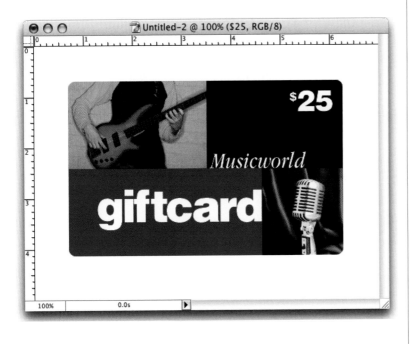

Step Nine:
It's time to add some white type with the Type tool. Click on your blue rectangle layer in the Layers palette, then press the letter "d" then "x" to set your Foreground to white. Press "t" to switch to the Type tool, then click on the image to add your type. The word "Musicworld" is set in Garamond Condensed Italic, and the word "gift-card" is set in Helvetica Black.

Continued

Step Ten:

We'll add a perspective effect to finish the project, but before we can apply the perspective, we have to get the card on a single layer. Go to the Layers palette and hide the Background layer from view by clicking on the Eye icon to the left of the Background layer. Then, go to the palette's flyout menu and choose Merge Visible (as shown here) to merge all the card layers into one single layer.

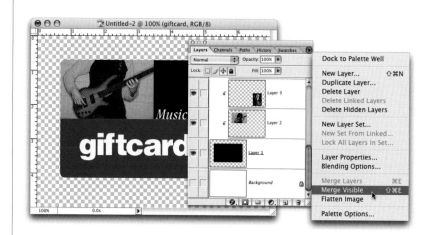

Step Eleven:

Now that the card is on one layer, press Command-T (PC: Control-T) to bring up the Free Transform command. Hold Shift-Option-Command (PC: Shift-Alt-Control), then click on the top-left transform handle and drag straight downward to create a perspective effect (as shown here). The card looks fairly stretched and distorted, but you'll fix that in the next step.

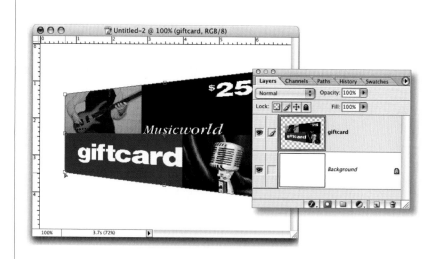

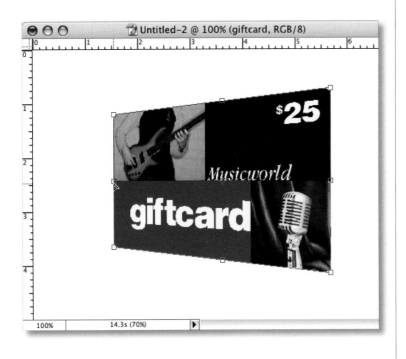

Step Twelve:
Release the keys you were holding, then click on the left-center transform handle and drag to the right to remove the stretched effect and make the card look normal again—just with a little perspective. Don't press Return (PC: Enter) quite yet.

Step Thirteen:
Now just move your cursor outside the Free Transform bounding box to the right, and click-and-drag downward to rotate the card just a little. Press Return (PC: Enter) to lock in all your Free Transform changes, completing the effect (as shown here).

Sepia Tone Effect

The sepia tone effect (popular many decades ago) has been a staple Photoshop effect for years. In the project you're going to do here (creating a CD cover for a fictitious band), you get an added twist by using a gradient map to convert your image to grayscale, which gives you a more "contrasty" grayscale conversion. Once again, the sepia part is near the end, but along the way you'll learn some other cool tricks as you build the project.

Step One:

Open the image you want to apply the sepia tone effect to.

Step Two:

After we apply the sepia tone effect later in this project, we'll use the image for a CD cover, so we'll need to set that up in the next two steps. Press the letter "m" to switch to the Rectangular Marquee tool, hold the Shift key, and draw a large perfectly square selection in the image, leaving plenty of room around the shack (as shown here).

Step Three:
Create a new blank document (File>New) that is larger than your shack selection. Then, press the letter "v" to switch to the Move tool, go back to the shack photo, and drag the selected area onto your new, larger document (as shown here).

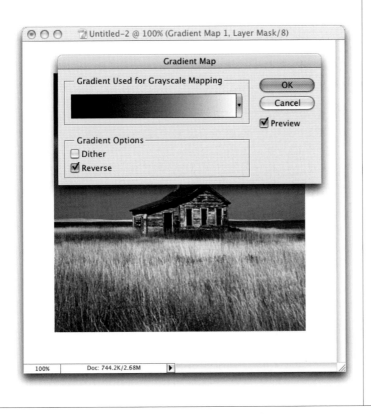

Step Four:
We're going to convert the photo to black-and-white (okay, grayscale), but we're going to do that using a gradient map so the conversion has more contrast. Set your Foreground to black by pressing the letter "d". Choose Gradient Map from the Create New Adjustment Layer pop-up menu at the bottom of the Layers palette. When the dialog appears, it immediately makes the photo look black-and-white, so just click OK. Next you'll add the sepia tone color over your black-and-white image.

Continued

Step Five:

Go under the Create New Adjustment Layer pop-up menu again, but this time choose Solid Color. When the Color Picker appears, click on the Custom button (it's right under the Cancel button). This brings up the Custom Colors dialog. In the Book pop-up menu, choose PANTONE Solid Coated and pick the color you want for your sepia tone (I chose Pantone 142) and click OK.

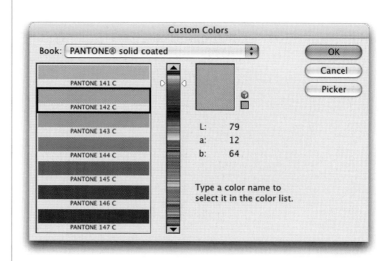

Step Six:

Once you click OK, you'll have just a solid block of color, so in the Layers palette change the layer blend mode of the Color Fill adjustment layer from Normal to Color, and you'll see the sepia tone effect shown here. Next, press the letter "m" to switch to the Rectangular Marquee tool, hold the Shift key, and draw a selection that's slightly larger than the shack photo (as shown here).

Step Seven:

Now that this selection is in place, you can add a thin stroke outside your photo. Click on the Background layer in the Layers palette to make it active, then go under the Edit menu and choose Stroke. When the Stroke dialog appears, choose black as your stroke color by clicking on the Color swatch to bring up the Color Picker, then choose 1 pixel for Width and Center for Location. Click OK to apply the stroke you see here.

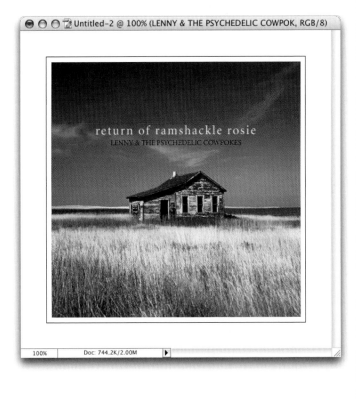

Step Eight:

To finish up the project, just add some text. Both the CD's name (all lowercase) and the band's name beneath it (all caps) are set in Minion.

Carved-in-Metal Effect

This is another one of those effects that's been around a while, even before layer styles were introduced in Photoshop 6 (we used to do this with channels "back in the old days"). The layer style version is much easier, and with the addition of the Fill opacity setting, it's even easier yet. In this project, you're going to build a poster for Z-107.5, a fictitious, classical music radio station.

Step One:

Open the object that you want to carve text or an icon into. (This technique works just as well with anything from leather to wood to a bar of soap.) Make sure your object is on its own layer. In this case, you can hold the Shift key and click on all the white background areas behind the lock using the Magic Wand tool from the Toolbox. Go under the Select menu and choose Inverse to select the lock instead of the background. Press Shift-Command-J (PC: Shift-Control-J) to cut the lock from the Background layer and copy it onto its own layer. Now, press "d" then "x" to set white as your Foreground color.

Step Two:

Press "t" to switch to the Type tool (the font used here is Times Bold), then click inside the image and create the type you want to carve into the lock. Click on the Move tool in the Toolbox. Press Command-T (PC: Control-T) to bring up the Free Transform command. Move your cursor just below the bounding box, and click-and-drag up and to the right to rotate the text so it matches the angle of the lock. Hold the Shift key and drag one of the corner points to resize your text, and then click inside the bounding box to drag it into position. When the angle, size, and position look about right, press Return (PC: Enter).

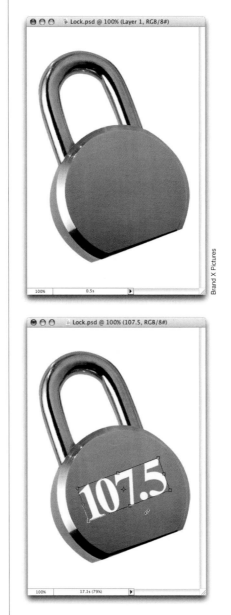

Step Three:
Choose Inner Shadow from the Add a Layer Style pop-up menu at the bottom of the Layers palette (it's the first icon from the left). When the dialog appears, increase the Opacity setting to 100% to make the shadow darker. Decrease the Distance to 3 so the letters don't appear as recessed, then click OK.

Step Four:
Go to the Layers palette and just below the Opacity field you'll see a field for Fill. Lower the amount of Fill to 0%, so the white fill is hidden, but the inner shadow stays at full strength (as shown here).

Continued

Step Five:

Go to the Layers palette, hold the Command key (PC: Control key), and click on your Type layer's thumbnail. This puts a selection around your type. Now, in the Layers palette click on the lock layer (Layer 1) to make it active, then press Command-L (PC: Control-L) to bring up Levels. In the Levels dialog, grab the bottom-right Output Levels slider and drag it a little to the left (as shown here) to darken the area inside the numbers. This makes the carving look deeper and more realistic. Don't deselect yet.

Step Six:

In the Layers palette click on the Type layer again. Then, click on the Create a New Layer icon at the bottom of the Layers palette to add a new layer above your Type layer (your selection will still be in place). Go under the Edit menu and choose Stroke. When the Stroke dialog appears, enter 1 pixel for Width, make sure the Color swatch is set to white, and choose Center for location. Click OK to apply a white stroke around your selection. Press Command-D (PC: Control-D) to deselect.

Step Seven:

In the Layers palette, lower the Opacity setting of this stroke layer to around 55%, which gives the impression of a highlight around the carved-in numbers, making it look even more realistic. At this point, the carved-into-metal effect is complete, but we're going to use the lock in a project—a poster for a classical radio station.

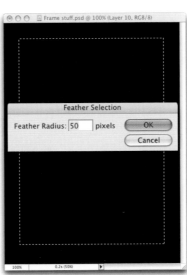

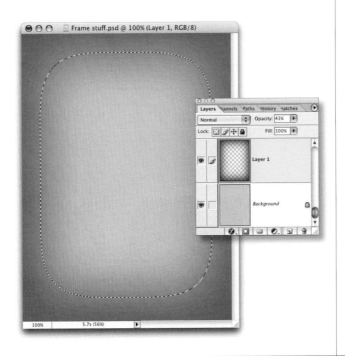

Step Eight:
Open a new document (File>New) that's 6x8" set at 72 ppi in RGB mode. Click on the Foreground color swatch in the Toolbox and pick a beige color in the Color Picker (I used R=217, G=215, B=170). Fill the background with this color by pressing Option-Delete (PC: Alt-Backspace).

Step Nine:
Now we'll add a burned-in edge effect (like we show elsewhere in this book). Click on the Create a New Layer icon in the Layers palette, then press "d" to set your Foreground color to black. Fill this new layer with black by pressing Option-Delete (PC: Alt-Backspace). Press the letter "m" to switch to the Rectangular Marquee tool and draw a selection just inside the borders of the entire image (as shown here). Go under the Select menu and choose Feather. When the dialog appears, enter 50 pixels (to soften the edges of your selection) and click OK.

Step Ten:
Press Delete (PC: Backspace) to knock a hole out of the black layer, revealing part of the Background layer. The effect will be a bit too dark, so go to the Layers palette and lower the Opacity of this layer to around 40% to give you the burned-in edge effect you see here. Press Command-D (PC: Control-D) to deselect.

Continued

Step Eleven:

Open the photo of a picture frame, and make sure that the frame is on its own layer (see Step One). Press the letter "v" to switch to the Move tool, and drag this frame onto your image with the burned-in effect (as shown here). If you need to resize the frame, press Command-T (PC: Control-T) to bring up the Free Transform command and press Command-Zero (PC: Control-Zero) to see the entire bounding box. Hold the Shift key and drag one of the corner points. Press Return (PC: Enter) to lock in your transformation. To add some depth, we'll add a drop shadow. Choose Drop Shadow from the Add a Layer Style pop-up menu at the bottom of the Layers palette. When the dialog appears, lower the Opacity to 36%, increase the Size to 6, and click OK to apply a soft shadow.

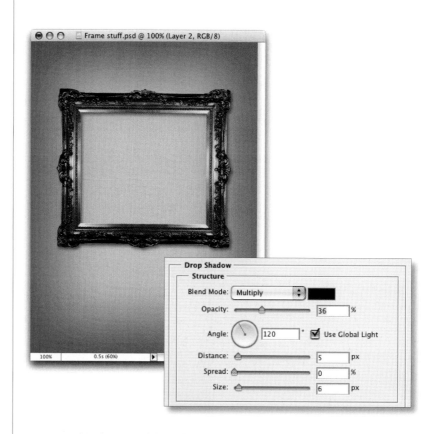

Step Twelve:

Hold the Command key (PC: Control key) and click on the Create a New Layer icon at the bottom of the Layers palette to create a new blank layer directly beneath your frame layer. Press the letter "m" to switch to the Rectangular Marquee tool and draw a rectangular selection that's a little larger than the opening of the frame. Press the letter "x" to set white as your Foreground color, then press Option-Delete (PC: Alt-Backspace) to fill your rectangular selection with white (as shown here). Deselect by pressing Command-D (PC: Control-D).

Step Thirteen:

Now back to the lock document (remember that one?). In the Layers palette, hide the Background layer from view by clicking on the Eye icon in the left-hand column of the palette. Then choose Merge Visible from the palette's flyout menu. Switch to the Move tool and drag-and-drop the lock onto your frame image. To scale it down so it fits in the frame, press Command-T (PC: Control-T) to bring up the Free Transform command, hold the Shift key, grab a corner point, and drag inward (as shown here). When the size is right, press Return (PC: Enter) to lock in your transformation.

Step Fourteen:

In the Layers palette, click on the frame layer to make it active, hold the Command key (PC: Control key), then click on the Create a New Layer icon to create a new blank layer directly beneath your frame layer. Press the letter "d" to set your Foreground color to black, and then press Shift-U until you have the Line tool (it's one of the Shape tools). In the group of three icons on the left side of the Options Bar, click on the third icon from the left so your line will be made of pixels, rather than a path or a shape layer. You're going to draw some wire as if the picture were hanging, so near the top left of your frame, click-and-drag up and to the right to draw a diagonal line. Release the mouse button, then click on the end of this line and drag down and to the right to draw another line back to the right-hand side of the frame, as shown here.

Continued

Step Fifteen:

Press Shift-U again to switch to the Custom Shape tool. Then up in the Options Bar, click on the icon next to the word "Shape" to bring up the Custom Shape Picker. In the default set of shapes, click on the one that looks like a pushpin (as shown here). Hold the Shift key, and click-and-drag out a pushpin shape at the apex of the two lines that you drew in the previous step (as shown here).

Step Sixteen:

The two lines and pushpin need a drop shadow, so choose Drop Shadow from the Add a Layer Style pop-up menu at the bottom of the Layers palette. When the dialog appears, lower the Opacity to 26% and the Size to 3 so the shadow is less blurry. Click OK to apply your shadow (as shown here).

Step Seventeen:
To finish the project, we'll just add a black bar at the bottom along with some type, so create a new layer, then use the Rectangular Marquee tool to draw a rectangular selection at the bottom of your image area. Fill this rectangle with black by pressing Option-Delete (PC: Alt-Backspace), then deselect by pressing Command-D (PC: Control-D). All the type is set in one font—Trajan Pro (which comes with Photoshop CS)—using the Type tool and Character palette.

Soft-Edged Vignette

Designers have been using this technique probably since Photoshop version 1.0, and it's still just as popular today. It's generally used for creating a sense of elegance for an image, so it's often used in high-end jewelry ads, golf course ads for high-priced homes and condos, or just about anything that could use that luxurious look.

Step One:

Open the photo that you want to apply the soft-edged vignette effect to.

Step Two:

Press the letter "m" to switch to the Rectangular Marquee tool, and draw a large rectangular selection just inside the border of your entire photo (as shown here), leaving a 1/2" to 3/4" border outside your selection.

Step Three:

To soften the edges of your selection, go under the Select menu and choose Feather. In this case, you'll enter 10 pixels (if you want a softer, wider edge, use a higher number—the higher the Feather Radius, the softer the edge), and click OK. You'll see the corners of your selection become rounded (reflected in the capture shown in the next step).

Step Four:

Go under the Select menu and choose Inverse. That way, that little border area around the photo now becomes the area that's selected. Press the letter "d" to make your Background color white, then press Delete (PC: Backspace) to delete those edge areas, which gives you the soft-edged effect you see here. Press Command-D (PC: Control-D) to deselect. Now you'll put that soft-edged photo to work in an ad for a high-rise beach condo.

Step Five:

Create a new blank document (File>New) that's 6x8" set at 72 ppi in RGB mode, then go back to the pool photo, press the letter "v" to switch to the Move tool, and click-and-drag the photo onto your new document. Press Command-T (PC: Control-T) to bring up the Free Transform command. Hold the Shift key, grab a corner point, and drag inward to scale your photo down so it fits easily within the image area (as shown above), then press Return (PC: Enter) to lock in your transformation. *Tip*: If you can't reach the Free Transform handles, press Command-Zero (PC: Control-Zero) and the window will resize so you can see them.

Step Six:

Now all you have to do is use the Type tool and the Character palette to add some text (and add the photo of the high-rise beach condo, which is downloadable at www.scottkelbybooks.com/classicphotos). The headline text is set in the font Papyrus, as is the phone number. The condo name (a tribute to *Seinfeld*) is set in CG Phenix American (the "got milk?" font), and the body copy is set in Adobe Caslon Pro (which comes with Photoshop CS).

Torn Edge Effect

If there's ever been an effect that was a real classic—this is it. It's supposed to look like you've ripped out the middle of a photo to reveal what's beneath it (although you'll often see this effect with nothing but white behind the tear). You find this used in print ads, on the Web, on TV, and in posters. However, we're going to take this technique one step further, adding a white edge to your rip, to make it look even more realistic.

Step One:
Open the photo you want to appear inside your torn edge. In other words, this photo will be revealed when you tear a chunk out of the photo that you'll place on the layer above it in the next step (if that makes any sense—and I can't swear that it does, even to me).

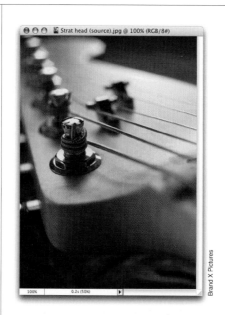

Step Two:
Now open the photo that you want to apply the tear to—in this case a piece of sheet music. Press the letter "v" to switch to the Move tool, and click-and-drag this sheet music image on top of your guitar image. It will appear on its own layer above the guitar photo (as shown here).

Step Three:

Press the letter "L" to switch to the Lasso tool and draw a loose, jaggy selection around the area you want "torn away" (as shown here). The best way to make this look realistic is to draw the selection very quickly. If you spend too much time drawing it, it will look "planned" and "stiff," so just click and think jaggy. (By the way, this would be an ideal time for a Will Smith "Gettin' Jaggy With It" pun, but I would never stoop to that form of desperate humor. That comes later, in Chapter 9.)

Step Four:

Now press Delete (PC: Backspace) to knock a hole out of your sheet music layer, revealing the guitar image on the layer beneath it. Now you can deselect by pressing Command-D (PC: Control-D).

Continued

Step Five:

To add a feeling of depth between the sheet music layer and the guitar layer, choose Outer Glow from the Add a Layer Style pop-up menu at the bottom of the Layers palette. When the dialog appears (shown here), change the Blend Mode pop-up menu from Screen to Normal, and then click on the beige color swatch and change the glow color to black in the Color Picker. Then, increase the Size to 16 to make the glow larger and softer. Click OK to apply this black glow inside your sheet music (as shown here). Next, we'll pull a trick that makes the tear look more realistic.

Step Six:

Take the Lasso tool and draw another jaggy selection that's just a tiny bit bigger than the one you originally drew back in Step Three (as shown here). You want to loosely trace the edge of the first rip—not exactly, mind you—just kind of like the first rip, but a little looser and let it extend a tiny bit into the sheet music, just like what you see here.

Step Seven:

Once your new selection is in place, press Command-L (PC: Control-L) to bring up Levels. Grab the bottom-left Output Levels slider and drag it almost all the way to the right (as shown here), to make your paper rip look almost white, then click OK. Press Command-D (PC: Control-D) to deselect. See how much more realistic the tear looks with that extra white area? Ahhh, it's the little things, isn't it? Well, that's the tear effect—now let's use it in a poster.

Step Eight:

Go under the Image menu and choose Canvas Size. First, make sure the Relative checkbox is turned on, then enter 1 inch for both Width and Height, and choose Black from the Canvas Extension Color pop-up menu (as shown here).

Continued

Step Nine:

When you click OK, a black border is added around your photo (as shown here). Next, you'll need to add a little more space at the bottom of the poster for the headline and the music school's name, so go back under the Image menu and choose Canvas Size. For Height enter .75 inches with the Relative checkbox turned on, and in the Anchor grid, click the top-center square (this tells Photoshop to add the extra canvas size only to the bottom, by anchoring your image to the top of the document).

Step Ten:
When you click OK, three-quarters of an inch of black border is added to the bottom of your poster, enough for you to add some type with the Type tool. The headline is set in the font Helvetica Black (with the horizontal scaling set to 120% in the Character palette to make the letters look wider). The Web address is set in the same font. The name of the school is set in Trajan Pro, which comes with Photoshop CS.

Adding Glints

I hate to admit it, but this is one of my favorite effects because it's actually a lot of fun applying it (try it once, and pretty soon you'll be applying glints to things that have no business having glints). What's nice is that the "glint" brush tip is already within Photoshop, you just have to find it, load it, and then add one little twist (in Step Four) that will make all the difference.

Step One:

Open your background image that has an object that you want to add glints to (in this example, we're going to add glints to a diner's jukebox, then we're going to use that in a DVD menu). Press the letter "d" then "x" to set your Foreground to white.

Brand X Pictures

Step Two:

Press the letter "b" to switch to the Brush tool, then click on the icon next to the word "Brush" in the Options Bar to bring up the Brush Picker. In the Brush Picker's flyout menu, choose Assorted Brushes (as shown here). When the dialog appears, click the Append button and these brushes will be loaded to your default set of brushes in the Picker. Scroll down in the Picker until you see the 48-pixel brush that looks like an "X" and click on it to select it (as shown here).

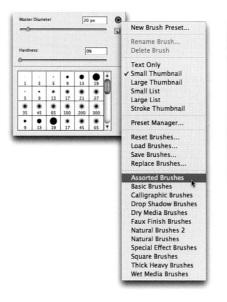

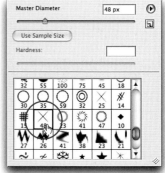

Step Three:

Create a new blank layer by clicking on the Create a New Layer icon at the bottom of the Layers palette. Then take the Brush tool and click once directly over the areas where you want to add a glint (I usually click over areas that already have a bright highlight). Don't paint—just click and an "X" glint will be added. (In the example shown here, I clicked in five different spots—four on the jukebox and one on a shiny spot on the spoon.)

Step Four:

Once your glints are in place, go up to the Brush Picker again, scroll back up toward the top, and choose the 17-pixel, soft-edged brush (as shown here). Click once in the center of each glint to enhance the effect (as shown).

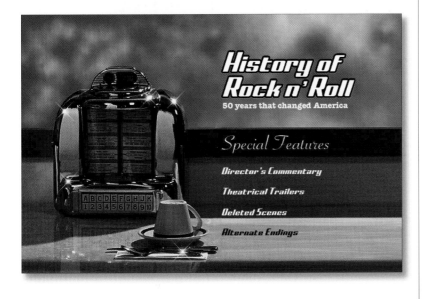

Step Five:

Now that your glints are in place, it's time to finish off the DVD menu by adding some text with the Type tool. The title and features are set in the font Bullet (from House Industries). I added a black stroke to the DVD's title by choosing Stroke from the Add a Layer Style pop-up menu at the bottom of the Layers palette. Just change the stroke color from red to black by clicking on the Color swatch and choosing black in the Color Picker, and then click OK. The "50 years" slogan is set in the font Americana Bold, and the "Special Features" text is set in the font Savoye.

Chapter

FIVE

TIME PASSAGES
TIMELESS EFFECTS

Okay, remember Al Stewart? (No, he's not a racecar driver.) He had a hit with the song "Time Passages," which was a decent song, but it paled in comparison to his hit "Year of the Cat." Unfortunately, there was no easy way to work "Year of the Cat" in as a chapter title, so I had to go with a backup plan and use his song "Time Passages," which fits better for a chapter on some of Photoshop's timeless special effects. There was always one thing that bothered me about "Year of the Cat" anyway. The line where he sings, "She comes in incense and patchouli." I have to be honest. I have no idea what in the wide world of sports "patchouli" even is. I always assumed it was some sort of pasta, but when I started thinking about it, I couldn't imagine why she'd come in wearing pasta. Hey, I've worn pasta numerous times, but never, never with incense. Think about it—incense and pasta. Not me, my friend. Either way, what does this all have to do with a chapter on timeless techniques? Not a whole bunch, but I have to admit, I'm really glad to have that whole patchouli thing off my chest.

Changing the Color of an Object

There's a number of different techniques for changing the color of an object, but this particular version gives you the most flexibility because it uses an adjustment layer. This way, if you decide you want to change the color again, it just takes a few seconds—just double-click on the adjustment layer in the Layers palette and pick a new shade. Check it out!

Step One:
Open the image that has an object whose color you want to change. In this case, we're building a spread inside a brochure, and our fictitious client wants the guitar to be blue, instead of its current cream color.

Step Two:
Choose Hue/Saturation from the Create New Adjustment Layer pop-up menu at the bottom of the Layers palette. When the Hue/Saturation dialog appears (shown here), click the Colorize checkbox. Move the Hue slider to find the color you want (in this case, slide the Hue slider to 215 to set a nice blue hue over the entire image and increase the Saturation to around 33). Click OK.

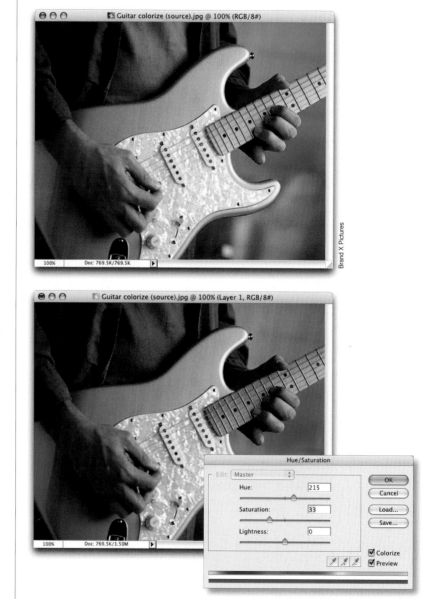

Step Three:

In the Layers palette you'll see the adjustment layer appear above your Background layer, and it will have a white layer mask thumbnail to the right of it. Click once directly on this layer mask thumbnail to select it. Press "x" until your Foreground color toggles to black. Then press Option-Delete (PC: Alt-Backspace) to fill this mask with black. When you do this, the blue tint is hidden (masked) from view.

Step Four:

Press "x" again to toggle your Foreground color to white. Press "b" to access the Brush tool. Click on the icon next to the word "Brush" in the Options Bar to bring up the Brush Picker, and choose a medium-sized, hard-edged brush. Begin painting over the body of the guitar, and as you paint, a blue version will be revealed. If you make a mistake—no sweat—just toggle your Foreground color back to black by pressing "x" again and paint over the mistake; the original color will return in that area. That's part of the beauty of using an adjustment layer.

Step Five:

While you're painting, you'll have to shrink the brush size when you come to tight areas. You can shrink the brush by pressing the Left Bracket key ([) on the keyboard. Continue painting until the entire guitar body is blue. If your client suddenly decides that he wants the guitar to be a different color, simply double-click on the Hue/Saturation thumbnail in the Layers palette to bring up the Hue/Saturation dialog. Move the Hue slider until you get the color you want.

Continued

Step Six:

Now we're going to use the image in a brochure layout, but first we have to flatten the image, so go to the Layers palette's flyout menu and choose Flatten Image. Click the Background color swatch in the Toolbox and pick a light gray in the Color Picker. The photo is 8 inches wide, so go under the Image menu and choose Canvas Size. In the dialog, turn on the Relative checkbox, then enter 8 inches for Width. In the Anchor grid, click the left-center square, so the extra canvas area will be added to the right of your image. In the Canvas Extension Color pop-up menu choose Background, then click OK. Now go under the Window menu and choose Character palette. Press the letter "t" to switch to the Type tool and add your type (we selected Helvetica Regular and Helvetica Bold using the Character palette).

Canvas Size

Current Size: 770.8K
Width: 8.014 inches
Height: 6.333 inches

OK
Cancel

New Size: 1.50M

Width: 8   inches
Height: 0   inches
☑ Relative
Anchor:

Canvas extension color: Background

"The quality, craftmanship, and design of our guitars has made them a legend around the world."

MICHAEL REED
PRODUCT MANAGER

TV Scan Lines

This is an incredibly popular technique for making an image look as though it's been viewed on a TV screen (because when photographed in real life, TV screens often show a series of horizontal lines, called scan lines). It's very popular for creating high-tech effects, video walls, and dozens of other uses. In the project below, you're going to re-create the look of the U.S. Army's TV spots for a free Special Forces video offer—in which they used a scan lines effect for the high-tech feel of military binoculars.

Step One:
Open the photo that you want to apply a scan lines effect to. Go to the Layers palette and create a new layer by clicking on the Create a New Layer icon at the bottom of the Layers palette.

Step Two:
Press the letter "m" to switch to the Rectangular Marquee tool and drag a thin horizontal selection at the top of your image (as shown). Click your Foreground color swatch to select a dark green in the Color Picker (I used R=57, G=65, B=31), and fill your selection with this dark green color by pressing Option-Delete (PC: Alt-Backspace). Stay on the same layer and do the exact same thing at the bottom of the image area (so it looks like the image shown here). Then deselect by pressing Command-D (PC: Control-D).

Continued

Step Three:

Click on the Create a New Layer icon again to create another new layer, and in the Layers palette drag it below your green bars layer. You're going to do the same thing as in Step Two—draw a thin horizontal selection, but make it start just below your top green bar and make it smaller. Fill this bar with a muddy yellow-orange color (I used R=169, G=136, B=0) by clicking the Foreground color swatch in the Toolbox and pressing Option-Delete (PC: Alt-Backspace). Do the same thing at the bottom (as shown here). Press Command-D (PC: Control-D) to deselect.

Step Four:

In the Layers palette, click on the green bars layer, and create another new layer above it by clicking on the Create a New Layer icon. Press the letter "d" to set your Foreground color to black, then press Option-Delete (PC: Alt-Backspace) to fill this layer with black. Next, lower the Opacity of this black layer to 50% in the Layers palette so you can see the rest of your image through it. Now press the letter "x" to set your Foreground color to white.

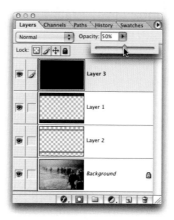

Step Five:

In the Army TV spot, they used a very clever trick to make it look like you were seeing this scene through military field binoculars. Here's how it's done: First, select the Rounded Rectangle tool from the Toolbox (as shown here), then go to the Options Bar and click on the third icon from the left in the group of three icons near the left side (to create pixels, rather than a shape layer or a path).

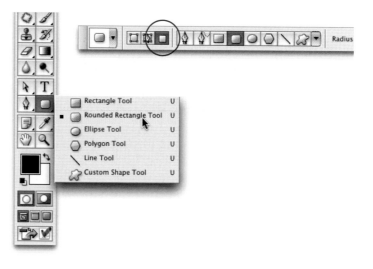

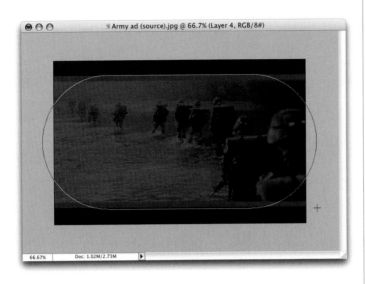

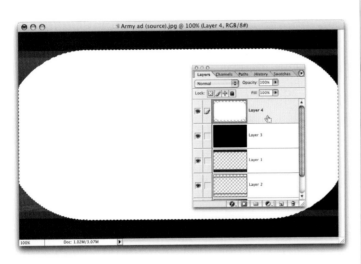

Step Six:

Click the Create a New Layer icon in the Layers palette to create another new layer, but before you use the Rounded Rectangle tool, go to the Options Bar and set the Radius (the roundness of the corners) to 200 pixels. Drag out the right-hand corner of your document window so you can see the gray canvas area outside your image area. Now, drag out a huge pill shape (like the one shown here), with the top and bottom of the pill extending into the gold area, and the ends extending off the sides a bit. To help you position the shape, press the Spacebar after you start dragging it out and reposition it as you drag. Release the Spacebar to finish drawing your shape. When you release the mouse button, your huge pill shape will be filled with white.

Step Seven:

Next, hold the Command key (PC: Control key), go to the Layers palette, and click on the white pill layer to put a selection around the pill shape. You only need this shape to create a selection, and now that you have it, drag this white shape layer into the Trash icon in the Layers palette to delete it.

Step Eight:

Don't deselect yet, but go to the Layers palette, click on the black-filled layer, and raise its Opacity back to 100%. Go under the Select menu and choose Feather. When the dialog appears, enter 10 pixels for the Feather Radius (to soften the edges of your pill-shaped selection) and click OK. Now press Delete (PC: Backspace) to knock a soft-edged pill shape out of your black layer, which creates the first part of the binocular look. Now you can deselect using Command-D (PC: Control-D).

Continued

Step Nine:

Now for the scan lines (finally!). In the Layers palette, drag your black binoculars layer beneath the yellow-orange bars layer, then click the Create a New Layer icon to add a new blank layer above it. Click the Foreground color swatch to select a medium gray from the Color Picker, and fill this layer with gray by pressing Option-Delete (PC: Alt-Backspace). Next, go under the Filter menu, under Sketch, and choose Halftone Pattern. When the dialog appears (shown here), set the Size to 1, Contrast to 5, and for Pattern Type choose Line.

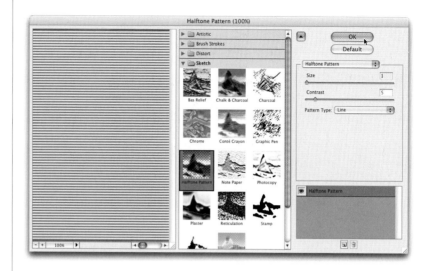

Step Ten:

Click OK and a pattern of lines is applied to your gray layer. Now, to get those lines to blend into your binocular-shaped image, in the Layers palette change the blend mode of this gray layer from Normal to Multiply (as shown) and lower the Opacity of this layer to around 40% to give you the scan lines effect. So that's basically it—create a gray layer, run the Halftone Pattern filter set to Lines, change the layer blend mode to Multiply, and lower the Opacity. Now for some high-tech goodies.

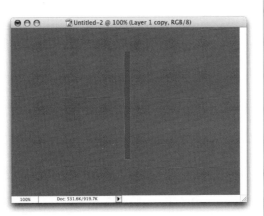

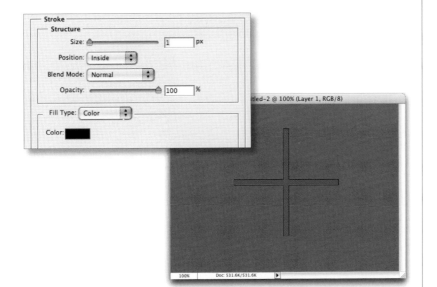

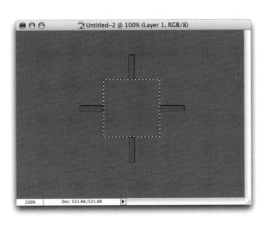

Step Eleven:

To create the center of the binoculars, we created a new document from the File menu. Click the Foreground color swatch in the Toolbox, pick a gray color, and press Option-Delete (PC: Alt-Backspace) to fill the background to help you see the effect better as you create it. Then create a new layer by clicking the Create a New Layer icon in the Layers palette. Press the letter "m" to switch to the Rectangular Marquee tool and draw a tall vertical selection. Click the Foreground color swatch in the Toolbox and select a red color. Fill the selection with red by pressing Option-Delete (PC: Alt-Backspace), and press Command-D (PC: Control-D) to deselect.

Step Twelve:

Now draw another rectangle, but make this one horizontal and fill it with red too using Option-Delete (PC: Alt-Backspace), making a large plus sign (like the one shown here). Press Command-D (PC: Control-D) to deselect. Next, choose Stroke from the Add a Layer Style pop-up menu at the bottom of the Layers palette. Set the Size to 1, Position to Inside, click the Color swatch and select black in the Color Picker, and click OK.

Step Thirteen:

Using the Rectangular Marquee tool, hold the Shift key, and draw a square selection over the center of the plus sign (as shown here), then press Delete (PC: Backspace) to knock out a portion of the plus sign. (The stroke will automatically adjust itself to fit the new shape.) Press Command-D (PC: Control-D) to deselect.

Continued

Step Fourteen:

Click the Create a New Layer icon in the Layers palette to create a new blank layer. Press Shift-M to switch to the Elliptical Marquee tool in the Toolbox, hold the Shift key, and draw a circular selection that fills the space you just knocked out. Press "d" then "x" to set your Foreground color to white, and press Option-Delete (PC: Alt-Backspace) to fill this circular selection with white. Lower the Opacity of this layer to 40% in the Layers palette. Then Press Command-D (PC: Control-D) to deselect.

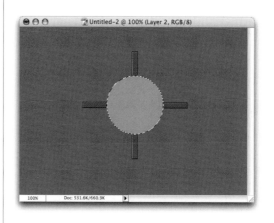

Step Fifteen:

Click the Create a New Layer icon in the Layers palette to add another new layer. This time draw another circular selection that is about half as big as the first circle. Press "d" to set your Foreground color to black, and fill this circle with black by pressing Option-Delete (PC: Alt-Backspace). Then lower the Opacity of this layer to 40% in the Layers palette, and deselect using Command-D (PC: Control-D).

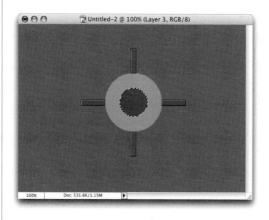

Step Sixteen:

Add yet another new layer by clicking the Create a New Layer icon in the Layers palette. Press Shift-U until you've selected the Line tool (it's one of the Shape tools in the Toolbox). In the Options Bar, set the Weight to 1 pixel, then hold the Shift key and draw a straight line between the two horizontal red rectangles. Do the same between the two vertical rectangles (as shown here).

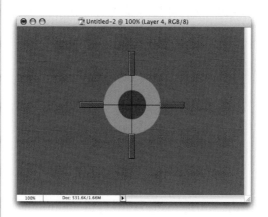

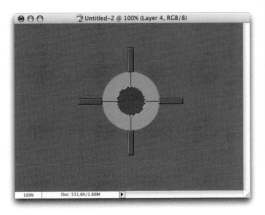

Step Seventeen:
Don't change layers, but hold the Command key (PC: Control key), and in the Layers palette click on the small black circle layer to put a selection around it. Press Delete (PC: Backspace) to knock a hole out of the two black lines. Deselect by pressing Command-D (PC: Control-D). Now you're ready to bring this into your main document.

Step Eighteen:
In the Layers palette, link all the "binocular sight" layers (omitting the Background layer) by clicking in the second column beside each layer's name. Now click on the center circle with the Move tool and drag the whole shebang over onto your scan lines document. Click on the red lines layer in the Layers palette and lower the Fill to around 20%.

Step Nineteen:
Finally, go to the Layers palette and drag the scan lines layer above the "binocular target" layers, so they have scan lines over them as well. To finish the project, you can add three other elements: (1) Set the headline type to the font Helvetica Bold, with a slight gold outer glow behind it (choose Outer Glow in the Add a Layer Style pop-up menu at the bottom of the Layers palette). (2) Add some random red coordinates in the lower-right corner using the font Helvetica Regular. (3) On the left center, I drew a 2-point vertical line with the Line tool and added a few 1-point horizontal lines, like a ruler. I also added some vertical Helvetica text with the Type tool. These seem silly, but they make a big difference in this project (but obviously, they're not necessary for the scan lines effect—it just happens to work wonderfully for the Army ad).

Speed Blur

This is another one of those effects you see everywhere—a massive zoom blur. Creating this effect is not as obvious as it might seem because there's no "zoom" filter. Instead, you use the zoom setting of the Radial Blur filter. In this project you'll create an ad for an insurance company that caters to drivers with a lead foot.

Step One:
Open the photo you want to apply a speed blur effect to. (In this case, we're using a photo of a lonely country road. You'll lose the "lonely country" part when you apply the effect.)

Step Two:
Go under the Filter menu, under Blur, and choose Radial Blur. Set the Amount to 100 and the Blur Method to Zoom.

Step Three:
Click OK and the classic speed blur effect is applied to your photo. Now, we'll take it a step further by using the photo in an ad layout.

Step Four:
You're going to need to add some room beneath the photo so you can add some body copy. Go under the Image menu and choose Canvas Size. Click the Relative checkbox, then for Height enter 2 inches. In the Anchor grid, click the top-center square so the 2 inches of extra canvas area will be added below the photo, and choose White in the Canvas Extension Color pop-up menu. Click OK to add the extra white space (as shown here).

Step Five:
Next you're going to add a sign in front of your speedy road, so open the sign image (you can download this image along with the rest of the photos used in this book from scottkelbybooks.com/classicphotos). Once open, press the letter "w" to switch to the Magic Wand tool and click once in the white background area, then go under the Select menu and choose Inverse, which will put a selection around the sign (as shown here).

Continued

Step Six:

Press the letter "v" to switch to the Move tool, and then click-and-drag the selected sign into your road image. The sign will be a bit too big, so press Command-T (PC: Control-T) to bring up Free Transform. Hold the Shift key, click on a corner point of the bounding box, and drag inward to scale your sign down to size (as shown here). Press Return (PC: Enter) to lock in your transformation. Next, you'll add a shadow to create some depth between the sign and the road.

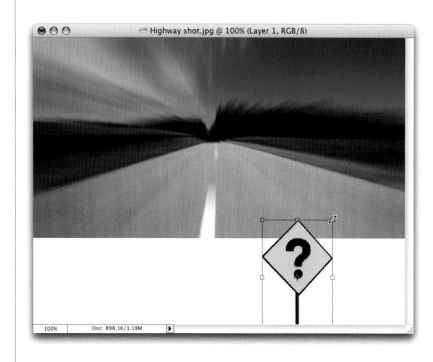

Step Seven:

Choose Drop Shadow from the Add a Layer Style pop-up menu at the bottom of the Layers palette. When the dialog appears, move your cursor outside the dialog into your image area, and click-and-drag the shadow a bit to the left (as shown here). Lower the Opacity of the shadow to around 30% in the Drop Shadow dialog and click OK. Press the letter "t" to switch to the Type tool and add a headline on the photo using a font such as Helvetica Bold (in other words, Arial Bold will do).

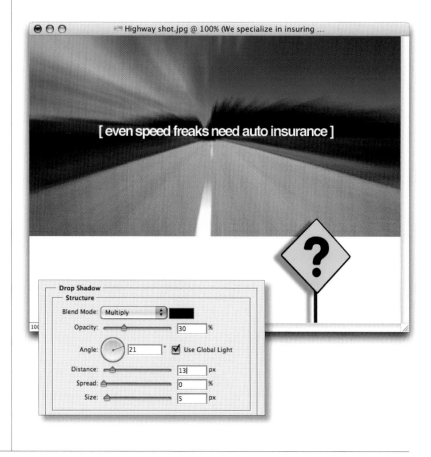

To complete the ad, you just need to add a subhead and some body copy. The "Got speeding tickets..." is set in the font Minion, and the text right below it is in Minion Italic. "Citation Insurance" is set in Optima (from Adobe) and the text below it is in Helvetica. The little logo shape above "Citation Insurance" is one of Photoshop's built-in custom shapes—I just erased the bottom of the circle. Pretty sneaky, eh?

Filter Edge Effects

If you want to add some visual interest to the edges of your photos, this is a very effective technique. It's quick, simple, and because it uses filters, it's very flexible—if you want a different look, just try the technique using different filters. In this project, we'll create an edge effect, and then place the final image into a calendar layout.

Step One:
Open the photo you want to apply an edge effect to.

Step Two:
Press the letter "m" to switch to the Rectangular Marquee tool and draw a rectangular selection about 1" inside the border of your image (as shown here).

Step Three:

Go near the bottom of the Toolbox and click on the Quick Mask icon (as shown here) to enter Quick Mask mode. (Incidentally, you can also press the letter "q" to enter Quick Mask mode.) In the next step, you'll apply an effect to the edge, and because you're in Quick Mask mode, you'll get a preview of how the edge will look before you apply it.

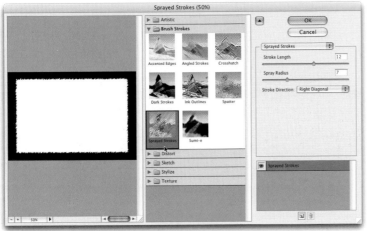

Step Four:

Go under the Filter menu and choose Filter Gallery. In the middle of the Filter Gallery dialog, click on the Brush Strokes folder, then from the list of filters that appears, choose Sprayed Strokes (as shown). Set the Stroke Length to 12, Spray Radius to 7, and for Stroke Direction choose Right Diagonal to create a nice ragged edge. Don't click OK yet.

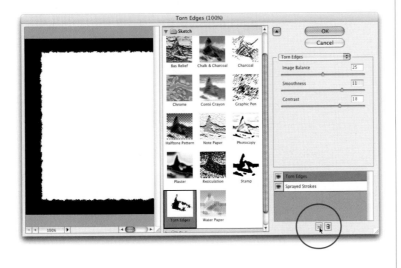

Step Five:

At the bottom right-hand side of the Filter Gallery you'll find two icons that look like the Layers palette's New Layer icon and the Trash icon. Click on the one that looks like the New Layer icon (the New Effect Layer icon) to add another filter (this actually duplicates the Sprayed Strokes filter, but you'll change that next). Go back to the center column and click on the Sketch folder to reveal its filters. Click on Torn Edges, then set the Image Balance to 25, Smoothness to 11, and Contrast to 18, and then click OK.

Continued

Step Six:

Once you click OK, you'll see that the edges of your Quick Mask are now somewhat jagged and torn (as shown here).

Step Seven:

Go to the Toolbox and click the icon to the left of the Quick Mask icon (or better yet, just press the letter "q") to return to Standard mode. When you do this, the jagged edge selection you created with the Filter Gallery will appear around your image. While the selection is in place, go under the Select menu and choose Inverse. That way, everything outside your main image is now selected (as shown here).

Step Eight:

Now press the letter "d" to set your Background color to white and then press Delete (PC: Backspace) to erase everything around your selection, leaving you with your own custom edge effect (as shown here). Now you can deselect by pressing Command-D (PC: Control-D). Now that you have the edge effect, let's do something cool—let's use it in a calendar. You'll start by simply expanding the canvas area downward, where you'll add your calendar dates.

Step Nine:
Go under the Image menu and choose Canvas Size. As for how much space to add, add approximately as much space as the current document's height (so if your image is 6 inches high, add another 6 inches of canvas size). Click the Relative checkbox and in the Height field enter 6 inches. For the Anchor position, click in the top-center square of the grid so the canvas area will be added below your photo, and of course, for the Background Extension Color, choose White from the pop-up menu, then click OK.

isla del sol at sunset   *catherine frank*

Step Ten:
The rest is simply adding your calendar dates and text. The captions under the photo are in the font Cochin Italic (from Adobe). The month and the days of the week are set in Copperplate Gothic (also from Adobe). The dates are set in the font CG Phenix American. The rest are just some lines I added between the dates using the Line tool. By the way, when you're setting your dates, most calendars set the days using right justification so the letters line up much easier—just a tip from someone who learned the hard way. Here's the final calendar with the edge effect up top.

Painted Edge Effects

Outer edge effects are particularly popular right now because they add the power of "presentation" to our photos. This particular version makes use of Photoshop's built-in brushes to paint an edge around your photo—but don't worry, Photoshop will do most of the hard work for you.

Step One:
Open the document that you want to add a custom black edge effect to. Press Command-A (PC: Control-A) to put a selection around the entire image (as shown here).

Step Two:
Press Shift-Command-J (PC: Shift-Control-J) to cut your photo off the Background layer and copy it onto its own layer (as shown here).

Step Three:
To add this black edge you'll need to have some open space around your photo to accommodate it, so go under the Image menu and choose Canvas Size. Click the Relative checkbox, then enter 2 inches for both the Width and Height, and for Canvas Extension Color choose White in the pop-up menu. Click OK to add 2 inches of white space around your photo.

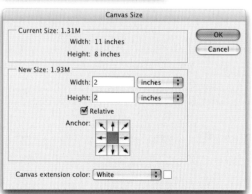

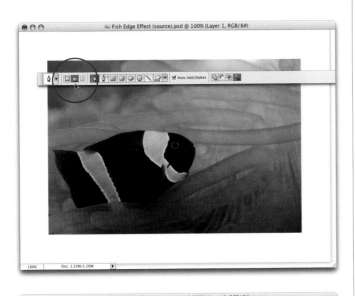

Step Four:
Press the letter "p" to switch to the Pen tool and then go up to the Options Bar and click on the second icon in the group of three icons near the left (as shown here), which makes the Pen tool draw a path, rather than a shape layer. This is important because you'll need a path for this particular technique.

Step Five:
Take the Pen tool and click once on the bottom-left corner of the photo. Hold the Shift key, then move your cursor to the top-left corner of the photo and click once. This draws a straight path up the left side of your photo. Now move your cursor to the top-right corner of your photo and click once to draw a straight path to there. Continue this until you have a path around your entire photo (as shown here).

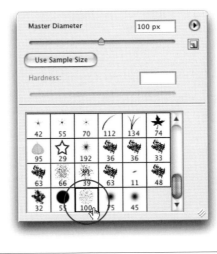

Step Six:
Now press the letter "b" to switch to the Brush tool, then go up to the Options Bar and click on the icon next to the word "Brush" to bring up the Brush Picker. Scroll to the bottom of the Picker, and from the default set of brushes, choose the 100-pixel Rough Round Bristle brush. (*Note:* For high-res, 300-ppi images, use the Master Diameter slider to increase the size of this brush to 250 pixels.)

Continued

Step Seven:

Go to the Layers palette and create a new layer by clicking on the Create a New Layer icon at the bottom of the Layers palette.

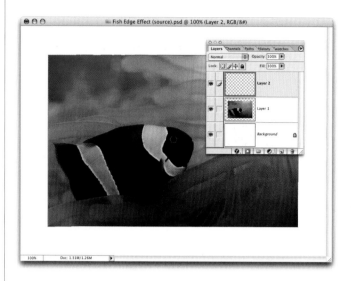

Step Eight:

Go to the Paths palette (you'll see your path highlighted here, named "Work Path" by default). From the Paths palette's flyout menu, choose Stroke Path.

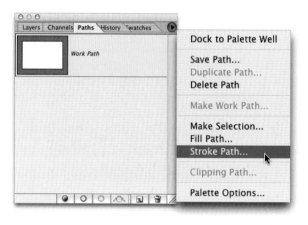

Step Nine:

When the Stroke Path dialog appears, from the Tool pop-up menu choose Brush and turn on the Simulate Pressure checkbox (as shown here). It's important to turn on Simulate Pressure so the stroke is varied as it is applied, starting with a small stroke and getting larger as it progresses around your photo. It's this checkbox that makes all the difference.

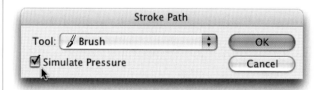

Step Ten:

When you click OK in the Stroke Path dialog, that 100-pixel Rough Round Bristle brush traces right around your path (as shown here) and the size is varied as it paints—starting small, going to full size, and then getting small again at the end of the path, creating a very cool effect except for two things: (1) The ripped edge extends into your photo area, and (2) the edge isn't solid black, and parts of it are dropping out to transparent. But you'll fix that next.

Step Eleven:

We'll deal with the second problem first. To get rid of the dropout problem, just duplicate the edge layer by pressing Command-J (PC: Control-J). See, that was easy—it's fixed. If you think that was easy, wait until you read Step Twelve.

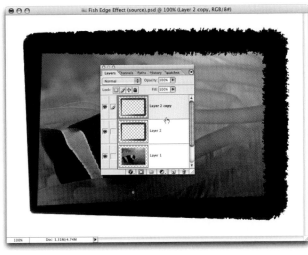

Step Twelve:

To fix the first problem (the edge extending into the photo), just go to the Layers palette and drag the fish layer above the two brush stroke layers so it's at the top of the stack. That's it—you're done, bunky! (*Note:* This is a great technique to experiment with—try it again but with different brush tips.)

Fitting Your Image into Their Sign

This is actually somewhat of a collage technique because you're taking an image you create and you're placing it into an existing image. In this example, you're going to build a sign (well, more like a poster), and you're going to place it realistically over a sign that appears in a photograph. The trick is the sign is not perfectly perpendicular to the viewer (which would be too easy); instead, the sign is on an odd angle, but once you learn this technique, even that becomes easy!

Step One:

We're going to start by creating the poster that we'll later put into another photo of a sign. Create a new document (File>New) that is 5x6³/₄". Click the Foreground color swatch in the Toolbox to select a light beige from the Color Picker (I used R=232, G=219, B=159), and fill your document with this beige color by pressing Option-Delete (PC: Alt-Backspace). Now, open the object you want on this background (in our case it's an entryway, as shown here).

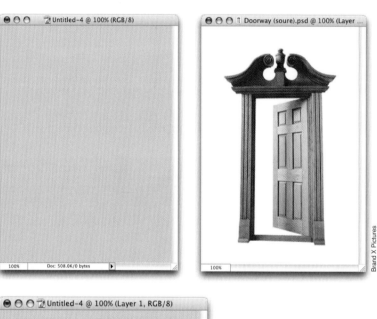

Step Two:

Select just the entryway by pressing the letter "w" to switch to the Magic Wand tool, holding the Shift key, and clicking on all the white background areas. Then choose Inverse from the Select menu. Press the letter "v" to switch to the Move tool and drag the entryway onto your beige background (as shown here). Now, go to the Layers palette, hold the Command key (PC: Control key) and click on the Create a New Layer icon. This creates a layer directly beneath the entryway layer.

Step Three:

Now you're going to add a black area behind the open door, so press the letter "m" to switch to the Rectangular Marquee tool and draw a rectangular selection that is just slightly larger than the door opening (as shown). Press the letter "d" to set your Foreground color to black and press Option-Delete (PC: Alt-Backspace) to fill your selection with black (as shown here). You can deselect by pressing Command-D (PC: Control-D). Now let's use a burned-in portrait effect.

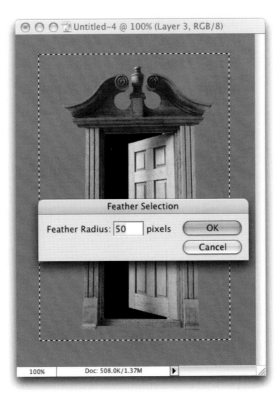

Step Four:

In the Layers palette, click on the Background layer, then click on the Create a New Layer icon to add a new layer above your Background layer. Click the Foreground color swatch in the Toolbox to select a darker beige (I used R=176, G=165, B=113), and fill this layer with that color by pressing Option-Delete (PC: Alt-Backspace). Using the Rectangular Marquee tool, draw a selection that is approximately a half-inch inside the borders of your image area (as shown here). Then go under the Select menu and choose Feather. Enter 50 pixels to greatly soften the edges of your selection, and click OK.

Continued

Step Five:

Press Delete (PC: Backspace) to knock a soft-edged hole out of your dark beige layer, revealing the lighter layer beneath (as shown here). Now you can deselect by pressing Command-D (PC: Control-D). Next, we'll need to create some space below this image so we can add some text.

Step Six:

Go under the Image menu and choose Canvas Size. Turn on the Relative checkbox and for Height enter 2.5 inches. In the Anchor grid, click the top-center square so the extra canvas area will be added below your image. In the Canvas Extension Color pop-up menu, choose White, and click OK. Now that you have that extra space, you can add your text with the Type tool. (The font shown here is Minion, from Adobe, set in lowercase with lots of space [tracking] between the letters, which was set in the Character palette under the Window menu.)

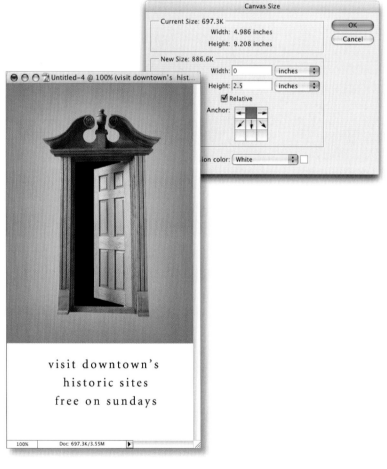

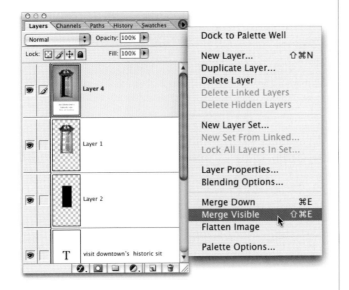

Step Seven:

Go to the Layers palette, click on the top layer, and add a new layer above it by clicking on the Create a New Layer icon. With the Option key (PC: Alt key) held down, choose Merge Visible from the Layers palette's flyout menu (as shown). This converts that blank layer into a layer that contains a flattened version of all your layers. Press Command-A (PC: Control-A) to select this entire layer; then press Command-C (PC: Control-C) to copy this layer into memory.

Step Eight:

Open the photo that has the sign you want to cover with your poster. Press Shift-L until you have the Polygonal Lasso tool selected, and click once on the bottom left-hand corner of the existing sign. Move your cursor to the top-left corner of the sign and click again. A straight selection line is drawn between the two corners. Continue clicking around the sign just like that—making straight-line selections—until the entire sign is selected (as shown here). It should only take you about a minute or so.

Continued

Step Nine:

Once your sign is selected, go under the Edit menu and choose Paste Into. Your poster will be pasted inside your sign selection. However, the sign is pasted in flat—it's up to you to give it the perspective to properly fit the sign. But luckily, that's easy (and this is what this tutorial is really all about). Press Command-T (PC: Control-T) to bring up the Free Transform function. Hold the Command key (PC: Control key), grab the top-left control point, and drag it until it meets the top-left corner of the sign in the photo. Release only the mouse button, grab the top-right corner point and drag until it touches the top-right corner of the original sign. Repeat for the bottom corners. The sign will look distorted until you move all four points.

Step Ten:

You can press Return (PC: Enter) to lock in your transformation and complete the effect (as shown here). There's one extra thing you might do to help the poster look like it's really in the photo. Command-click (PC: Control-click) on your poster layer in the Layers palette, go to the Create New Adjustment Layer pop-up menu, and choose Photo Filter. When the dialog appears, click on the color swatch to access the Color Picker. Then move your cursor outside the dialog and click once on the sky to sample that color and click OK in the Color Picker. With the Preview checkbox selected in the Photo Filter dialog, adjust the Density slider to an amount you think looks good. This will add a bit of blue tint to your poster, so it looks like it's really under the sky. Try it and see what you think.

Chapter SIX

SERIOUS SIDE EFFECTS
EFFECTS THAT DIDN'T FIT ANYWHERE ELSE

Is that the best I could come up with—effects that didn't fit anywhere else? Apparently so. Or you'd have read something clever there instead. Look, I'm going to be straight with you. This entire book is about special effects, and technically there are really three categories of classic effects: type effects, photo effects, and...okay, there are only two categories of classic effects. But if this book had just two huge chapters, nobody would buy it. Apparently people don't buy books with just two chapters, even if they're two massively huge chapters. So book publishers (commonly referred to as "the evil overlords") make you write a bunch of chapters so you'll actually sell the books you write. Now, I could go against this "make-a-bunch-of-chapters" theory and force a major paradigm shift in the publishing industry by writing the first book with only two chapters. But if they're right and the book doesn't sell, then they'd unleash the "I-told-you-so" clause hidden deep within all book publishing contracts, which generally means "you no longer write books for us." So...in short: Enjoy these nine chapters.

Digital Pixel Effect

This is one of those classic effects that's used every time the word "digital" appears on a magazine cover or spread, a book cover, or a billboard. It makes the image (in our example, a person) look like they're becoming "digital" because half of their face is turning into pixels.

Step One:

Open the photo you want to apply the effect to (it's usually applied to photos of people, but I've seen it used on product shots as well). Duplicate the Background layer by pressing Command-J (PC: Control-J). You'll apply the effect to this duplicate layer (Layer 1, as shown here).

Step Two:

Go under the Filter menu, under Pixelate, and choose Mosaic. When the dialog appears, for Cell Size enter 10 pixels (this isn't an "official" size, so if you'd like smaller or larger pixels, feel free to experiment), then click OK to pixelate the entire layer (as shown here).

Step Three:
The secret to smoothly blending from a crisp photo into a pixelated mess is to use a layer mask, so click the Add a Layer Mask icon at the bottom of the Layers palette (as shown here).

Step Four:
Press the letter "g" to switch to the Gradient tool, then press Return (PC: Enter) and the Gradient Picker will appear right where your cursor is within the image area. Choose the Black to White gradient (as shown here).

Step Five:
Take the Gradient tool, click on the man's right ear and drag horizontally to his left ear (as shown here) and the photo will then blend gradually from the clean photo on the left to the pixelated photo on the right. What you're really doing here is revealing the clean photo on the layer underneath on the left, and then blending to the pixelated version on the right, giving you the classic pixelated "digital" look. To finish the effect, go to the Layers palette's flyout menu and choose Flatten Image. Now to put the photo to use, let's put it in a two-page editorial spread.

Continued

Step Six:

Create a new document (File>New) that's twice as wide as your photo. Press Command-R (PC: Control-R) to make your rulers visible, then click on the left ruler and drag out a guide to the center of your two-page spread. (*Note:* If you have Snap turned on under the View menu, the guide should visibly "snap" to the center of the document.) Get the Gradient tool again, but this time go up to the Options Bar and click on the fourth gradient style (the Reflected Gradient) as shown in the Options Bar here. We're going to use this gradient to create what looks like the natural bend in the center of the two-page spread in a magazine.

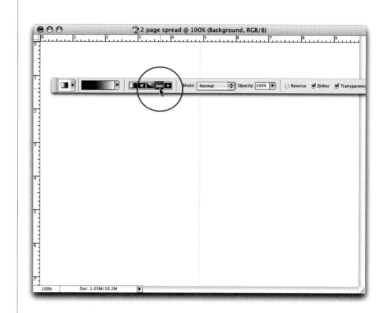

Step Seven:

Click on the Create a New Layer icon at the bottom of the Layers palette to create a new layer above the Background layer. Then, click the Gradient tool in the center, right on the guide, and drag a very small distance to the right (as shown here) to create a gradient that's solid in the middle and then quickly blends off into white.

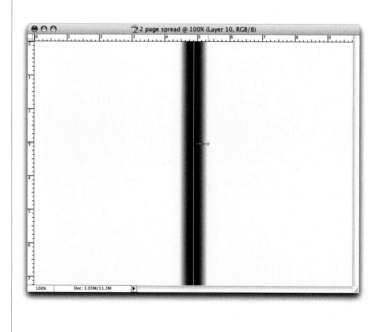

Step Eight:

Go back to your pixelated photo, press the letter "v" to switch to the Move tool, drag the image onto your two-page spread document, and position it on the left side of the spread (as shown here). In the Layers palette, drag it below the gradient layer, then in the Layers palette click on the gradient layer (Layer 1). Lower the Opacity of this layer to around 25%, then change the layer blend mode from Normal to Darken, so you can see the pixelated image beneath (as shown here).

Step Nine:

All that's left to do now is add some text on the right page of the spread to complete the project. The top line is set in Helvetica. The word "digital" is set in CG Phenix American (the "got milk?" font), as is the author's byline. The body copy is set in Adobe Minion.

Creating Stamps

This is a slick little technique for making any photo look like a postage stamp. Versions of it have been around for a while, but in this particular technique, Photoshop does most of the work for you by using a pretty fascinating path trick—and the whole thing is much faster and easier than it looks.

Step One:
Open the photo you want to turn into a stamp.

Step Two:
Press Command-A (PC: Control-A) to put a selection around the entire photo, and press Shift-Command-J (PC: Shift-Control-J) to cut that photo off the Background layer and copy it onto its own separate layer (as shown here).

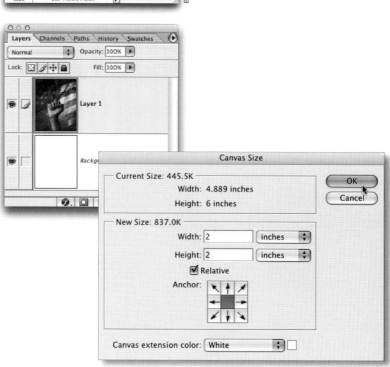

Step Three:
You'll need to add some white space around your stamp so you'll have room to create the stamp edge, so go under the Image menu and choose Canvas Size. In the dialog (shown here), turn on the Relative checkbox, and for both Width and Height enter 2 inches. Set the Canvas Extension Color pop-up menu to White and click OK.

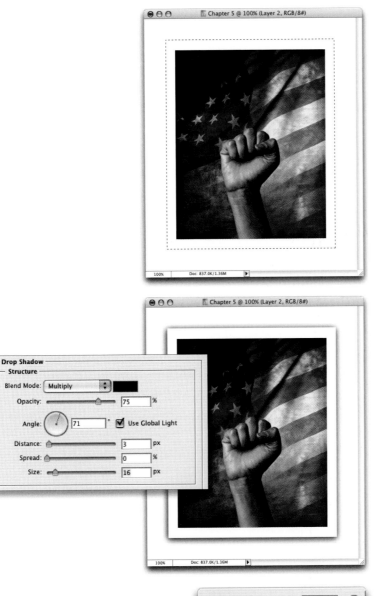

Step Four:

Now go to the Layers palette, hold the Command key (PC: Control key), and click on the Create a New Layer icon to create a new blank layer directly beneath your photo layer. Press the letter "m" to switch to the Rectangular Marquee tool and draw a rectangular selection that is about a half-inch larger than your photo (as shown here). Press the letter "d" then "x" to set your Foreground color to white, and fill this large rectangular selection with white by pressing Option-Delete (PC: Alt-Backspace). Now you can deselect by pressing Command-D (PC: Control-D).

Step Five:

You won't be able to see the white rectangle you just created because, after all, it's on a white background, but this will help—choose Drop Shadow from the Add a Layer Style pop-up menu at the bottom of the Layers palette. When the dialog appears, increase the Size setting to around 16 so the shadow peeks out around all sides of the white rectangle. Center your shadow on the box by changing the Angle to 71° and the Distance to 3 (as shown here). Click OK to apply the shadow.

Step Six:

Next, you're going to knock holes out of your white border (well, actually Photoshop is going to do this for you). Press the letter "e" to switch to the Eraser tool, and in the Options Bar make sure the Mode pop-up menu is set to Brush. Then, click on the icon next to the word "Brush" in the Options Bar to bring up the Brush Picker. When it appears, choose the 19-pixel, hard-edged brush (as shown here).

Continued

Step Seven:

Go under the Window menu and choose Brushes to bring up the Brushes palette (shown here). In the list of controls on the left side of the palette, click on the words "Brush Tip Shape" to bring up those options. Near the very bottom of the palette (right above the preview box) is a Spacing slider. Make sure the Spacing checkbox is turned on and increase the slider to 190% (this is what worked for me—if the holes in your stamp edges start to run into each other, you can come back here later and try a higher number).

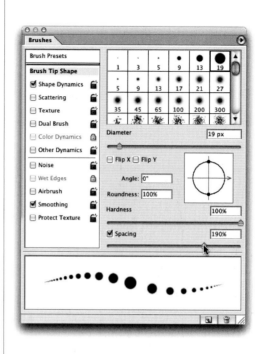

Step Eight:

Go to the Layers palette, hold the Command key (PC: Control key), and click on the white rectangle layer to put a selection around just that white rectangular box. Now that your selection is in place, press the letter "p" to select the Pen tool from the Toolbox, and go under the Window menu and choose Paths. From the Paths palette's flyout menu, choose Make Work Path (as shown here). When the Make Work Path dialog appears, just click OK and your selection will be replaced with a path (as if you had drawn it yourself with the Pen tool).

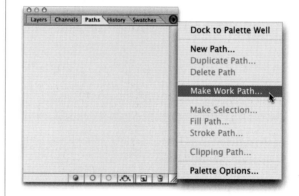

Step Nine:

Go back to the Paths palette, and you'll see the path you just created (by default it's named "Work Path"). Click on that path in the palette, and from the palette's flyout menu choose Stroke Path (as shown here).

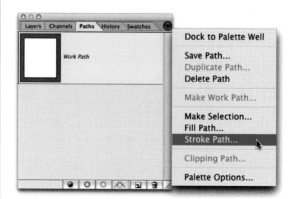

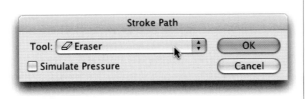

Stroke Path

Tool: ✐ Eraser

☐ Simulate Pressure

OK

Cancel

Step Ten:

Here's where Photoshop kicks in and does the work. When the Stroke Path dialog appears (shown here), choose Eraser from the Tool pop-up menu and turn off the Simulate Pressure checkbox.

Step Eleven:

When you click OK, the Eraser tool will trace around that rectangular path on the edge of your white box, knocking out little half-circles (half of that 19-pixel brush). It's half a circle because the Eraser erases half inside the path where the white box is visible and half outside the path (which isn't visible). Speaking of visibility, at this point you'll still see the thin black path around your stamp, so hide that from view—go to the Paths palette and click just below the Work Path to deselect it.

Step Twelve:

The reason there's a gap between the eraser strokes (instead of being one continuous stroke as usual) is because of that spacing you added back in Step Seven in the Brushes palette. If these little half-circles are touching each other, all you have to do is press Command-Z (PC: Control-Z) to undo the Stroke Path. Now press the letter "e" to get the Eraser tool again. Go back to the Brushes palette, increase the amount in the Spacing slider and try Steps Nine through Eleven again. It may take a couple of tries to get the spacing right, but you'll get it evenly spaced rather quickly. Finally, add text with the Type tool (I used Minion Regular and Helvetica Condensed) to complete the effect.

Curling Type Around Objects

Nothing looks worse than when you see straight type on a product that's obviously rounded or curved. It screams, "This was done in Photoshop." Here's a classic technique for bending your type around an object, so it really looks as if the type is on the product, not "stuck on" using Photoshop.

Step One:

Open the object that you want to wrap text around (and by wrapping text, I mean that the text follows the contours of the object). In this case, we're using a tube of hair gel, so the text should look rounded around the tube. The tube needs to be on its own layer above the Background layer, so press the letter "w" to switch to the Magic Wand tool and click once on the white background. Go to the Select menu and choose Inverse to select the tube. Press Shift-Command-J (PC: Shift-Control-J) to cut the tube from the Background layer and copy it onto its own layer.

Step Two:

The name of this fictitious hair gel is "Sample" so press the letter "t" to switch to the Type tool. Press the letter "d" to set your Foreground color to black, and then click on the document and type the word "sample" (we used the font Optima in all lowercase set in the Character palette found under the Window menu).

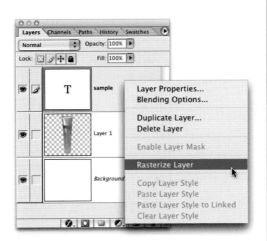

Step Three:

In the next step you're going to apply a filter, but you can't apply a filter to a Type layer so you have to convert it into a regular pixel-based image layer. To do that, go to the Layers palette, hold the Control key and click (PC: Right-click) on your Type layer's name. When the contextual pop-up menu appears, choose Rasterize Layer (as shown here).

Step Four:

You want to apply the filter only to the word (and not the entire layer), so before you choose the filter, press the letter "m" to switch to the Rectangular Marquee tool and draw a selection around your rasterized type (as shown here). Now go under the Filter menu, under Distort, and choose Shear. This is the filter you're going to use to create the wraparound effect. It works perfectly in this example because it bends items horizontally to the left or right, which is exactly what we need.

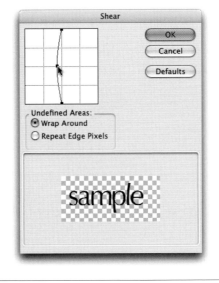

Step Five:

When the Shear dialog appears, click on the middle of the line in the center of the grid and a point will appear. Drag this point just a little to the left (as shown), and you'll see your text curve just a bit in the large preview area at the bottom of the filter dialog.

Continued

Step Six:

Once it's bent a little, click OK to apply the bend to your text. You can see the result shown here—the text is a bit curved. Press Command-D (PC: Control-D) to deselect.

Step Seven:

Press Command-T (PC: Control-T) to bring up Free Transform. Move your cursor outside the Free Transform bounding box to the right, and click-and-drag upward to rotate your curved text until it's vertical (hold the Shift key while you rotate and it will snap into place). Click inside the bounding box to drag the text into position. While you're still in Free Transform, hold the Shift key, grab a corner point and drag either inward or outward to resize your text as needed to fit the tube. Once it's rotated and in place, press Return (PC: Enter) and you can see how that little bend in the type makes it look like it curves around the tube. You can also lower the Opacity of this type in the Layers palette to around 55%, so it blends in with the tube (as shown here).

Step Eight:

Next you'll create some text for the top of the tube. Get the Type tool and use the same font (Optima) but this time type in all caps (as shown here). In the next step you'll use the Shear filter again to curve this type as well, so go ahead and rasterize it in the Layers palette. Unfortunately, because this text will appear horizontally on the tube, we can't run the Shear filter without rotating the text first. That's because the filter only shears to the left or the right, so we have to rotate the text before we shear it. Start by using Free Transform to rotate the text on its side as we did in the previous step. Then using the Rectangular Marquee tool, put a selection around your rotated text.

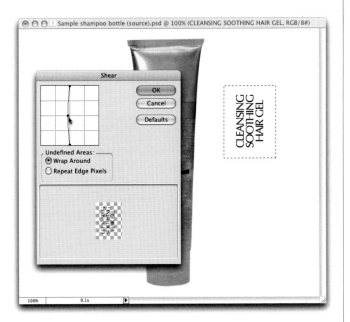

Step Nine:

Now that it's rotated and selected, go under the Filter menu, under Distort, and choose Shear. You can apply the same amount of Shear, so just click OK and this text will be curved (you can see a preview at the bottom of the Shear dialog). Press Command-D (PC: Control-D) to deselect. Once curved, you can go back to Free Transform to rotate it, resize it, and position it. You can add more text as well, just remember to rotate it before you shear it. Keep in mind that the smaller the type, the less amount of shear it needs, so you may need to click on the grid point in the Shear dialog and move it back to the right a little.

Continued

Step Ten:

In a moment, you'll add this bottle to an ad, but to do that you'll need the bottle and all the text on just one layer with no white background. Here's what to do: First, click on the Create a New Layer icon in the Layers palette to create a new blank layer. Then, in the Layers palette, click on the Eye icon in the first column beside the Background layer to hide it from view. Hold the Option key (PC: Alt key) and choose Merge Visible from the Layers palette's flyout menu (as shown here). This makes your top layer a flattened version of your bottle, but leaves all the other layers still intact. Sweet!

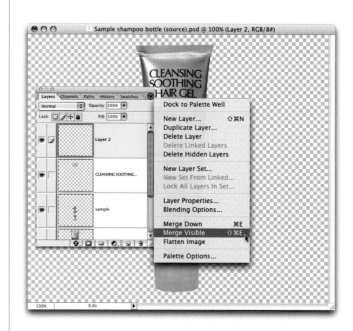

Step Eleven:

Open the image that you want to add the tube to. In this example we're using a spread with a close-up image of a woman with space to the right of her face for the tube and some body copy. In the tube image, press the letter "v" to switch to the Move tool, go the Layers palette, click-and-hold on the flattened tube layer, and drag it onto the spread. Scale it down to size using the Free Transform command. When the size is right, press Return (PC: Enter). Now we want to make a reflection for the tube: Press Command-J (PC: Control-J) to duplicate the hair gel tube layer. Next, bring up Free Transform, then Control-click (PC: Right-click) within the bounding box and choose Flip Vertical from the pop-up menu (as shown here). Click inside the bounding box and drag this flipped layer straight down until the two caps touch, making a mirror reflection. Press Return (PC: Enter) to lock in your transformation.

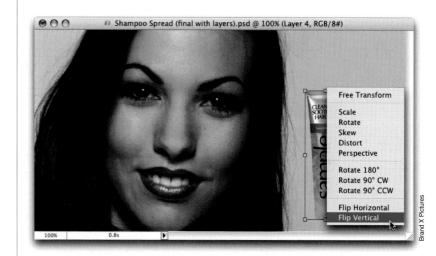

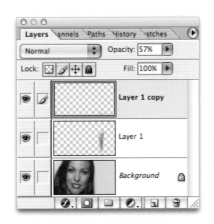

Step Twelve:
Lastly, lower the Opacity of this flipped layer to 57% to create the reflection shown here below the gel tube. I also added a shadow below the tube by adding a new layer below the tube and using a small, soft-edged brush with the Foreground color set to black to paint the shadow. I lowered the Opacity of the shadow layer in the Layers palette to make it more realistic. Now you can add some text to finish the ad. I made it easy—all the type is set in Optima. I created the white line below "Pantone" using the Line tool set to 2 pixels in the Options Bar and the Foreground color set to white. *Note*: The name "Pantone" is a tribute to one of my favorite companies—Pantone, the color people. Plus, the name is close enough to the real hair-care product Pantene® to make you look twice. ;-)

Blind Emboss Effect

Here's how to re-create the classic blind emboss effect. This technique makes it look as though an object, such as a logo, type, or an icon, is raised up off the background, but the object itself is not actually there. It's somewhat similar to the effect used on network logos that you see in the bottom right-hand corner of your TV screen.

Step One:
We're going to build the cover of a wine list for this project, so start by creating a new document (File>New) that's 6x8" at 72 ppi. Click on the Foreground color swatch in the Toolbox, and choose a light beige color in the Color Picker (I used R=236, G=232, B=166). Fill your background with this color by pressing Option-Delete (PC: Alt-Backspace).

Step Two:
To add some texture to your background, go under the Filter menu, under Texture, and choose Texturizer. When the dialog appears (shown here), choose Canvas in the Texture pop-up menu, enter 130% for Scaling, and enter 4 for Relief. In the Light pop-up menu choose Top Right, and then click OK to apply the texture to your Background layer.

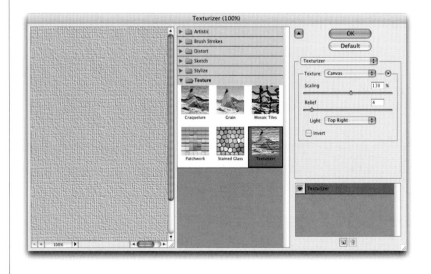

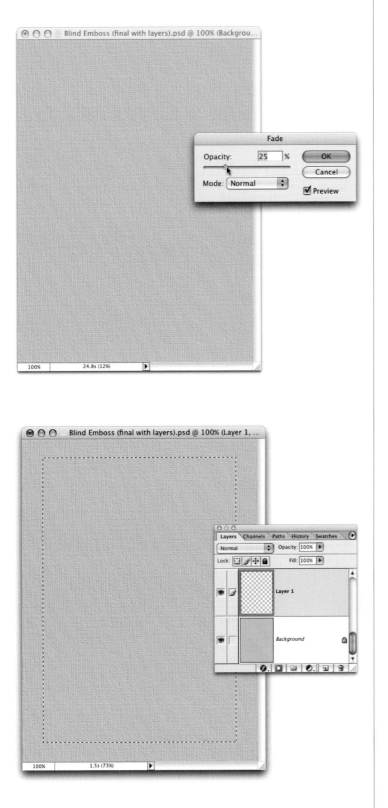

Step Three:
When the texture is applied, it will probably look too intense (especially if you're going to put text over it later), so go under the Edit menu and choose Fade Texturizer. This is kind of like an "undo on a slider." When the dialog appears, drag the Opacity slider to the left until it's set at 25% (as shown here), and click OK to soften the intensity of the texture.

Step Four:
Create a new layer by clicking on the Create a New Layer icon at the bottom of the Layers palette. Now press the letter "m" to switch to the Rectangular Marquee tool and draw a rectangular selection that is about three-quarters of an inch inside your document's borders (as shown here).

Continued

Step Five:

You're now going to add a thin black stroke to your selection, so go under the Edit menu and choose Stroke. When the dialog appears, click on the Color swatch and choose black in the Color Picker. Set the Width to 1 pixel, and choose Center for Location. Click OK to add your stroke to the selection.

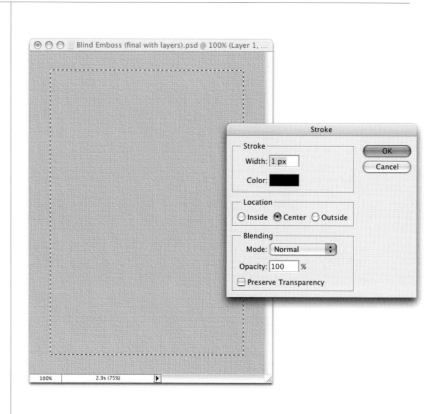

Step Six:

With your selection still in place, go under the Select menu, under Modify, and choose Contract. Enter 4 pixels in the dialog and click OK. Add the same stroke to this selection by going under the Edit menu and choosing Stroke. Just click OK and the stroke will be added. Don't deselect just yet.

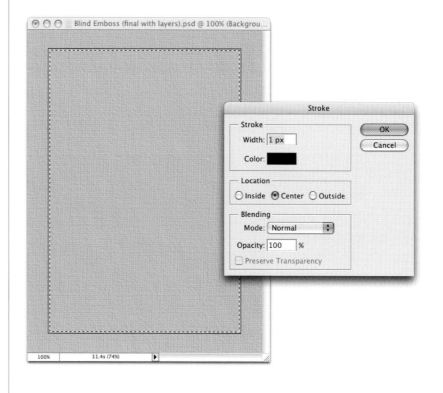

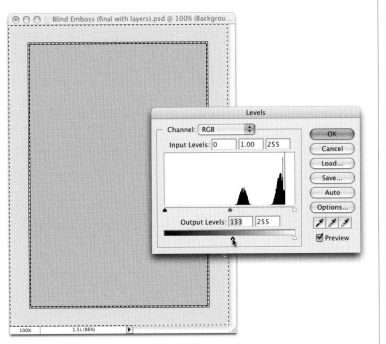

Step Seven:

Go under the Select menu and choose Inverse, so everything outside the center stroke is selected. In the Layers palette, click on the Background layer to make it active, then go under the Image menu, under Adjustments, and choose Levels. When the Levels dialog appears, click on the bottom-left Output Levels slider and drag it to the right until it reads 133 (about halfway to the right) to lighten the area around your center rectangle. Click OK, then deselect by pressing Command-D (PC: Control-D).

Step Eight:

Click on the Foreground color swatch and choose a medium gray (the shade of gray isn't that critical, so any middle gray will do). Press the letter "t" to switch to the Type tool and create a large letter (in this case, a capital "B") in a script font. (The font I used was Savoye, but you can use any fancy script you like.) Position your letter in the center of your image area (as shown here).

Continued

Step Nine:

Choose Bevel and Emboss from the Add a Layer Style pop-up menu at the bottom of the Layers palette. When the dialog appears, you only have to change two things: (1) At the bottom of the dialog, drag the Highlight Mode Opacity slider to 100%, and (2) lower the Shadow Mode Opacity slider to 50%. This makes the whites in the bevel brighter, and the shadows in the bevel less dark. Click OK to apply your bevel to your type (as shown here).

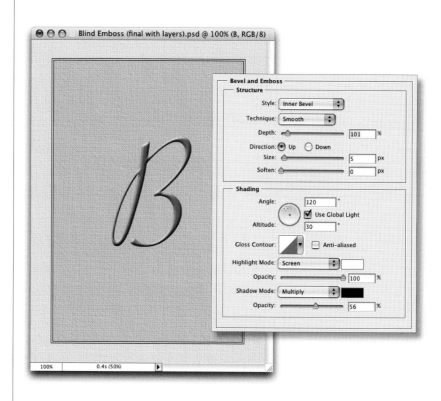

Step Ten:

Go to the Layers palette, and just below the Opacity field you'll see a field for Fill. Lower the amount of Fill to 0%, and the gray color inside your text will disappear, but the Bevel and Emboss effect will remain, giving you the look of a blind emboss (as shown here). If you think the embossing looks a bit strong, go to the Layers palette again, but this time lower the regular Opacity to around 65%.

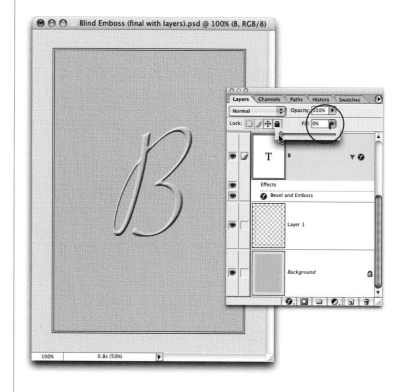

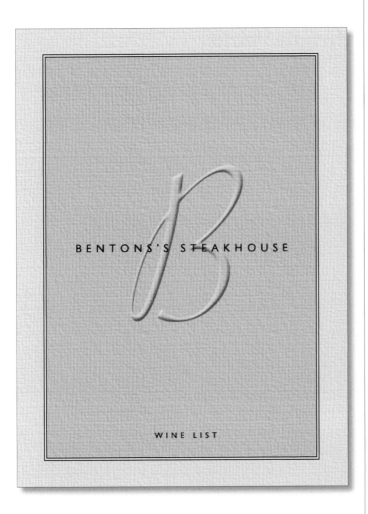

Step Eleven:
The final step is to add some type with the Type tool. I used the font Gill Sans in uppercase, and I increased the tracking (the space between the letters) by going to the Tracking field in the Character palette and entering 420 for the amount.

Adding Fireworks to Nighttime Photos

Here's a trick that has been in use ever since Photoshop 3.0. It enables you to add a photo of fireworks to any night shot and have it blend seamlessly with the photo. Better yet, it also teaches you a great layer mask trick that makes the fireworks appear as if they are behind the foreground buildings. In our project, we're taking a shot of Times Square and making it look like New Year's Eve, and then placing the final image into an editorial layout.

Step One:

Open the image you want to add fireworks to.

Step Two:

Open a photo of fireworks (you can use your own, or download this one from this book's companion website at www.scottkelbybooks.com/ classicphotos).

Step Three:

Press the letter "v" to switch to the Move tool, drag your fireworks image on top of your Times Square photo, and position the fireworks at the top of the image area (as shown here). As you can see, the black area behind the fireworks blocks out the buildings, but you'll fix that in the next step.

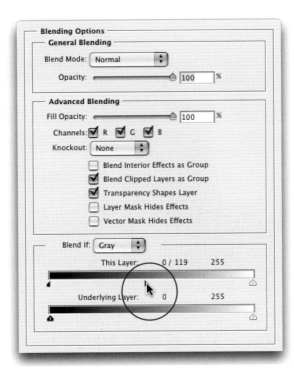

Step Four:
To get the fireworks to blend into your background, go to the Layers palette and double-click on your fireworks layer (double-click just to the right of the name "Layer 1"). This will open the Layer Style dialog set to the Blending Options. Go to the bottom of the dialog, hold the Option key (PC: Alt key), then click on the left triangle under the This Layer slider and drag it to the right.

Step Five:
As you drag to the right, the black background behind your fireworks will drop out and blend in with the background, leaving just the color of the fireworks (as shown here). The reason you hold the Option/Alt key is that the blend would otherwise look harsh and jaggy, but by holding that key before you drag, it splits the triangle under the slider, giving you a dramatically smoother blend. Once you have a good blend, click OK in the Layer Style dialog. If you look closely at the photo, there's still a problem—the fireworks appear in front of the buildings, rather than behind them.

Continued

Step Six:

To make it appear as though the fireworks are behind the buildings, go to the bottom of the Layers palette and click on the Add a Layer Mask icon (it's the second icon from the left). Then lower the Opacity of this layer to around 25% in the Layers palette so you can see the buildings clearly through the fireworks. Press the letter "b" to switch to the Brush tool, click on the icon next to the word "Brush" in the Options Bar to bring up the Brush Picker, and choose a hard-edged brush. Press the letter "x" until your Foreground color is set to black, then start painting over the buildings. As you do, it erases the shape of the buildings from the fireworks. In the example shown here, I'm painting over the tall thin signs on the left.

Step Seven:

Make sure you paint over all the buildings. (Remember, you're not painting on the photo itself, but on the mask, so if you make a mistake, just press the letter "x" to switch your Foreground color to white, then paint over the mistake and the original fireworks photo will reappear.) In the example shown here, I'm painting over the tall building in the center. Once you've "knocked out" the buildings, return to the Layers palette and raise the Opacity setting of the fireworks layer back to 100%.

Times Square (source).jpg @ 100% (Layer 1, Layer Mask/8)

100%   6.4s (65%)

Step Eight:

To make the fireworks even more vibrant, just duplicate the fireworks layer by pressing Command-J (PC: Control-J). Below is the final image used in a magazine spread. I created it by first going to Image>Canvas Size. (*Note:* When I dragged the fireworks image over in Step Three, part of it was extending out into the canvas area. So before I increased the canvas size in this step, I had to press Command-A [PC: Control-A] to Select All and then choose Crop from the Image menu to crop away the extra parts of the fireworks image.) In the Canvas Size dialog, I turned on the Relative checkbox, entered 6 inches in the Width field, clicked on the left-center square in the Anchor grid, clicked on the Canvas Extension color swatch, and sampled the color of the Samsung sign in the photo using the Color Picker. The fonts used are Garamond Condensed for all the large type and body copy and Helvetica for the page number and author's byline.

Continued

Step Nine:

Here is the exact same fireworks file applied to a totally different image. Use the same technique to blend the fireworks into the background and the layer mask trick to paint over the towers to make it look as if the fireworks are behind them, not in front of them. However, this photo poses a new problem—the Thames River. There should be a reflection of the fireworks in the water, right?

Step Ten:

To create the illusion of a reflection in the water, duplicate the fireworks layer by pressing Command-J (PC: Control-J). Then press Command-T (PC: Control-T) to bring up Free Transform. Control-click (PC: Right-click) within the bounding box and a contextual pop-up menu will appear. Choose Flip Vertical (as shown) to flip the duplicate layer. Click inside the bounding box and drag the fireworks down to the water. Press Return (PC: Enter) to lock in your transformation. Go under the Filter menu, under Blur, and choose Gaussian Blur.

Step Eleven:

When the Gaussian Blur dialog appears (shown in Step Ten), enter 3.5 pixels to blur the fireworks and make their colors appear to be reflected in the water. You'll have to do the layer mask trick again and paint over the lampposts in black to make the reflection appear behind the posts, not in front. If the reflection looks too intense, try lowering the Opacity of the flipped fireworks layer in the Layers palette. The final image, with reflected fireworks, is shown here.

Lightning Effect

This is about the quickest, easiest, time-tested way to add a lightning effect to your photo without having to draw a bunch of paths or jump through a lot of time-consuming hoops. In our project, we're going to add some lightning to a TV news weather-watch screen against a backdrop of a city at night.

Step One:

Create a new document (File>New) that's 7x5" at 72 ppi in RGB mode, then create a new blank layer by clicking on the Create a New Layer icon at the bottom of the Layers palette. Press Shift-M until you have the Elliptical Marquee tool, hold the Shift key, and draw a large circular selection (like the one shown here). Press "d" to set your Foreground color to black, then fill your selection with black by pressing Option-Delete (PC: Alt-Backspace). Press Command-D (PC: Control-D) to deselect.

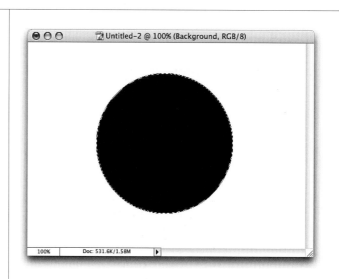

Step Two:

You need to mark the exact center of this circle, so press Command-T (PC: Control-T) to bring up the Free Transform bounding box around your circle. Press Command-R (PC: Control-R) to make your rulers visible, then click directly on the top ruler and drag a guide down until it reaches Free Transform's center point, and then release. Drag another guide to the center from the left ruler. Where these two guides cross is the exact center of your circle.

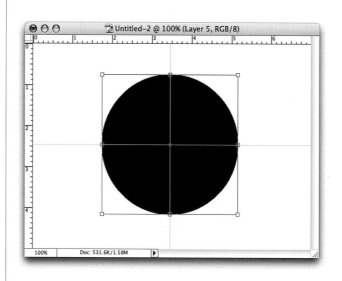

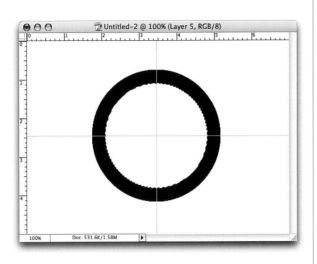

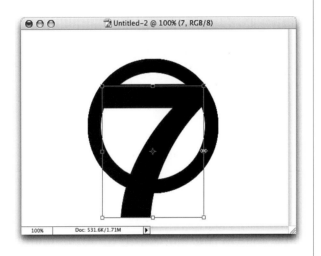

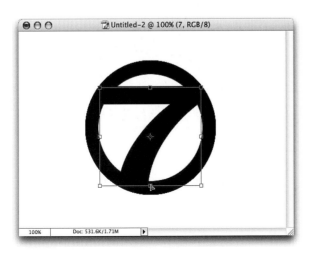

Step Three:

Now that the center point is marked with guides, you don't need Free Transform any longer, so press the Escape key. Hold Shift-Option (PC: Shift-Alt) and click the Elliptical Marquee tool directly on the point where those two guides cross and drag outward to create a smaller concentric circle (like the one shown here). Press Delete (PC: Backspace) to knock a hole out of your black circle (as shown), and press Command-D (PC: Control-D) to deselect. You're done with the guides, so you can remove them by going to View>Clear Guides.

Step Four:

Press the letter "t" to switch to the Type tool, click on your document, and type the number "7" (the font shown here is Helvetica Bold, but any thick, sans serif typeface will do). Click on the Move tool in the Toolbox, and press Command-T (PC: Control-T) to bring up the Free Transform command. Hold the Shift key, grab a top-corner point of the bounding box, and drag upward until the top of the 7 extends from the left side of the circle to the right. If you need to make it wider, release the Shift key, grab the right-center point (as shown) and drag to the right. Don't press Return (PC: Enter) yet.

Step Five:

Once the width is right (and the top of the 7 touches both sides of the circle), you'll have to fix the part of the number that extends below the circle (you can see the problem in the previous step). Just grab the bottom-center point of the bounding box and drag upward until the bottom of the number is tucked up into the black circle (as shown here). Now press Return (PC: Enter) to lock in your transformation.

Continued

Step Six:

Now press Command-E (PC: Control-E) to merge your "7" layer with the black circle layer directly beneath it, creating just one layer (as shown here) for the logo. In the Layers palette, click on the first icon to the right of the word "Lock" to lock the transparent pixels on this layer. (You need to do this because in the next step you'll add a gradient to your logo. If you don't lock the transparent pixels, the Gradient tool will fill your entire layer with a gradient, not just the logo.)

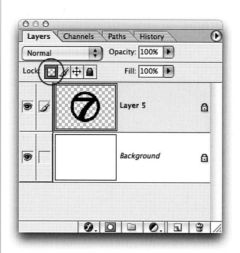

Step Seven:

Press the letter "g" to switch to the Gradient tool, then click on the down-facing arrow next to the gradient thumbnail in the Options Bar to bring up the Gradient Picker. From the Picker's flyout menu, choose Metals. Click the Append button in the resulting dialog to add the Metallic set of gradients to your default set of gradients. Once loaded, click on the Silver gradient in the Picker, then take the Gradient tool and drag diagonally through the logo (as shown).

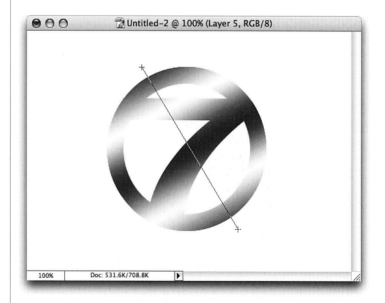

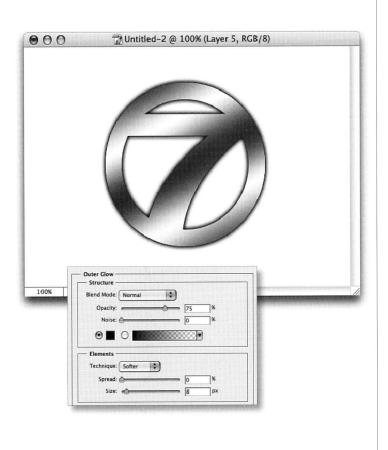

Step Eight:

Choose Outer Glow from the Add a Layer Style pop-up menu at the bottom of the Layers palette (it's the first icon from the left). Change the Blend Mode pop-up menu from Screen to Normal, then click on the beige color swatch and change the glow color to black in the Color Picker. Lastly, increase the Size to 8 and click OK to add a black glow around your logo (as shown here).

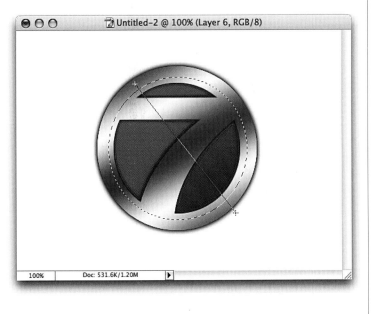

Step Nine:

Go to the Layers palette, hold the Command key (PC: Control key) and click on the Create a New Layer icon to create a new blank layer directly beneath your circle layer. Get the Elliptical Marquee tool, hold the Shift key, and draw a selection that's just a bit larger than the inner part of the circle (as shown here). (*Tip:* To position your selection as you draw, press-and-hold the Spacebar, move your selection, release the Spacebar, and continue to drag out your selection.) Click on the Foreground color swatch in the Toolbox and choose a bright red in the Color Picker, and then change your Background color to a darker red. Get the Gradient tool, open the Gradient Picker from the Options Bar, choose the first gradient in the default set (Foreground to Background), and drag the Gradient tool diagonally through your selection (as shown here). Deselect by pressing Command-D (PC: Control-D).

Continued

Step Ten:

Now we need to add some room for text. Go under the Image menu and choose Canvas Size. In the dialog, turn on the Relative checkbox, enter 4 inches for Width, click on the left-center square in the Anchor grid, choose White in the Canvas Extension Color pop-up menu, and click OK to add 4 inches of white canvas space to the right of your logo. Press the letter "d" to set your Foreground color to black, then switch to the Type tool and enter your type. The font shown here is Helvetica Black with the horizontal scaling set to 130% in the Character palette for the word "Storm"; 160% for the word "Crew"; and only 105% for the tag line below it. Now go to the Layers palette, and click in the second column beside the logo layer, the red gradient layer, and all your Type layers to temporarily link them together.

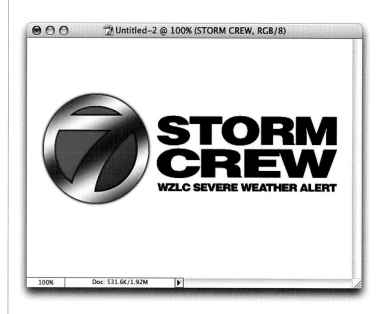

Step Eleven:

Open the photo you want to use as your background (in this case, a photo of a city at night). Go back to your logo document, press the letter "v" to switch to the Move tool, click directly on your logo, and drag it right onto your city photo. All the other linked layers will come right along with it. *Note:* If your logo is too large, resize it by pressing Command-T (PC: Control-T) to bring up Free Transform. Now, double-click directly on the Type layer's thumbnail (it has a "T" on it) in the Layers palette to highlight your type and to switch to the Type tool at the same time. In the Options Bar, click on the black color swatch and choose white in the Color Picker to change your copy to white. Click OK in the Color Picker and then press Enter to lock in your color change. Do this on all Type layers. Now we'll add the lightning to your project.

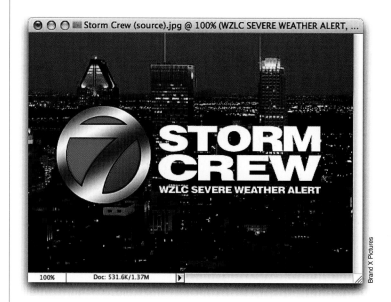

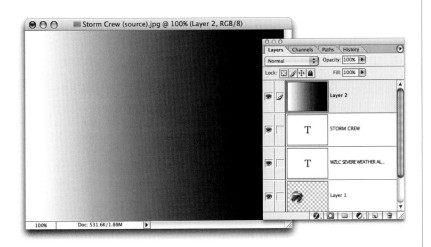

Step Twelve:

Press "d" then "x" to set your Foreground color to white and your Background color to black. Go to the Layers palette and click on the Create a New Layer icon to add a new blank layer and drag it to the top of the stack of layers (as shown here). Get the Gradient tool, bring up the Gradient Picker from the Options Bar, and choose the Foreground to Background gradient (it's the first gradient in the Picker). Drag the Gradient tool from the left side of your image area all the way to the right.

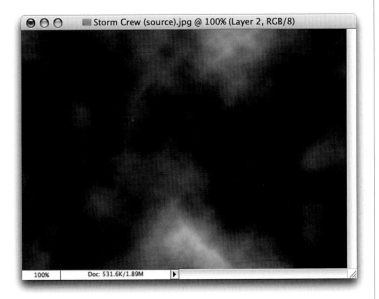

Step Thirteen:

Now go under the Filter menu, under Render, and choose Difference Clouds to apply a random cloud pattern over your gradient (as shown here). *Note:* Each time you apply this filter, you get a different look, so if you don't like the way your lightning looks in Step Fifteen, just go back to this step, and try applying Difference Clouds again or even try applying it two or three times until you come up with a lightning pattern that looks better.

Continued

Step Fourteen:
Press Command-I (PC: Control-I) to invert your clouds (as shown here).

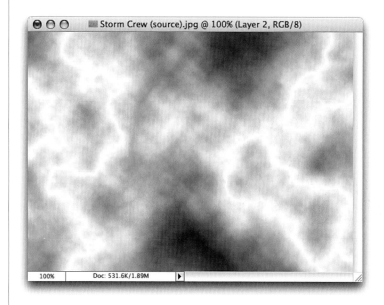

Step Fifteen:
Press Command-L (PC: Control-L) to bring up the Levels dialog. Grab the top-center Input Levels slider (the midtones slider) and drag it to the right. When you're almost all the way to the right, you'll see your lightning appear (as shown here). Click OK.

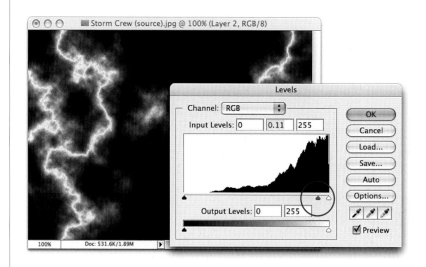

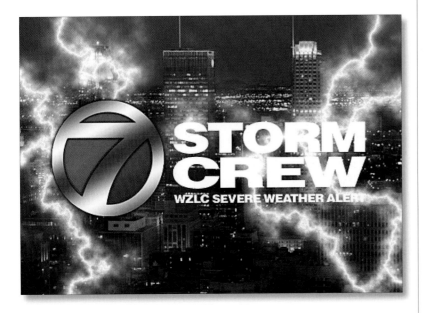

Step Sixteen:
To make your lightning blend in with your photo, go to the Layers palette and change the blend mode of your lightning layer from Normal to Screen (as shown here).

Step Seventeen:
The lightning goes right over the logo, but if you don't want that, you can do this: Hold Shift-Command (PC: Shift-Control) and in the Layers palette click once on both the logo layer (don't change layers, just click on it) and the red gradient layer to put a selection around your logo. Now press Delete (PC: Backspace) to erase the lightning that appears over the logo (you're basically knocking a round hole out of the lightning layer), then press Command-D (PC: Control-D) to deselect, which completes the effect.

Chapter SEVEN

DANGEROUS TYPE
CLASSIC TYPE EFFECTS

Finally, a chapter name that makes sense—"Dangerous Type," which is perhaps the ultimate name for a chapter on classic type effects. Now, is there really a song, TV show, or movie title named "Dangerous Type"? You know it. It's a song by one of the coolest bands of the '80s—The Cars. Now, it wasn't a big hit for them, but that wasn't one of my criteria for being a chapter name. It just had to be a real song, TV show, or movie title—not a big song—so the song "Dangerous Type" fits that bill. Now, what about the previous chapter, the one named "Serious Side Effects." Is there really a song named "Serious Side Effects"? Well, there is a song named just "Side Effects" (it's by Parliament) but I added the word "serious" myself to give a little more impact to the title. Now, how was I able to get away with that? Well, there's a little-known loophole within my chapter naming rules that allows me to add a word to a legitimate song title in the event that it needs a little more impact. I know what you're thinking: "Oh, how convenient. You can just add a word whenever you see fit. Is that it?" That's right. It's great to be me.

Chrome Beveled Type

This is actually two classic techniques in one: a chrome beveled edge effect and an "airbrushy" fill, which is often used with the chrome bevel to create a reflected look. Photoshop comes with a gradient that's often used for this airbrushed look, but you're going to create your own custom airbrush gradient for this project, which is a logo for a custom wheel dealer.

Step One:

Create a new document (File>New) that's 9x4.5" set at 72 ppi in RGB mode, and press the letter "d" to set your Foreground color to black. Press the letter "t" to switch to the Type tool, click on your document, then type in the word you want to apply the effect to at a very large point size (which you can set in either the Options Bar or the Character palette in the Window menu). In the example here, I'm using the font Savoye.

Step Two:

Go to the Layers palette and Control-click (PC: Right-click) directly on the Type layer's name. From the contextual menu that appears, choose Rasterize Layer (as shown here) to convert your Type layer into a regular image layer.

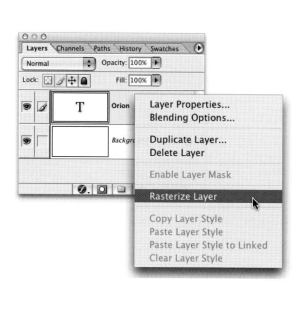

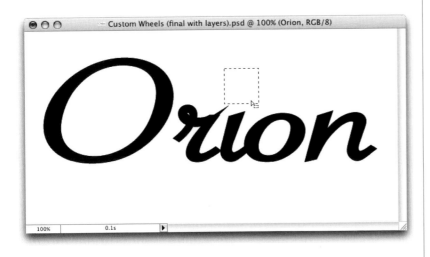

Step Three:
The reason you needed to rasterize the Type layer in the previous step is because you're now going to edit one of the letters. Press the letter "m" to switch to the Rectangular Marquee tool and draw a square selection encompassing the "dot" over the "i" in "Orion" (as shown), and press Delete (PC: Backspace) to remove the dot (don't worry, you'll add a dot of your own later in the project). Press Command-D (PC: Control-D) to deselect.

Step Four:
Press the letter "g" to switch to the Gradient tool, then click on the gradient thumbnail on the left side of the Options Bar to bring up the Gradient Editor. You're going to create a gradient similar to the one you see here (it doesn't have to be exact, just similar). Start by double-clicking on the far-left color stop under the gradient ramp to bring up the Color Picker. Choose white and click OK in the Color Picker. To add the next color, just click right below the gradient ramp to add another color stop, then double-click on it and choose a bluish gray color. If you want to add a color stop of the same color, hold down Option (PC: Alt), click on the color stop, and drag out a new color stop where you want it beneath the gradient ramp. Continue adding the other stops and choosing colors until it's similar to the gradient you see here. Click the New button to save your custom gradient, then click OK.

Continued

Step Five:

Choose Gradient Overlay from the Add a Layer Style pop-up menu at the bottom of the Layers palette. When the dialog appears, click on the down-facing triangle to the right of the Gradient thumbnail to bring up the Gradient Picker. The last gradient in the Picker is the one you created in the previous step. Click on that one (as shown), and the gradient is applied to your type. Don't click OK yet.

Step Six:

Click on the word "Stroke" in the Styles list on the left side of the Layer Style dialog. Change the Fill Type pop-up menu to Gradient, then click on the down-facing arrow to the right of the Gradient thumbnail to bring up the Gradient Picker. From the Picker's flyout menu, choose Metals and click Append in the resulting dialog to load the metallic gradients (they'll appear in the Gradient Picker right after the custom gradient you made earlier). Click on the Silver gradient (as shown), then increase the Size to 7 to apply a metallic gradient stroke outside your letters. Don't click OK yet.

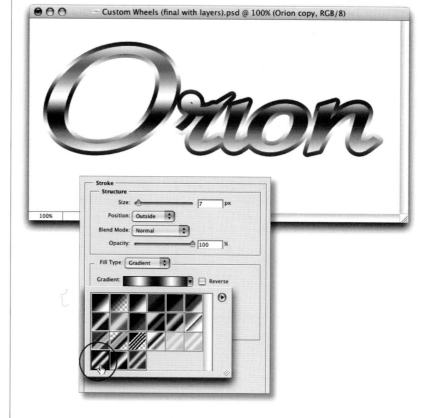

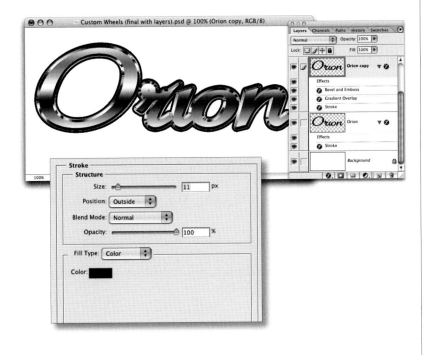

Step Seven:

Now to make the stroke look more metallic, click on the words "Bevel and Emboss" in the Styles list on the left side of the Layer Style dialog. Change the Style pop-up menu to Stroke Emboss (so it only affects the stroke), change the Technique pop-up menu to Chisel Hard, and increase the Depth to around 350%. Lower the Size to 4, then click on the down-facing arrow to the right of the Gloss Contour thumbnail to bring up the Contour Picker and choose a contour with two or three hills (like the one shown in the thumbnail here). Now you can click OK to add the gradient overlay and metallic-looking stroke to your type.

Step Eight:

Now press Command-J (PC: Control-J) to duplicate your layer, along with all three of the layer styles you applied to it. This copied layer appears above your original, so go to the Layers palette and click on the original text layer to make it active (as shown here). On that layer, click directly on the words "Bevel and Emboss" and drag that effect to the Trash icon at the bottom of the Layers palette to delete it. Do the same for Gradient Overlay, but not for Stroke. Instead, double-click on the word "Stroke" to bring up the Layer Style dialog and set the Size to 11, change the Fill Type pop-up menu to Color, click on the Color swatch, and change the color from red to black in the Color Picker to add a black stroke around your type (as shown here). Click OK in the Color Picker but not in the Layer Style dialog yet.

Continued

Step Nine:

Now click on the words "Drop Shadow" in the Styles list on the left side of the Layer Style dialog. Set the Angle to 116°, the Size to 10, and the Distance to 15. Now click OK to apply the edited stroke and a soft shadow to your type (as shown here).

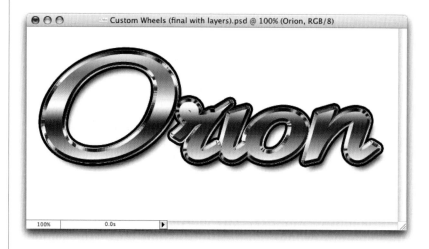

Step Ten:

Open the wheel photo, press the letter "w" to switch to the Magic Wand tool, and Shift-click on all the white background areas. In the Select menu, choose Inverse to select the wheel instead of the white background. Now press "v" to switch to the Move tool and drag the wheel over onto your type image and position it over the "i" where the dot used to be (as shown here). Press Command-T (PC: Control-T) to bring up Free Transform. Hold the Shift key, grab a corner point, and drag inward to scale the wheel down to size. Release the Shift key, move your cursor outside of the bounding box to the right, click-and-drag downward to rotate the wheel a little (as shown here), and press Return (PC: Enter) to lock in your transformation.

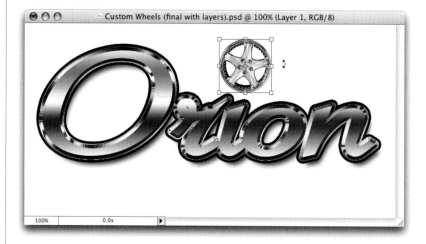

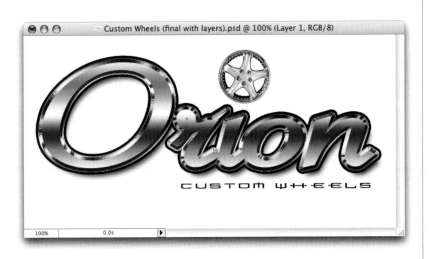

Step Eleven:

To finish the logo part of this project, just add the type under the logo with the Type tool (which is set in the font Mata from House Industries).

Step Twelve:

Here's the logo used on a webpage. The navigation type at the top of the page is set in the font Myriad Pro (which comes with Photoshop CS), and the type at the bottom of the page is set in Verdana.

Gel Type

The gel look, introduced by Apple Computer in its Mac OS X operating system, took the design world by storm a few years back. Here's a variation of the gel effect based on a technique created by my good friend Jack Davis (Photoshop guru and author of the *Photoshop WOW!* book series). Jack is "King of the Gel," and this simplified version pays homage to this "Layer Styles Master."

Step One:

Create a new document (File>New) that's 7x5" at 72 ppi in RGB mode. Press the letter "d" to set your Foreground color to black, then press the letter "t" to switch to the Type tool. Click on the document and type in what you want to appear in a gel look. (In this example, I'm building a Web banner for a fictitious TV news station, Channel 5, so type in a large "5" using the font Impact, or you could use another sans serif font.)

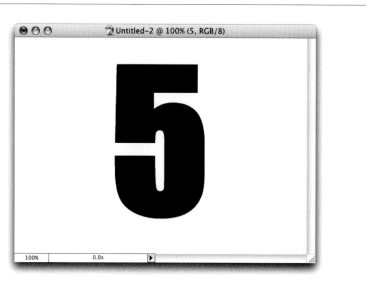

Step Two:

Choose Color Overlay from the Add a Layer Style pop-up menu at the bottom of the Layers palette. When the dialog appears, click on the color swatch to the right of the Blend Mode pop-up menu and choose a bright yellow (as shown here) in the Color Picker. Click OK in the Color Picker, but leave the Layer Style dialog open. (*Note:* We're using Color Overlay, rather than just starting with yellow type, so we can easily change the color later if we need to.)

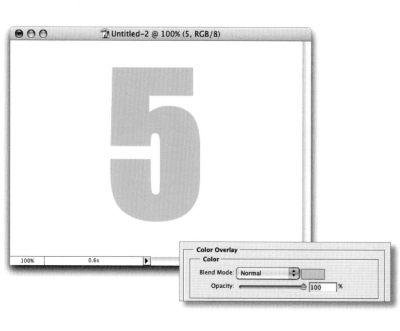

Step Three:

Click on the words "Inner Shadow" in the Styles list on the left side of the Layer Style dialog. Turn off the Use Global Light checkbox, increase the Distance to 7, set the Choke to 20%, and the Size to 10. This creates a shadow inside your letters (as shown here), but don't click OK yet.

Step Four:

Now click on the words "Inner Glow" in the Styles list (this will put what looks like a thin stroke around the inside of the number). Click on the beige color swatch and choose black in the Color Picker for your inner glow color. Lower the Opacity to 50%, and change the Blend Mode pop-up menu from Screen to Multiply. Don't click OK yet.

Continued

Step Five:

Click on the words "Bevel and Emboss" in the Styles list. Increase the Size to 7 and set Soften at 1. In the Shading section, turn off Use Global Light, turn on the Anti-aliased checkbox, and set the Angle to 90° and the Altitude to 67°. Increase the Highlight Opacity slider to 100% and then lower the Shadow Opacity slider to 0% to give you the gel effect that you see here. Before you click OK, click on the New Style button (it's just below the Cancel button), give your style a name, and click OK. This gel style will be saved in the Styles palette (under the Window menu), so in the future you can just click on this style in the Styles palette and it will apply the gel look, rather than going through all these steps every time. Click OK to close the Layer Style dialog and to apply all of your effects.

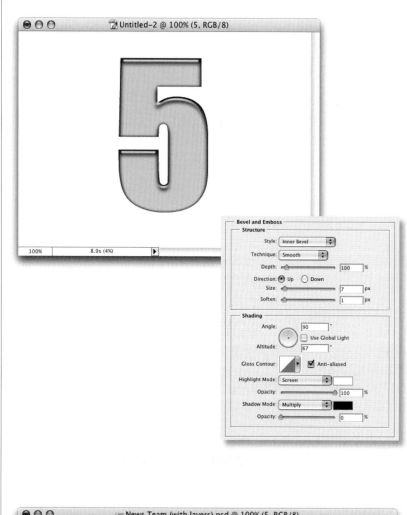

Step Six:

Now that we have the gel look down, let's put it to work in our Web banner for the TV news channel. Create a new document (File>New) that's 9x2.5" at 72 ppi in RGB mode. Press the letter "d" to set your Foreground color to black, then fill the Background layer with black by pressing Option-Delete (PC: Alt-Backspace).

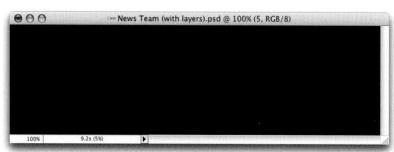

Step Seven:
Open the downtown photo and press the letter "v" to switch to the Move tool. Drag the image over onto your black background, and position it in the top-right corner (as shown here).

Step Eight:
Add a new blank layer by clicking on the Create a New Layer icon at the bottom of the Layers palette. Press the letter "m" to switch to the Rectangular Marquee tool and draw a square selection around the left side of the banner (as shown here). Click the Foreground color swatch to select a gray color in the Color Picker, and fill your selection with this gray by pressing Option-Delete (PC: Alt-Backspace). Press Command-D (PC: Control-D) to deselect.

Step Nine:
Open the photo of the news team, press the letter "w" to switch to the Magic Wand tool, and click on the white background area (you may need to uncheck Contiguous in the Options Bar and adjust the Tolerance for a better selection). If any white areas are not selected, press "L" to switch to the Lasso tool, hold down the Shift key, and click-and-drag to include those white areas in your selection. Once you've selected just the white background, choose Inverse from the Select menu, press "v" to switch to the Move tool, and click-and-drag that image over onto your downtown photo, positioning it as shown here.

Continued

Step Ten:

Now go back to your "5" document, switch to the Move tool, and click-and-drag that layer over onto your Web banner document, positioning the "5" on the left side (as shown here). If you need to resize the "5," press Command-T (PC: Control-T) to bring up the Free Transform command, hold the Shift key, drag a corner handle of the bounding box, and press Return to lock in your transformation. The edges around the number look a little too dark, but you'll fix that in the next step.

Step Eleven:

Below your "5" layer in the Layers palette, double-click directly on the words "Inner Shadow" to be able to edit its settings. Click on the black color swatch, and when the Color Picker appears, move your cursor outside the Picker and it will change to the Eyedropper tool. Click the Eyedropper in the sky of the downtown image to make your shadow color light purple, which changes that hard, black edge to the softer, more gel-like edge you see here. Click OK to apply your change. (And by the way, if you don't like the look of your yellow-colored text, just double-click on the words "Color Overlay" below your Type layer in the Layers palette. Then click on the color swatch to bring up the Color Picker and try out any color you want. It's magic.)

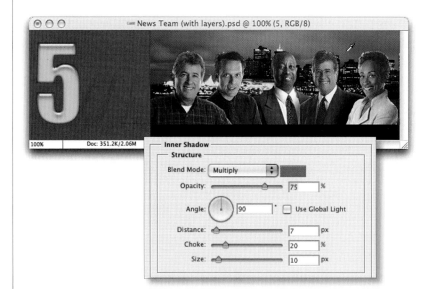

Step Twelve:
Now you'll add the news team text. Press the letter "d" then "x" to set your Foreground color to white, and click on the Create a New Layer icon at the bottom of the Layers palette to add a new blank layer. Then, press "t" to switch to the Type tool and add the words "NEWS TEAM" (I used the font Compacta Bold here, but you can use any tall, thick font).

Step Thirteen:
To finish off the project, just add the station's info and tag line in the thin black bar just below the newscasters' photo. The font shown here is Helvetica Condensed Bold Italic.

Putting a Photo into Type

This is one of the all-time most-requested effects, and luckily, it's one of the easiest. The coolest thing about this effect is that it's so flexible—once you get the photo into the type, not only can you change the position, size, and most other attributes of the photo, but you can also change the type—even type in new letters—and the effect updates instantly.

Step One:

In this project, we're going to build a cover for a video game, so create a new document (File>New) that's 7x5" at 72 ppi in RGB mode. Press the letter "d" to set your Foreground color to black, then press the letter "t" to switch to the Type tool. Click on the document and type in the letter or number in which you want your photo to appear (in this case, it's the number 3, set in the font Bullet from House Industries, but you can use any thick, italic, sans serif typeface).

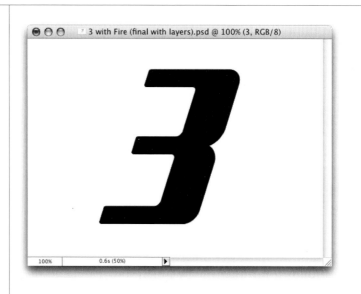

Step Two:

Open the photo you want to appear within your type (in this case, we want the fire from this photo to appear inside the "3"). *Note:* Although we're applying this to just one number, the technique works just the same using multiple letters or numbers.

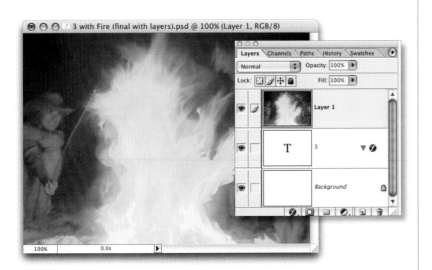

Step Three:

Press the letter "v" to switch to the Move tool and drag this photo over onto your number document. It will appear above your number "3" layer in the Layers palette (as shown here).

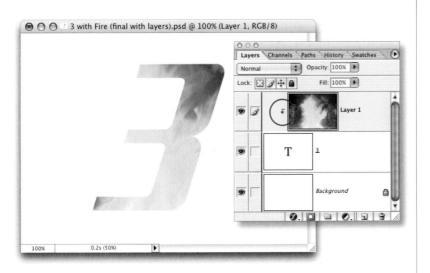

Step Four:

You've done all the hard parts—getting the photo inside the type is easy. Just press Command-G (PC: Control-G), which is the shortcut for Create Clipping Mask, and basically everything outside your number "3" is "clipped off." In the Layers palette, a small arrow pointing downward will appear to the left of your photo's thumbnail image, indicating that the photo is clipped into the layer directly beneath it (as shown).

Continued

Step Five:

Now that the photo is inside your number, you can get the Move tool from the Toolbox and reposition the photo so the tips of the flames are a little more visible (here I dragged the photo just a little bit to the left).

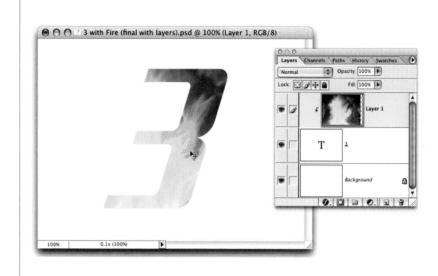

Step Six:

Because white and light-colored areas of a photo clipped into type can blend in when used over lighter backgrounds, it's fairly common to see a black stroke around type that has a photo clipped into it. To add a black stroke, go to the Layers palette and click on your Type layer. Choose Stroke from the Add a Layer Style pop-up menu at the bottom of the Layers palette. When the dialog appears, click the Color swatch, select black in the Color Picker, and click OK. Then click OK in the Layer Style dialog to apply a black stroke around your type (as shown here). Now we'll take this fiery "3" and put it to use on the cover of a video-game box.

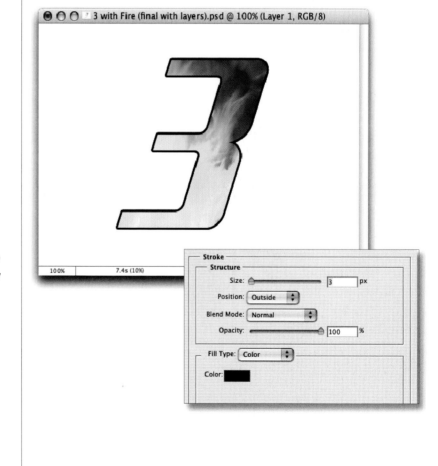

Brand X Pictures

Step Seven:

Create a new document (File>New) that's 5x7" at 72 ppi in RGB mode. Then open the photo you want to use as the background for your video box (in this case, a futuristic soldier). Press the letter "v" to switch to the Move tool and drag-and-drop this photo onto your blank document, positioning it at the bottom of the image window (as shown here). (You may need to use Command-T [PC: Control-T] to bring up the Free Transform command to resize your image. If so, just press-and-hold the Shift key as you drag a corner point, then press Return [PC: Enter] to lock in your transformation.)

Step Eight:

Add a new layer by clicking on the Create a New Layer icon at the bottom of the Layers palette. Press the letter "m" to switch to the Rectangular Marquee tool and draw a rectangular selection across the white area above your photo. Press the letter "d" to set your Foreground color to black, then fill this selection with black by pressing Option-Delete (PC: Alt-Backspace). Now deselect by pressing Command-D (PC: Control-D).

Continued

Step Nine:

Click the Foreground color swatch in the Toolbox and select a bright red in the Color Picker. Then press Shift-U until you get the Line tool (it's one of the Shape tools). Up in the Options Bar, click on the third icon in the left set of three icons so the line you draw will be made up of pixels, rather than a path or a shape layer, and enter 2 pixels in the Weight field. Hold down the Shift key and with the Line tool draw a horizontal line separating the black bar at the top from the photo below it (as shown here).

Step Ten:

Now go back to your fiery "3" document. Click on the fire photo layer in the Layers palette, hide the Background layer by clicking on the Eye icon to the left of the layer, then press Command-Shift-E (PC: Control-Shift-E) to permanently merge your fire and "3" layers into one single layer. Switch to the Move tool and drag-and-drop this merged layer over onto your video-game box image, positioning it near the bottom (as shown here). Use the Free Transform command (Command-T; PC: Control-T) to resize the "3" if necessary.

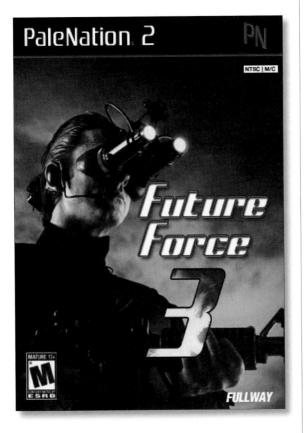

Step Eleven:

Now you'll add the title of the game (again, the font used is Bullet). Press "d" then "x" to set white as your Foreground color, then press "t" to switch to the Type tool and type in "Future Force." Now choose Stroke from the Add a Layer Style pop-up menu. When the dialog appears, lower the Size to 2 pixels, and then in the Styles list on the left side of the Layer Style dialog, turn on the checkbox for Drop Shadow to add its default settings. Then click directly on the words "Inner Shadow" so its options appear. Lower both the Size and Distance settings to 3, then click OK to apply all three layer styles (as shown).

Step Twelve:

Lastly, just add the finishing type to complete the project using the Type tool and Character palette. The type for the words "PaleNation 2" and the red "PN" on the top are set in the download-able shareware font Zrnic from Larabie fonts (www.larabiefonts.com). The word "Fullway" in the bottom-right corner is set in Helvetica Black Oblique, and the small type under the "PN" is set in the font Helvetica Regular.

Multiple Inline/Outline Type Effect

This technique was actually first born in Adobe Illustrator, where creating multiple inlines and outlines was an everyday design chore, but since the invention of layer styles back in Photoshop 6, creating multiple inline effects within Photoshop is a breeze. In our project here, we're going to use the multiple inline effect to create a cereal product box.

Step One:

In this project, we're going to build a cereal box, so create a new document (File>New) that's 7x5" at 72 ppi in RGB mode. Press the letter "d" to set your Foreground color to black, then press the letter "t" to switch to the Type tool. Click on your document and type the word "Honey" (the font shown here is Impact set at a large point size with its horizontal scaling set to 120% in the Character palette, but you can use any thick, italic, sans serif typeface).

Step Two:

Click the Foreground color swatch in the Toolbox to select a medium green in the Color Picker (I used R=3, G=143, B=82), and click your Background color swatch to pick a lighter shade of green (I used R=38, G=179, B=50). Choose Gradient Overlay from the Add a Layer Style pop-up menu at the bottom of the Layers palette. When the dialog appears, click on the down-facing arrow to the right of the Gradient thumbnail to bring up the Gradient Picker. Choose the first gradient in the Picker (the Foreground to Background gradient) and turn on the Reverse checkbox in the Layer Style dialog, but don't click OK yet.

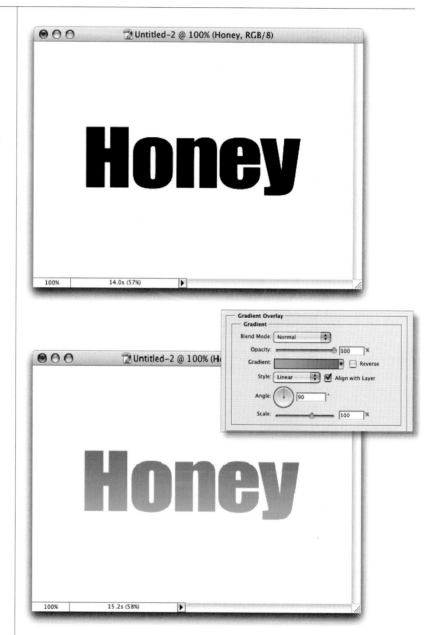

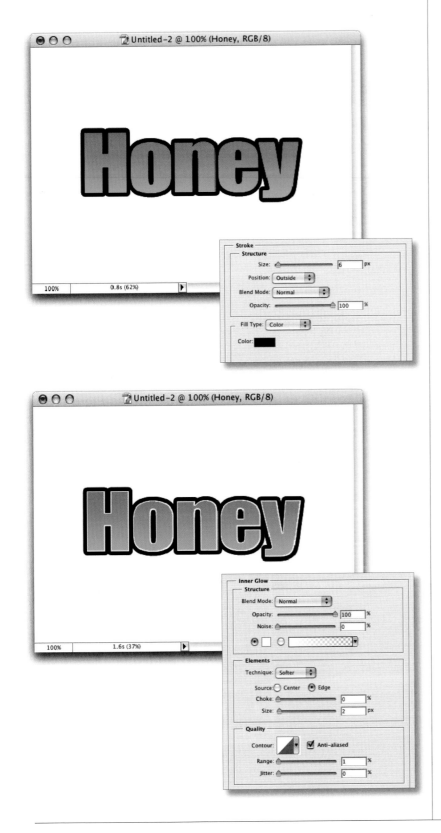

Step Three:

From the Styles list on the left side of the Layer Style dialog, click directly on the word "Stroke." When its options appear, click on the red Color swatch and change the stroke color to black in the Color Picker. Increase the Size to 6 to put a thick, black stroke around your letters (as shown here). Don't click OK quite yet. Instead, in the Styles list on the left of the dialog, click directly on the words "Inner Glow."

Step Four:

In the Inner Glow options, click on the beige color swatch and change the glow color to white in the Color Picker. Increase the Opacity setting to 100%, then lower the Size setting to 2. At the bottom of the dialog, lower the Range to 1 and turn on the Anti-aliased checkbox. Now when you click OK, the gradient, the black stroke on the outside, and the white stroke on the inside will all be applied to your type (as shown).

Continued

Step Five:

With the Type tool still selected, go up to the Options Bar and click on the Create Warped Text icon (it's just to the right of the color swatch in the Options Bar, and it has a capital "T" with a bent arrow under it). When the Warp Text dialog appears, for Style choose Wave, and with the Horizontal radio button selected, increase the Bend amount to +66% (as shown here). Click OK to bend your type.

Step Six:

Get the Move tool from the Toolbox, then press Command-J (PC: Control-J) to duplicate your bent Type layer in the Layers palette. With the Move tool, hold the Shift key, and click-and-drag the duplicate "Honey" text straight down until it appears below your original text (as shown here).

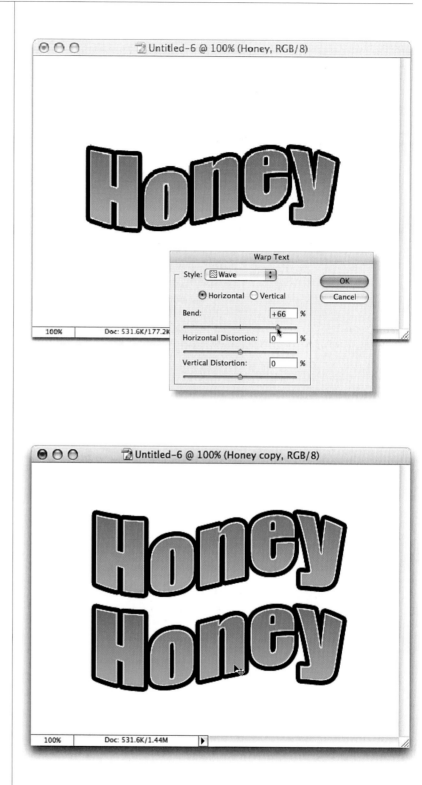

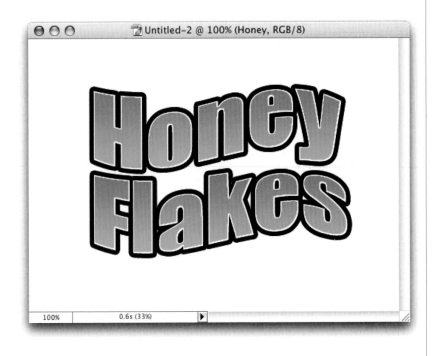

Step Seven:

Press the letter "t" to switch back to the Type tool, highlight the duplicate type, then type in the word "Flakes" over the old word "Honey," and it will automatically take on the same bend (as shown here). Now we'll take these two stroked Type layers and use them to create a fictitious cereal box.

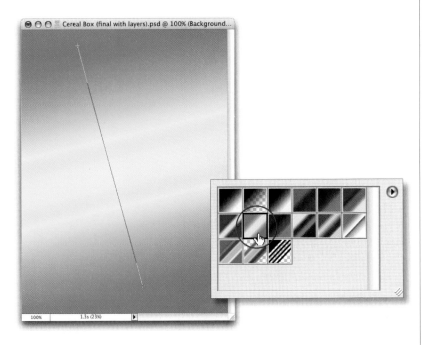

Step Eight:

Click on the Gradient tool in the Toolbox, and then create a new document (File>New) that's 6x8" at 72 ppi in RGB mode. In the Options Bar, click on the down-facing arrow to the right of the Gradient thumbnail to bring up the Gradient Picker and choose the Orange to Yellow to Orange gradient from the default set of gradients (as shown). Click the Linear Gradient icon in the Options Bar (it's the first in the set of five icons near the left). Now take the Gradient tool and click on the top of the new document, just left of center, and drag diagonally downward near the bottom right.

Continued

Step Nine:

Now go back to your inline type document. In the Layers palette, click in the second column beside your "Honey" layer (as shown here) to link your two layers together, then press Command-E (PC: Control-E) to merge these two layers together into one single layer. (The reason you have to link them together is that Photoshop won't let you merge Type layers unless they're linked.)

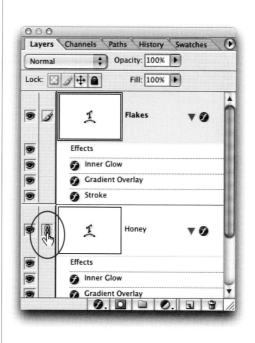

Step Ten:

Press the letter "v" to switch to the Move tool and drag-and-drop this merged layer on top of your gradient document, positioning your type in the top third of the document (as shown here).

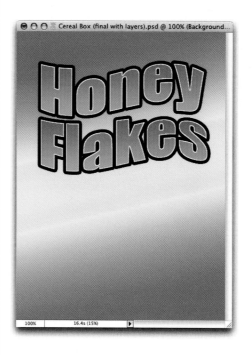

Step Eleven:
Open the photo of the cereal bowl. If your bowl isn't already on its own layer, press the letter "w" to switch to the Magic Wand tool, and click on the white background area. Choose Inverse from the Select menu, then press the letter "v" to switch to the Move tool, and drag-and-drop the image onto your gradient document. Press Command-T (PC: Control-T) to bring up the Free Transform bounding box (you may need to press Command-Zero [PC: Control-Zero] to zoom out so you can see all four handles), press-and-hold the Shift key, click a corner handle, and resize the image. Then move your cursor outside to the right of the bounding box, and click-and-drag upward to rotate the bowl and spoon a little bit, until the end of the spoon covers part of the letter "s" (as shown here). Click inside the bounding box to drag it into position. Press Return (PC: Enter) to lock in your transformation. Now you'll finish up by adding more type and applying the same text warp.

Step Twelve:
Here's the finished box with "CRUNCHY OAT FLAKES CEREAL!" added at the top in black (in the same font—Impact). To put a bend in that type, with the Type tool still selected, click the Create Warped Text icon again in the Options Bar, but this time for Style choose Flag instead of Wave, and increase the Bend amount to around +92%. The text at the bottom (with the weight info) is set in Helvetica Ultra Compressed using the Type tool and Character palette. The name of the fictitious company is set in the font Times, and the type under the product name is set in Times Italic.

3D Type Effect

Here's a twist on the classic technique of creating a 3D text effect right within Photoshop. In our project here, we're going to add a 3D type effect to an illustration that will be used on the cover of a software product box.

Step One:
Create a new document (File>New) that's set at 7x5" at 72 ppi in RGB mode. Click the Foreground color swatch in the Toolbox to select a medium green in the Color Picker (I used R=134, G=157, B=13), and then press the letter "t" to switch to the Type tool. Click on your document and enter your type (the large type here is set using the font Impact).

Step Two:
You're going to apply a perspective effect, but to do that you have to convert your Type layer into a regular image layer. So, go to the Layers palette, and Control-click (PC: Right-click) on the Type layer's name. From the contextual menu that appears, choose Rasterize Layer (as shown here).

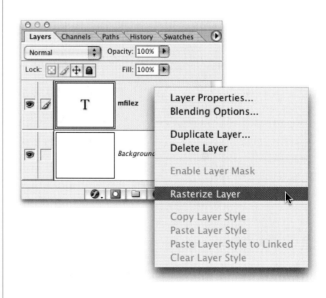

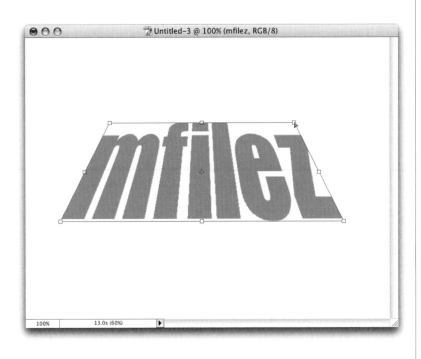

Step Three:

Now to create the perspective effect, press Command-T (PC: Control-T) to bring up the Free Transform bounding box. Hold Shift-Option-Command (PC: Shift-Alt-Control), grab the top-right corner point and drag inward to create a perspective effect (as shown here). Don't press Return (PC: Enter) yet.

Step Four:

Release the keys you were holding down, then grab the top-center point of the bounding box and drag straight down to make the type shorter (as shown here). Now press Return (PC: Enter) to lock in your transformation.

Continued

Step Five:

Duplicate your Type layer by pressing Command-J (PC: Control-J). Press the letter "d" to set your Foreground color to black, then Command-click (PC: Control-click) on your duplicate layer's thumbnail in the Layers palette to put a selection around it. Now fill your duplicate layer with black by pressing Option-Delete (PC: Alt-Backspace). Deselect by pressing Command-D (PC: Control-D), then in the Layers palette, drag this black layer beneath your original green Type layer (as shown here).

Step Six:

To create the 3D depth effect, press the letter "v" to switch to the Move tool, hold down (and keep holding) the Option key (PC: Alt key), then press-and-hold the Down Arrow key on your keyboard for just a few seconds, and the 3D effect will appear (as shown here). This creates the 3D effect by making numerous copies of your black layer in the Layers palette, each offset by just a pixel, giving the appearance that it's solid. In the example shown here, it created 30 copies of the black layer (just take a look in the Layers palette). So, are we stuck with 30 extra layers? We'll fix that in the next step.

Step Seven:

In the Layers palette, hide your original green Type layer from view by clicking on the Eye icon in the first column beside that layer (don't change layers, just click on the Eye icon). Then scroll down to the bottom of the palette and hide the Background layer by clicking its Eye icon, leaving only the black layers visible (as shown here).

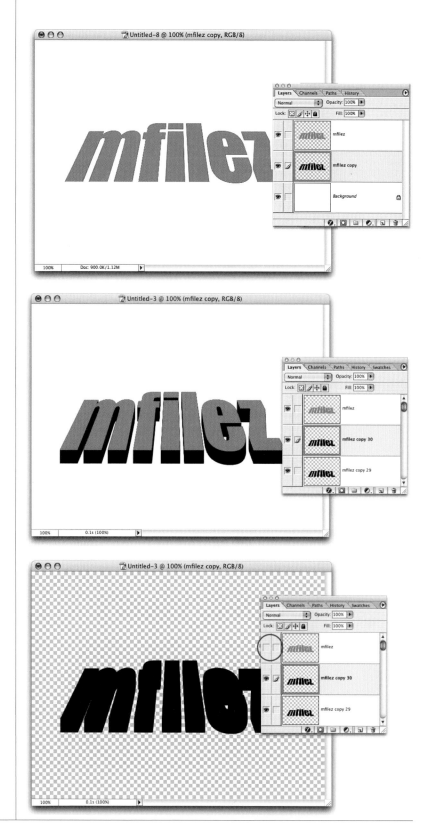

Step Eight:

In the Layers palette's flyout menu, choose Merge Visible to combine the 30 black 3D layers into one single layer (as shown here). Then in the Layers palette, click on the original green Type layer and press Command-E (PC: Control-E) to merge your green Type layer and the black 3D layer into one single layer.

Step Nine:

Now to enhance the 3D effect, press Command-T (PC: Control-T) to bring up the Free Transform bounding box. Grab the top-center point and drag straight down to compress the type and give you the 3D effect you see here. Press Return (PC: Enter) to lock in your transformation. Now we'll use this 3D type on the cover of a software product package.

Continued

Step Ten:

Create a new document (File>New) that's 6x8" at 72 ppi in RGB mode (this will be the cover of your software product box). Open a high-tech illustration, press "v" to switch to the Move tool, and drag-and-drop the image onto your blank document. Press Command-T (PC: Control-T) to bring up the Free Transform command. Hold the Shift key, grab a corner point, and scale the illustration down so it fits within the image area (as shown here). Then press Return (PC: Enter) to lock in your transformation.

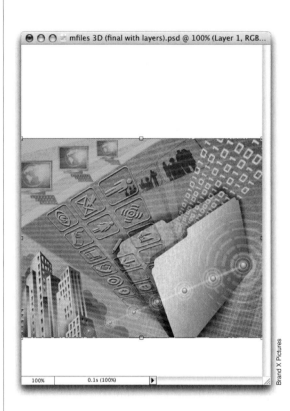

Step Eleven:

Go back to your 3D type document, and with the Move tool, click-and-drag your 3D type onto your illustration. Press Command-T (PC: Control-T) to bring up Free Transform. Hold the Shift key, grab a corner point, and scale the 3D text down so it fits within the image area. Then release the Shift key, move your cursor outside to the right of the bounding box, and click-and-drag upward to rotate your text (as shown). Click inside the bounding box and drag the type into position. Press Return (PC: Enter) to lock in your transformation.

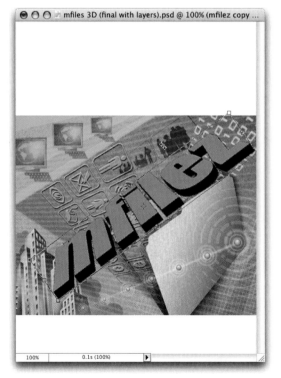

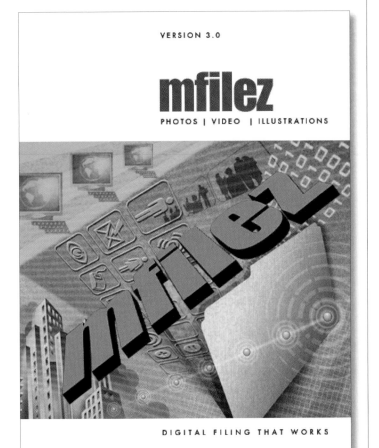

VERSION 3.0

mfilez

PHOTOS | VIDEO | ILLUSTRATIONS

DIGITAL FILING THAT WORKS

Step Twelve:

To make your type blend in with the illustration, go to the Layers palette and change the layer blend mode to Darken, then lower the Opacity to around 70%. Lastly, just add some text to finish off the box using the Type tool and Character palette. The product's name is set in the font Impact, but all the rest of the text is set in the font Futura Medium with the tracking set at 220 in the Character palette to add space between the letters.

Perspective Shadow Effect

This classic effect is a variation of the perspective shadow effect used on the logo for the old FOX TV show *The X-Files*. I saw it most recently used in the logo for the 2004 remake of the classic cult horror movie *Dawn of the Dead*, and that's the version we're showing here. The technique is quite simple—you actually spend more time tweaking the type to get it ready for the perspective shadow than you do applying the technique, which takes just seconds.

Step One:

Open the background image that you want to use for this technique. Press "d" then "x" to set your Foreground color to white. Press "t" to switch to the Type tool and type the word "DAWN" in all caps (I used the font Minion Pro). Highlight the letters "AW" in "DAWN" with the Type tool, then go to the Character palette (found in the Window menu) and lower the point size until it's just a little more than half the height of the "D." Now highlight the letter "N" and lower its point size until it's about three-quarters the size of the "D". (Hey, that's they way they did it.) Then create a separate line of type with the Type tool, and type the words "OF THE" at a smaller point size (as shown here). (You may have to get the Move tool from the Toolbox and position your type, as I did here.)

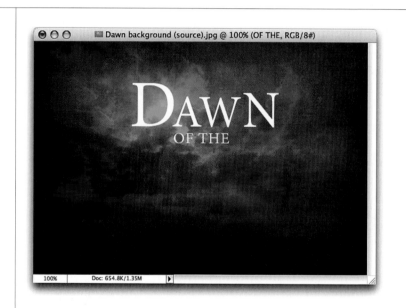

Step Two:

Go to the Layers palette, click on your "DAWN" layer, and press Command-J (PC: Control-J) to duplicate the layer. Press "v" to switch to the Move tool, hold the Shift key, and drag the duplicate text straight down. Press "t" to switch to the Type tool again, highlight the letters "AW" and change them to "UD", then highlight the letter "N" and change it to "E".

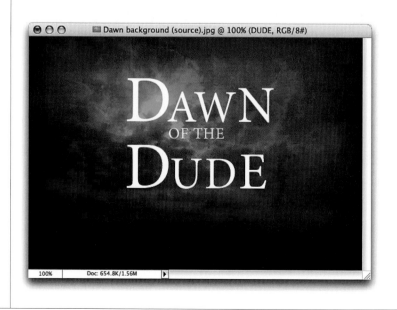

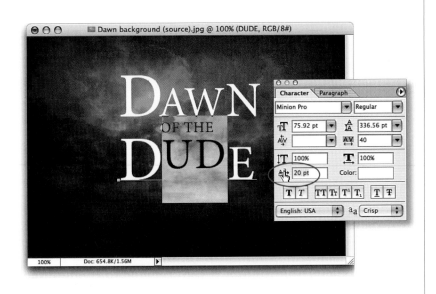

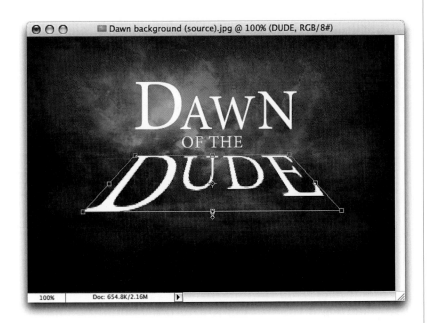

Step Three:

Now highlight the letters "UD" again with the Type tool and go to the Character palette. Click on the Set the Baseline Shift icon to highlight the field (as shown here), and use the Up Arrow key on your keyboard to move your type up off the baseline. Keep pressing the Up Arrow key until the tops of the letters "UD" align with the top of the letter "D" in the word "DUDE." Do the same thing with the letter "E"—highlight it and adjust the baseline shift until all four letters align across the top.

Step Four:

Go to the Layers palette and Control-click (PC: Right-click) on the "DUDE" Type layer's name. In the contextual menu that appears, choose Rasterize Layer. Now you can add a perspective effect by pressing Command-T (PC: Control-T) to bring up the Free Transform command. Then hold Shift-Option-Command (PC: Shift-Alt-Control), grab the bottom-right corner point and drag outward. Then release the keys, grab the bottom-center point (as shown here), and drag straight down to exaggerate the effect. Press Return (PC: Enter) to lock in your transformation.

Continued

Step Five:

Now soften this perspective type by going under the Filter menu, under Blur, and choose Gaussian Blur. When the dialog appears, enter 1 pixel for the Radius and click OK. Press the letter "m" to switch to the Rectangular Marquee tool and draw a selection around the bottom half of the type (as shown here). Soften the edge of this selection by going under the Select menu and choosing Feather. When the dialog appears, enter 10 pixels and click OK.

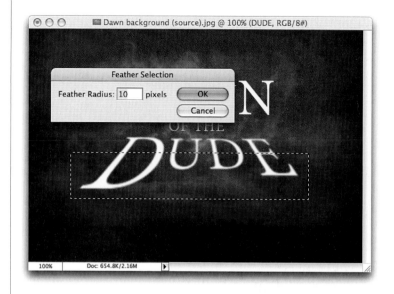

Step Six:

Now go back to Filter>Blur>Gaussian Blur, apply a 3-pixel blur to this rectangle, and click OK. By doing this, the tops of the letters have less of a blur, but then it looks like the letters get blurrier toward the bottom. The feathering you applied to the rectangular selection keeps you from seeing a hard edge. Deselect by pressing Command-D (PC: Control-D) to complete the effect (as shown here).

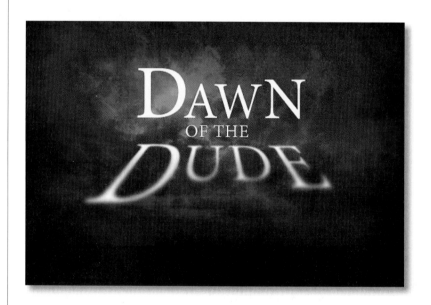

Distressed Type

It's not grunge type—it's distressed (damaged) type. This classic effect is as popular as ever, and it shows up in everything from store brands to clothing to movie posters, using a distressed look based on the technique you're going to learn here.

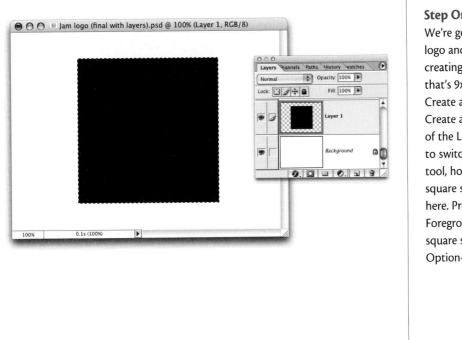

Step One:
We're going to create a radio station logo and put it on a T-shirt, so start by creating a new document (File>New) that's 9x7" at 72 ppi in RGB mode. Create a new layer by clicking on the Create a New Layer icon at the bottom of the Layers palette. Press the letter "m" to switch to the Rectangular Marquee tool, hold the Shift key, and draw a square selection like the one shown here. Press the letter "d" to set your Foreground color to black, then fill your square selection with black by pressing Option-Delete (PC: Alt-Backspace).

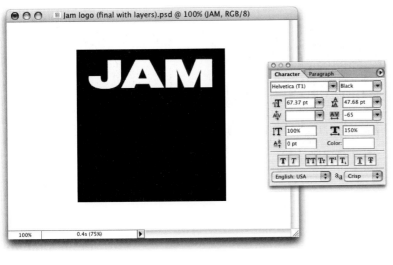

Step Two:
Deselect by pressing Command-D (PC: Control-D). Press the letter "x" to set your Foreground color to white, then press the letter "t" to switch to the Type tool. Click on the document and type the word "JAM" in a thick typeface. (The font shown here is Helvetica Black with the horizontal scaling set to 150% in the Character palette.) Press Enter to lock in your text.

Continued

Step Three:

You're going to add more text, and to make sure it lines up correctly you'll need to use guides. Press Command-R (PC: Control-R) to make your rulers visible. Then click directly on the left ruler, drag out a guide, and position it on the left edge of the "J". Drag out a second guide and position it on the right edge of the "M" (as shown here).

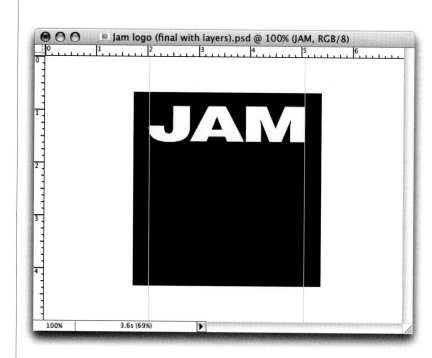

Step Four:

Press Command-J (PC: Control-J) to duplicate your Type layer. In the Layers palette, double-click directly on the duplicated Type layer's thumbnail (it has a big "T" on it) to highlight your text, then move your cursor away from your type and it will temporarily change into the Move tool. Click-and-hold on the document, press-and-hold the Shift key, and drag your duplicate layer down to the bottom of your black square (as shown). Release the Shift key, and with the type still highlighted, type in "FM." Press Enter to lock in your text change. Press Command-T (PC: Control-T) to bring up the Free Transform command, then grab the right-center point and drag it to the guide on the right. Next, grab the left-center point and drag it to the guide on the left so your type fits perfectly within the two guides. Then, grab the top-center point and drag downward to make the type shorter (as shown here). Press Return (PC: Enter) to lock in your transformation.

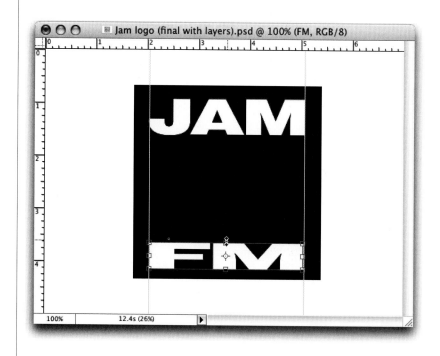

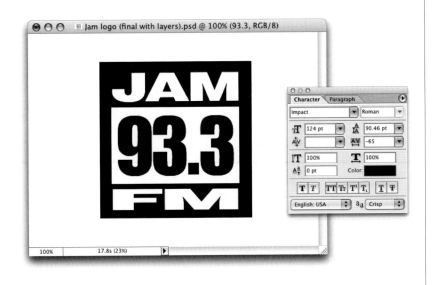

Step Five:
Click on the Create a New Layer icon at the bottom of the Layers palette to add a new blank layer, then press the letter "m" to switch to the Rectangular Marquee tool. Make a rectangular selection in the center of your black box between your two lines of type that's aligned with your left and right guides. Press Option-Delete (PC: Alt-Backspace) to fill your selection with white, then press Command-D (PC: Control-D) to deselect. Press the letter "d" to set your Foreground color to black, then get the Type tool and type in "93.3" in a tall, thick typeface (the font Impact was used here). Go under the View menu and choose Clear Guides, then press Command-R (PC: Control-R) to hide your rulers.

Step Six:
Go to the Layers palette and hide the Background layer from view by clicking on the Eye icon in the left column beside it. Then, choose Merge Visible from the palette's flyout menu (as shown here) to merge all the layers into just one layer above the Background layer. Doing this will also rasterize your Type layers into regular image layers.

Continued

Step Seven:

Now to add the distress: Press the letter "b" to switch to the Brush tool and press the letter "x" to set white as your Foreground color. Click on the icon next to the word "Brush" in the Options Bar to bring up the Brush Picker. In the Brush Picker, choose the 39-pixel Dry Brush from the default set of brushes (as shown here).

Step Eight:

Move this brush over black areas of your image and start clicking your mouse button. Don't paint strokes—just click your mouse button a number of times. Try ten or twelve clicks in one spot, then move your cursor to another spot, click seven or eight times, and move to another spot, keeping your locations and number of clicks random.

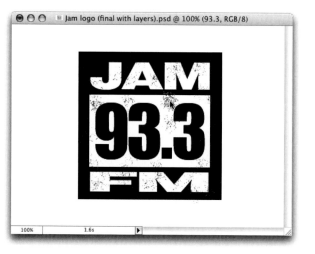

Step Nine:

Now, go back up to the Brush Picker and pick a different size and shaped brush. In this case, try the 48-pixel Oil Heavy Flow Dry Edges brush highlighted here, and do the same thing you did in the previous step—click multiple times over black areas in your logo (as shown here).

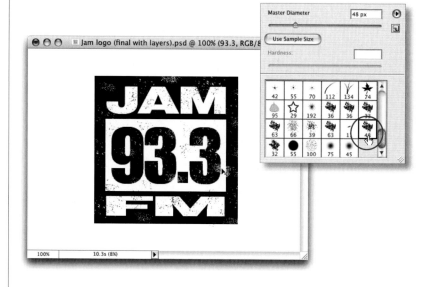

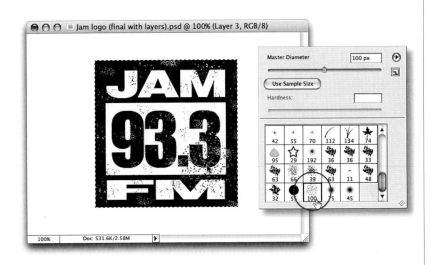

Step Ten:

Go to the Layers palette, hold the Command key (PC: Control key), and click on your logo layer to put a selection around it (by doing this, it ensures that you won't accidentally paint outside the black borders of the logo). Press the letter "d" to set your Foreground color to black, then get the Brush tool again, switch to the 100-pixel Rough Round Bristle brush in the Brush Picker, and start clicking multiple times over white areas in your image area until the logo looks pretty distressed (like the one shown here). In the next step, we'll add this logo to a T-shirt.

Step Eleven:

Open the photo that has a T-shirt you want to apply your logo to. Go back to the logo image, press the letter "v" to switch to the Move tool, and drag your logo onto the T-shirt image. Press Command-T (PC: Control-T) to bring up the Free Transform command. Hold the Shift key, grab a corner point, and drag inward to scale the logo down so it fits comfortably on the shirt. Then let go of the Shift key, move your cursor outside the bounding box to the right (as shown), and click-and-drag downward to rotate the logo so it has a similar angle to the shirt. Don't press Return (PC: Enter) yet.

Continued

Step Twelve:

Now hold Shift-Option-Command (PC: Shift-Alt-Backspace) and drag the bottom-right corner point of the bounding box inward (as shown here) to create a perspective effect (so the top of the logo appears wider than the bottom).

Step Thirteen:

Let go of those keys, then just hold the Command key (PC: Control key) and take the top-right corner point and drag outward a bit (as shown) to distort that corner of the logo (we're trying to make it look like the logo is really on the shirt). If necessary, move your cursor outside the bounding box, and click-and-drag to rotate the logo until its angle looks more realistic on the shirt. Now press Return (PC: Enter) to lock in your transformations.

Step Fourteen:
To help the logo blend into the shirt, go to the Layers palette and change the blend mode of your logo layer from Normal to Multiply and lower the Opacity of this layer to around 80% (as shown here).

Step Fifteen:
Now we need to put some bends in the logo so it looks like it's following the wrinkles and folds of the T-shirt. Go under the Filter menu and choose Liquify (it's near the top). At the bottom right of the Liquify dialog, turn on the checkbox for Show Backdrop so you can see the T-shirt image. Then get Liquify's Smudge tool (it's the top tool in the dialog's toolbar), go to one of the edges of your logo that falls near a fold in the shirt, and just paint a very short stroke along the edge (as shown here). To decrease the size of the Smudge tool, press the Left Bracket key on your keyboard.

Continued

Step Sixteen:

Repeat this short, simple stroke on a couple of different spots along the sides of your logo. Each time you do it, it will slightly bend the logo as if it was liquid, and this gives the impression that the logo is conforming to the bends in the shirt.

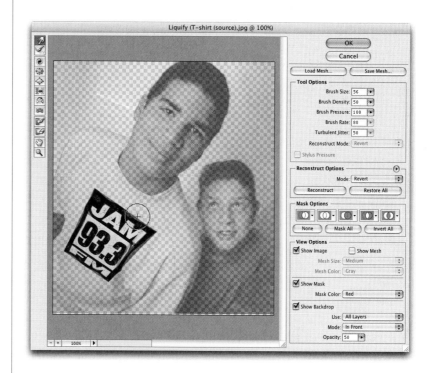

Step Seventeen:

After you've completed a few strokes, click OK in the Liquify dialog (you can see the results here). Although our five or six short strokes were in pretty random locations along the edges of the logo, it really looks like the shirt is affecting the logo, which helps "sell" the effect. Next, we'll take the photo and use it on a billboard. Just go to the Layers palette's flyout menu and choose Flatten Image. Open a billboard photo, and in your T-shirt image, get the Move tool, and drag it onto your billboard photo. Use Free Transform to scale it down to fit within the left side of the billboard.

Billboard 2 (final with layers).psd @ 100% (Layer 3, RGB/8#)

Step Eighteen:

To make it look like the photo is really in the sign, choose Inner Shadow from the Add a Layer Style pop-up menu at the bottom of the Layers Palette. When the dialog appears, just change the Angle to 120° and click OK to add that shadow across the top and left side of the photo. Press Shift-L until you have the Polygonal Lasso tool, and select the sign to the right of the photo. Set your Foreground color to black, and fill the selection with black by pressing Option-Delete (PC: Alt-Backspace), then deselect by pressing Command-D (PC: Control-D). Now add some text with the Type tool (the font is Helvetica Black with the horizontal scaling set to 150% in the Character palette). The "Your Hit Music Station" font is Helvetica Bold Condensed Oblique.

The Chapter Intro—Airbrushed Chrome

The spreads that introduce each chapter were designed by my good friend, and brilliant artist, Felix Nelson (he's the Creative Director for *Photoshop User* magazine). This "airbrushed-look" chrome effect uses one of Photoshop's default gradients, but Felix uses a cool trick for making the effect really look like an airbrushed version, and not so "digital."

Step One:

Create a new document (File>New) that's 10x5" at 72 ppi in RGB mode. Click on the Foreground color swatch in the Toolbox and choose a grayish green in the Color Picker (I used R=117, G=146, B=141), and fill the Background layer with this color by pressing Option-Delete (PC: Alt-Backspace). Press "d" to set your Foreground color to black, then press "t" to switch to the Type tool, and set your type. (The font used here and in the chapter intros is Bullet Regular Script from House Industries with the tracking [space between the letters] set to 300 in the Character palette.)

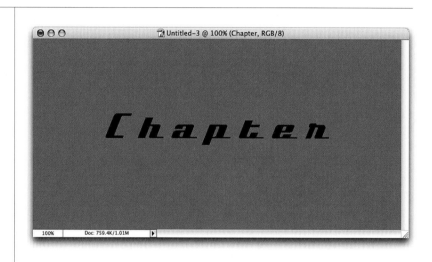

Step Two:

The font (Bullet Regular Script) is actually an italic font, but Felix wanted the letters to be upright (or roman). Here's how to make that happen: Click on the Move tool in the Toolbox, then press Command-T (PC: Control-T) to bring up Free Transform. Hold the Command key (PC: Control key), click on the top-center point of the bounding box, and drag to the left to skew the letters until they're straight up and down (as shown here). Press Return (PC: Enter) to lock in your straightening.

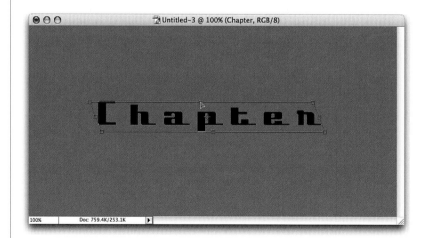

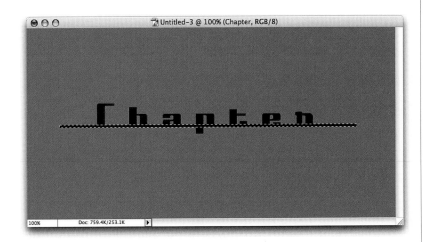

Step Three:
Go to the Layers palette and Control-click (PC: Right-click) on the Type layer's name, and from the contextual menu that appears, choose Rasterize to convert your Type layer into a regular image layer. Then press the letter "m" to switch to the Rectangular Marquee tool and draw a long thin rectangular selection along the bottom of the letters (as shown here). Press Option-Delete (PC: Alt-Backspace) to fill the selection with black.

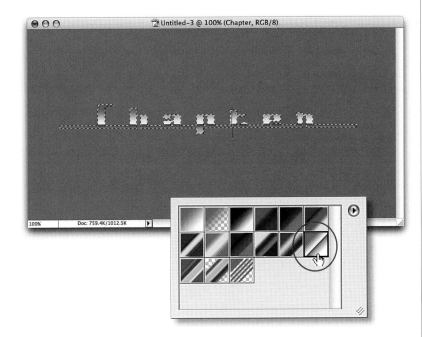

Step Four:
Deselect by pressing Command-D (PC: Control-D). Now, hold the Command key (PC: Control key), go to the Layers palette, and click on your "Chapter" layer to put a selection around your text and thin bar (as shown here). Then, press the letter "g" to switch to the Gradient tool, press Return (PC: Enter) to bring up the Gradient Picker, and choose the Chrome gradient from the default set of gradients (as shown here). Take the Gradient tool and drag it straight down from the top of the letter "t" to the bottom of the "p" (as shown here) to add the gradient. Don't deselect yet.

Continued

Step Five:

Now you're going to make the thin, dark brown line between the gold and white areas of your gradient even darker by using the Burn tool. Press Shift-O until you have the Burn tool; click on the icon next to the word "Brush" in the Options Bar to bring up the Brush Picker; and choose a very small, soft-edged brush. Drag the Burn tool all the way across the brown line, starting at the left and painting across to the right (and then back again). Hold the Shift key to make this easier as you paint. Don't deselect yet. Next we want to make the horizon between the brown and blue look less digital and more realistic, so you're going to smudge that line.

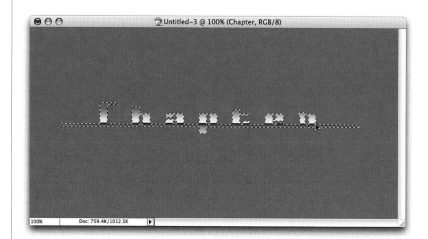

Step Six:

Go under the Filter menu and choose Liquify. Get the Zoom tool from Liquify's toolbar and zoom in real close on one of your letters. Then switch to the Smudge tool (it's the top tool in the toolbar) and decrease the size of the brush by entering a small number in the Brush Size field in the Tool Options section on the right side of the dialog. What you're going to do here is click and smudge upward at the outer edges of the letters at the horizon where the brown and the blue meet, and then smudge the horizon downward in the center of each of the letters (kind of making a "U" shape). Since Liquify puts a red mask around the transparent areas outside your type, it's a little bit hard to see when you smudge, but just have faith. Move from letter to letter and repeat this "U-shape" smudging, then click OK.

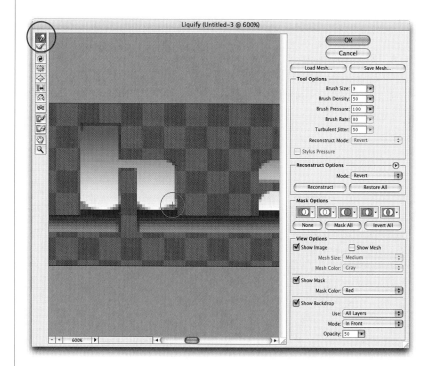

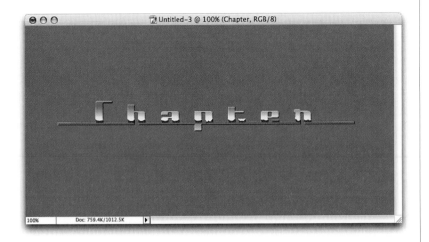

Step Seven:

Deselect by pressing Command-D (PC: Control-D). Then choose Bevel and Emboss from the Add a Layer Style pop-up menu at the bottom of the Layers palette. Change the Technique pop-up menu to Chisel Hard, increase the Depth to 171%, and lower the Size to 1. Also, increase the Highlight Opacity to 100% and turn on the Anti-aliased checkbox, then click OK to apply a bevel to your letters (as shown here).

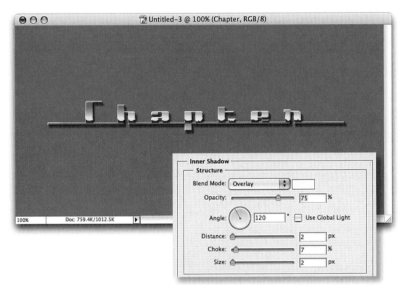

Step Eight:

To put a thin white line around the edge of the letters, choose Inner Shadow from the Add a Layer Style pop-up menu at the bottom of the Layers palette. Change the Blend Mode pop-up menu from Multiply to Overlay, and then click on the black color swatch and choose white in the Color Picker. Then set the Distance to 2, the Choke amount to 7%, and the Size to 2. Click on the checkbox next to the words "Drop Shadow" in the Styles list on the left side of the Layer Style dialog, and then click OK to add a thin white line around your type and a drop shadow (as shown here).

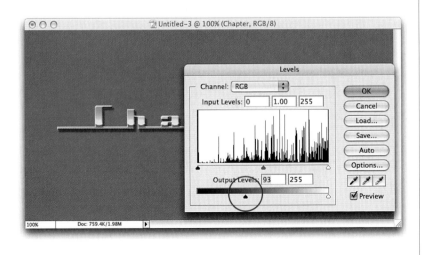

Step Nine:

Now you'll lighten the letters up a little by going under the Image menu, under Adjustments, and choosing Levels. In the Levels dialog, drag the bottom-left Output Levels slider to the right to lighten the overall tone of your type (as shown here), and then click OK. Now press Command-J (PC: Control-J) to duplicate your text layer and its three layer styles (the Bevel and Emboss, the Inner Shadow, and the Drop Shadow).

Continued

Step Ten:

In the Layers palette, click on the words "Drop Shadow" under the duplicated layer and drag it to the Trash icon at the bottom of the Layers palette to delete it. Then double-click on the words "Bevel and Emboss" for this layer. In the dialog, set the Angle to 128° and the Altitude to 42° (as shown here). Next, click on the down-facing arrow to the right of the Gloss Contour thumbnail to bring up the Contour Picker. From the Picker's flyout menu, choose Contours and then click the Append button in the resulting dialog to load an additional set of contours. Choose the contour with three hills (as shown), turn on the Anti-aliased checkbox, drag the Shadow Opacity slider to 100%, then click OK.

Step Eleven:

In the Layers palette, click on your original "Chapter" layer to make it active, then press Command-J (PC: Control-J) to make a duplicate of this layer, and drag it to the top of the layers stack. On this layer, click on the word "Effects" and drag it to the Trash icon to delete all the effects on it. Then change this layer's blend mode to Overlay and lower the Opacity setting to 50% (as shown here).

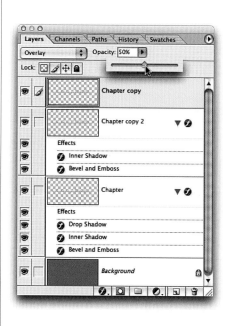

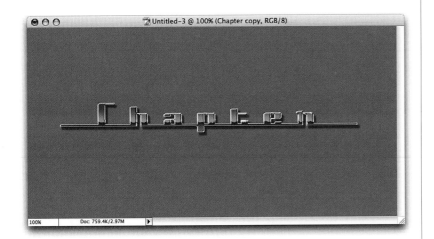

Step Twelve:

Here's the completed airbrushed chrome effect, as used in the opening of each chapter here in the book. Thanks to Felix Nelson for sharing his version of this classic effect. Now we'll create the big "V" part of the logo.

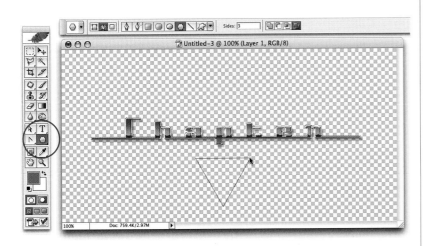

Step Thirteen:

Go to the Layers palette and hide the Background layer from view by clicking on the Eye icon to the left of the layer. Get the Polygon tool (highlighted here in the Toolbox—it's one of the Shape tools), and in the group of three icons on the left of the Options Bar, click on the second icon so your shape will create a path. Then enter 3 in the Sides field so your shape will form a triangle. Click-and-drag out your triangle path and position is as shown here.

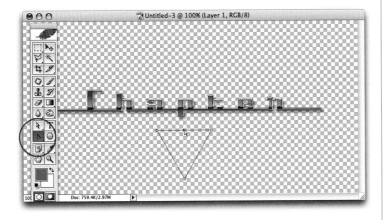

Step Fourteen:

Get the Add Anchor Point tool from the Toolbox (you'll find it in the Pen tool's flyout menu) and click once in the center of the top line of your triangle to add a curve point. To make it a straight point, get the Convert Point tool (shown here highlighted in the Toolbox) from the same flyout menu, and click once on the point you added to the triangle (as shown here).

Continued

Step Fifteen:
Press Shift-A until you have the Direct Selection tool (the white hollow arrow), and then click on your center point and drag it straight down (as shown here).

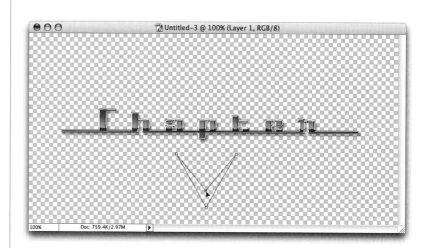

Step Sixteen:
Using the Direct Selection tool, grab the top-left corner point and drag outward, past the edge of your letters, and then do the same thing with the right corner point (as shown here). Click on the center point again and drag it down a little farther to give you the shape you see here.

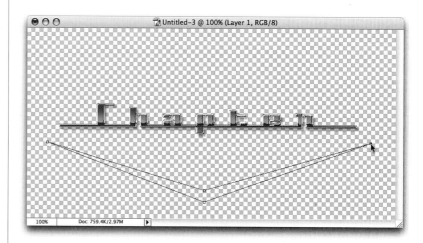

Step Seventeen:
Now go back to the Layers palette, make the Background Layer visible again by clicking in the empty box where the Eye icon used to be, and click on the Create a New Layer icon to create a new blank layer. Press Command-Return (PC: Control-Enter) to turn your path into a selection (as shown). Then get the Gradient tool, and using the same Chrome gradient, draw a gradient through the left side of your big "V" so the horizon between the brown and blue follows the shape of the "V." This might take you a few tries to get the angle of the gradient just right (it took me five or six tries to get what you see here).

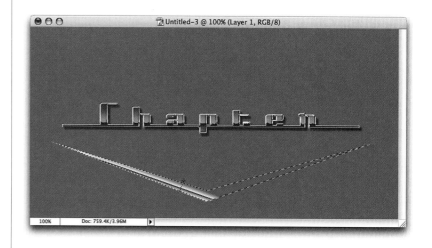

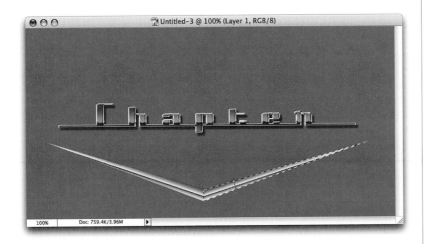

Step Eighteen:

Once the left side is correct, press the letter "m" to switch to the Rectangular Marquee tool, hold the Option key (PC: Alt key), and draw a selection over the entire left side of the big "V" to deselect that area, leaving just the right side selected (as shown here). Now you'll take the Gradient tool and drag a diagonal gradient so the horizon follows the right side of the "V." It took me about ten tries to get this side right. When it finally looks right, deselect by pressing Command-D (PC: Control-D).

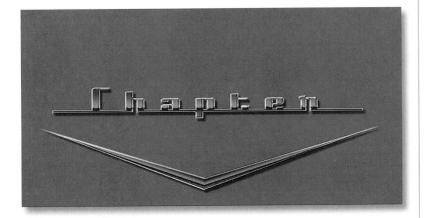

Step Nineteen:

Now you'll use the same layer technique that you used on the word "Chapter." Go to your original "Chapter" layer in the Layers palette, click directly on the word "Effects," and drag-and-drop it on to your big "V" layer to copy all three effects to that layer. You'll duplicate this layer and delete the drop shadow effect (sound familiar?), then you'll edit the Bevel and Emboss by adding a contour. Then you'll duplicate the original big "V" layer, move it to the top of the layers stack, trash all three effects, change the blend mode to Overlay, and lower the Opacity to 50% to give you the effect shown here.

Chapter EIGHT

FREEZE FRAME
CLASSIC PHOTOGRAPHIC EFFECTS

On some level, aren't all these classic effects photographic effects? I mean, this is Photoshop, right? It's all about photos, isn't it? Not so, my fast-to-judge friend. There are other classic effects that use no photos at all. What are these called? Lame effects. All right, they're not lame. They're type effects, but just about every other effect is photographic, so that's what we're celebrating in this chapter—the ubiquitousness of photographic effects (by the way, I have no way of knowing if "ubiquitousness" is really a word, but if it's not, don't you think it should be?). Okay, what about the chapter title "Freeze Frame"? It's from a J. Geils Band song of the same name. So, where are all the movie titles and TV show chapter names? I'm having a serious drought on those right now, so we're primarily going with song titles. It's a crutch, I know, but if I wait for a suitable movie title to come along, it could be a long night.

Sharp Foreground, Blurred Background

This is a technique that's usually done with a camera, but it doesn't have to be. Basically, you're blurring a copy of the photo, then erasing the detailed areas, giving you a simple depth-of-field effect.

Step One:

Open the photo that you want to apply the effect to. Press Command-J (PC: Control-J) to duplicate the Background layer in the Layers palette (as shown here).

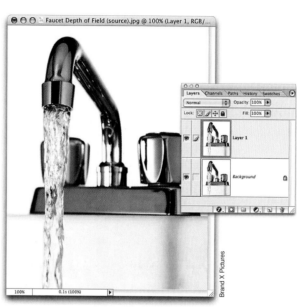

Step Two:

Go under the Filter menu, under Blur, and choose Gaussian Blur. When the dialog appears, increase the Radius to 4 pixels and click OK to put a blur over the entire image.

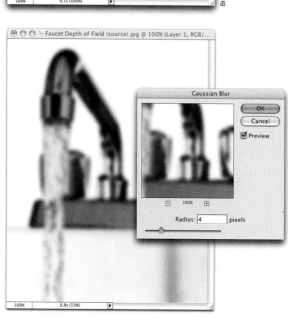

Step Three:

Press the letter "e" to switch to the Eraser tool. In the Options Bar, choose Brush in the Mode pop-up menu, then click on the icon next to the word "Brush," and choose a large soft-edged brush from the Brush Picker. Start erasing over the parts of the image that appear in the foreground (in this case, erase over the head of the faucet, as shown here). Erasing on this blurred layer reveals the original unblurred image on the Background layer.

Step Four:

Choose a smaller brush size in the Brush Picker and start erasing over the water, as it's also in the foreground of the photo. By making these areas sharp and leaving the background areas blurry, it creates a simple depth-of-field effect (as shown here). In the next step, you'll finish up by adding some text and some thin black lines, so go to the bottom of the Layers palette and create a new layer by clicking on the Create a New Layer icon.

Step Five:

Press Shift-U until you have the Line tool (it's one of the Shape tools), and up in the Options Bar, in the group of three icons on the left, click on the third icon from the left (so your lines are made of pixels, rather than paths or a shape layer). Then set your Weight to 1 pixel. Hold the Shift key and begin drawing straight lines (as shown here). The line at the top will go right across your faucet head, but you can use the Eraser tool and erase away that part of the line. Lastly, add some type using the Type tool and Character palette. The font for the company name is in Helvetica Black, and the rest is in Helvetica Medium Italic.

Blending Two Images

For years, blending images together has been one of the single most-requested Photoshop techniques. In our project here, we're not only going to blend from one image to another, but we're also going to show how the technique is used in Hollywood to create movie posters (plus, you get to learn some other cool tricks along the way).

Step One:

This first part isn't necessary for blending two images, but since we're doing a whole project (a movie poster), go ahead and create a new document (File>New) that's 6x8" at 72 ppi. Click on the Foreground color swatch in the Toolbox and choose a dark brown color in the Color Picker (I used R=92, G=59, B=1). Fill the Background layer with this dark brown by pressing Option-Delete (PC: Alt-Backspace).

Step Two:

Open the first image you want to use in your two-image blend. Press the letter "v" to switch to the Move tool, then click-and-drag the image onto your brown background, and position it as shown here. You may need to use Command-T (PC: Control-T) to bring up the Free Transform command to size your image.

Brand X Pictures

Brand X Pictures

Step Three:

Open the second photo you want to use in your two-image blend. Using the Move tool, drag this image on top of your first image. At the bottom of the Layers palette, click on the Add a Layer Mask icon (it's the second icon from the left) as shown here.

Step Four:

Press the letter "x" until your Foreground color is black. Press the letter "b" to switch to the Brush tool. In the Options Bar, click on the icon next to the word "Brush" and choose a large (200-pixel), soft-edged brush from the Brush Picker. Move over your photo, and begin painting (as shown), and as you paint, the photo beneath it (the three soccer players) will be revealed. Because you're using such a large, soft-edged brush, the blend is very smooth.

Continued

Step Five:

Continue painting with this large, soft-edged brush to reveal as much of the photo as you want (as shown here, where the top is softly blended into the other image, and the rest of the photo is revealed).

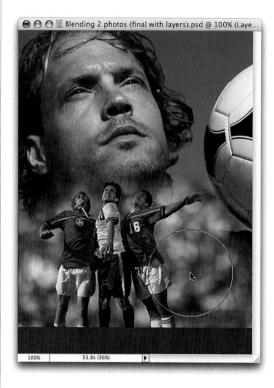

Step Six:

Now that the two photos are blended, you can blend the bottom photo right into the brown background. Go to the Layers palette, click on Layer 1 (the three soccer players) to make it active, then click on the Add a Layer Mask icon (as shown). Go up to the Brush Picker and lower the size of your 200-pixel brush to a 100-pixel brush (you'll need this smaller brush in the next step).

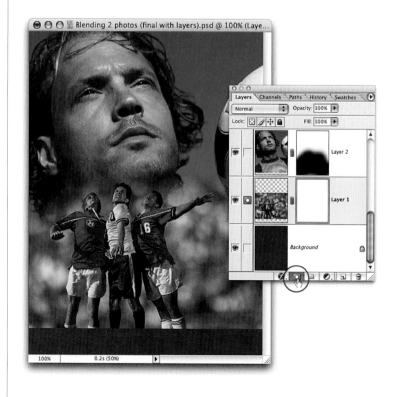

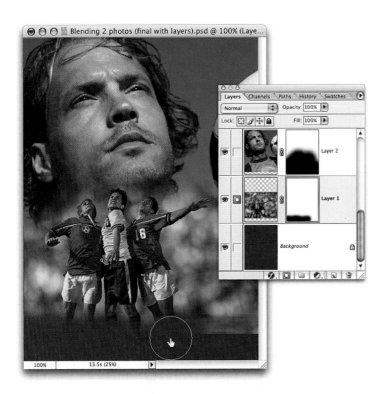

Step Seven:
Take the 100-pixel brush and paint a line along the bottom of your image of the three soccer players. This blends the bottom edge with the brown background (as shown here).

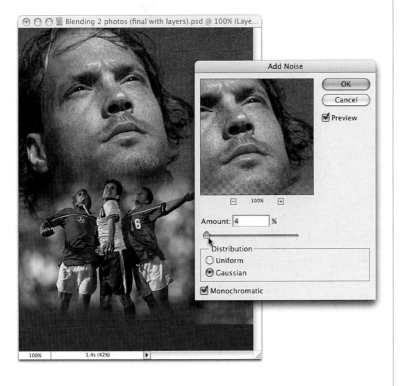

Step Eight:
Now to add a classic movie poster effect to your blended images: First, in the Layers palette click on the top layer (Layer 2) to make it active, then go under the Image menu, under Adjustments, and choose Desaturate to remove all the color from this top image. Then, go under the Filter menu, under Noise, and choose Add Noise. When the dialog appears, for Amount choose 4%, for Distribution choose Gaussian, and click on the Monochromatic checkbox (it's very important to turn on the Monochromatic checkbox so the noise is black and white, rather than colored dots). Click OK.

Continued

Step Nine:

In the Layers palette, click on Layer 1 to make it active. Just as we did in the previous step, desaturate this layer (remove the color) and apply the exact same Add Noise settings by choosing Filter>Noise>Add Noise.

Step Ten:

Now you'll add a brown tint to the entire image. In the Layers palette, click on the top layer (Layer 2), and choose Solid Color from the Create New Adjustment Layer pop-up menu (it's the fourth icon from the left at the bottom). When the Color Picker appears, set it to the same brown color that we used in Step One, then click OK. This creates a solid brown color on top of your layers, so to get this color to blend in with your other layers, change the layer blend mode from Normal to Color in the Layers palette (as shown here).

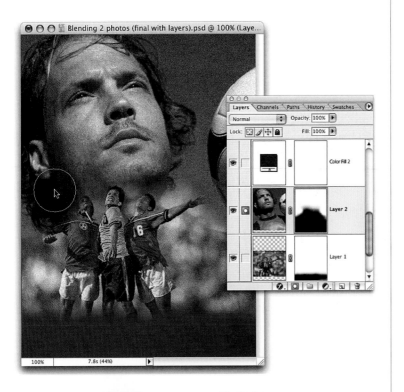

Step Eleven:

Now a little touch-up work: Click directly on the Layer 2 layer mask thumbnail to make it active. Press "x" until you've set your Foreground color to white, then paint over the entire soccer ball to make it visible. In the example shown here, I also switched to a smaller brush and painted over the right ear of the large soccer player to make it fully visible. Then I switched back to Layer 1, clicked on its layer mask thumbnail, pressed "x" until I changed the Foreground color to black, and painted another stroke inside the bottom of the photo to give me more room to add text.

Step Twelve:

Here's the image with type added. The actor's name and the name of the ficti-tious movie are set in Trajan Pro with the horizontal scaling set to 150% in the Character palette. The "IN THEATERS…" text is set in Helvetica Regular with the horizontal scaling set to 120%. That's it!

Making Splashy Product Shots

This is a popular technique for making one image (in this case a bottle of men's cologne) appear as though it is part of another image. We'll accomplish this by taking parts of the background image (in this case splashes of water) and placing them in front of the cologne bottle. It's easier than it looks, but the final effect makes it appear as if it took hours in a studio.

Step One:
Open the photo you want to add another photo into. In this example, our base photo is an image of fruit slices dropping into water (as shown here).

Step Two:
We're going to try to make it look like a bottle of cologne is splashing (bursting, etc.) through the water, so you'll need to rotate the photo on its side. Go under the Image menu, under Rotate Canvas, and choose Rotate 90° CW to rotate the image clockwise (as shown here).

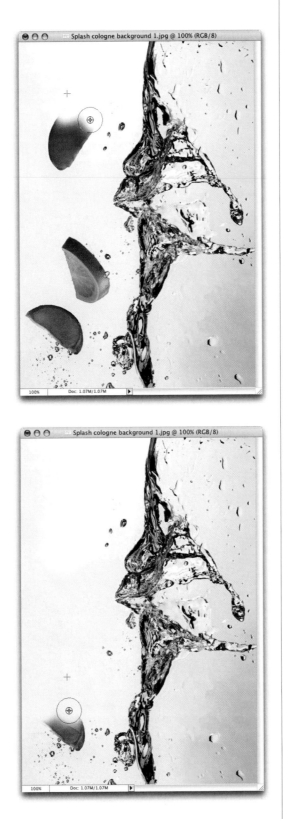

Step Three:
The first thing you'll want to do is remove the fruit slices, so press the letter "s" to switch to the Clone Stamp tool. Click on the icon next to the word "Brush" in the Options Bar to bring up the Brush Picker and choose a 45-pixel soft-edged brush. Option-click (PC: Alt-click) in an open area near one of the slices, then paint over the slice to clone the background area over the top fruit slice (as shown here).

Step Four:
Continue cloning over the slices by Option-clicking (PC: Alt-clicking) in open background areas near them and painting over them (as shown).

Continued

Step Five:

Open the photo you want to appear within the splash of water (in this case, a cologne bottle). Select the bottle's white background by clicking on it with the Magic Wand tool and from the Select menu choose Inverse. Then drag the cologne bottle onto your water splash using the Move tool. You'll need to rotate it a bit so it doesn't look so "stuck on there." Press Command-T (PC: Control-T) to bring up the Free Transform command. Move your cursor outside the bounding box to the right, and click-and-drag upward to rotate the bottle counterclockwise a little bit. Press Return (PC: Enter) to lock in the transformation.

Step Six:

Now that the cologne bottle is in place, you can crop the image down to size (it's a bit too big for such a small bottle). Press the letter "m" to switch to the Rectangular Marquee tool and put a selection around the area you want to keep, then go under the Image menu and choose Crop. Once the image area is cropped (as shown here), you'll need to deselect by pressing Command-D (PC: Control-D).

Step Seven:

In this step, you'll bring the water drops in front of the bottle by using a layer mask. Go to the bottom of the Layers palette and click on the Add a Layer Mask icon (as shown here).

Step Eight:

In the Layers palette, lower the Opacity setting of this cologne bottle layer to around 50% so you can see the water splashes through the bottle (as shown here).

Step Nine:

Press the letter "b" to switch to the Brush tool, set your Foreground color to black by pressing "x", click on the icon next to the word "Brush" in the Options Bar to bring up the Brush Picker, and choose a small hard-edged brush. Now start painting over the water behind the bottle. As you paint over the water, you will actually be painting on the mask, hiding those parts of the cologne bottle, making it appear that the water drops are in front of the bottle rather than behind. It helps if you zoom in close when doing this, so get the Zoom tool and click to zoom in a bit to make it easier.

Step Ten:

When you zoom out (press the Option key [PC: Alt key] and click with the Zoom tool), raise the Opacity level of your cologne bottle layer and you'll see that the water now looks like it's in front of the bottle. Unfortunately in our case, the water also completely covers the name of the cologne. I don't know why, but clients seem to get real…I don't know…cranky about little stuff like this, so you'll have to fix it in the next step.

Continued

Step Eleven:

You can reposition the bottle, without disturbing the water drops, by going to the Layers palette and clicking on the Link icon between the layer thumbnail and the layer mask thumbnail (as shown here). This unlinks the bottle and its mask, so you can move the bottle without disturbing the position of the mask.

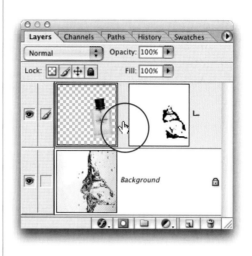

Step Twelve:

Now that the bottle and mask are unlinked, get the Move tool, click on the bottle's thumbnail in the Layers palette, and click-and-drag the bottle downward until the name of the cologne is clearly visible (as shown here).

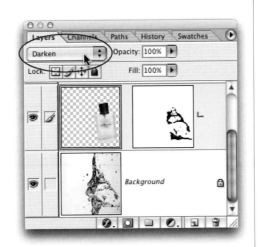

Step Thirteen:
Now that the water drops are in front and the bottle is positioned properly, you can make one more simple change to help the bottle blend more seamlessly into the background and water—go to the Layers palette and change the blend mode of this layer from Normal to Darken (as shown).

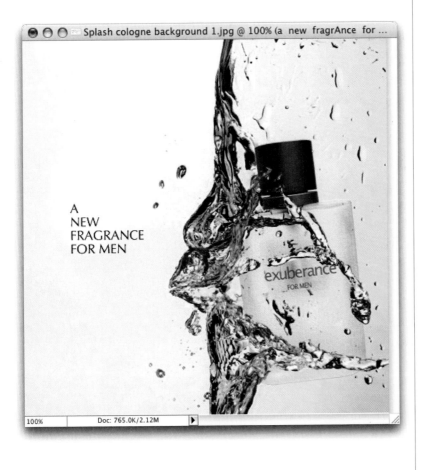

Step Fourteen:
Here's the final image with a headline added using the Type tool and set in the font Optima in all caps.

Creating Reflections

Here's the quickest, easiest way to create a reflection so it looks as though your object was photographed on a reflective background. The project you're going to build here uses the technique in a typical beauty product layout, and as usual, you get to learn some other helpful tricks along the way.

Step One:

Open a new document (File>New) that's 6x8" set at 72 ppi in RGB mode. Click on the Foreground color swatch in the Toolbox and choose a very light gray in the Color Picker (I used R=216, G=216, B=216). Click on the Background color swatch and pick an almost white color (I used R=234, G=234, B=234). Press "g" to switch to the Gradient tool, then press Return (PC: Enter) to bring up the Gradient Picker. Choose the very first gradient (the Foreground to Background gradient) in the Picker. Click the Linear Gradient icon in the Options Bar. Click in the top-right corner of your document and drag diagonally down to the bottom-left corner to add a light gradient to the Background layer.

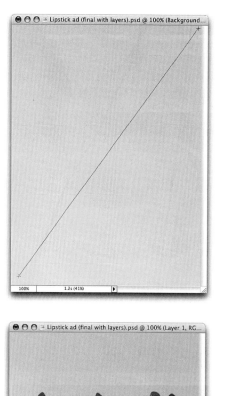

Step Two:

Open the photo you want to add a reflection to. Make sure your object is on its own layer. In this case, you can click on the white background behind the lipstick using the Magic Wand tool from the Toolbox. Go under the Select menu and choose Inverse to select the lipstick instead of the background. Press Shift-Command-J (PC: Shift-Control-J) to cut the lipstick from the Background layer and copy it onto its own layer. Press "v" to switch to the Move tool, and click-and-drag the lipstick onto your light-gray to white gradient background.

Brand X Pictures

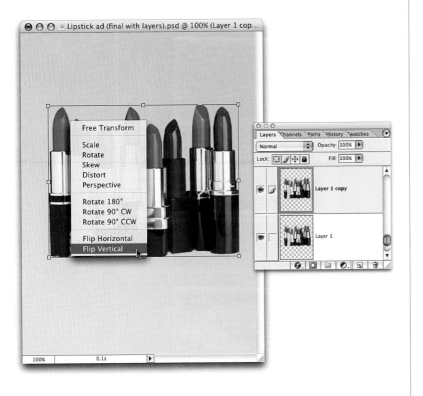

Step Three:
To create the reflection, start by pressing Command-J (PC: Control-J) to duplicate the layer. Then, press Command-T (PC: Control-T) to bring up the Free Transform command. When the Free Transform bounding box appears, Control-click (PC: Right-click) within the bounding box and a contextual menu will appear. Choose Flip Vertical (as shown here), then press Return (PC: Enter) to lock in your transformation.

Step Four:
You can see the flipped version here. Now, using the Move tool, hold the Shift key, click on the flipped image, and drag straight down (the Shift key will keep the flipped lipstick in the same horizontal position as you drag).

Continued

Step Five:

Keep dragging straight down until the bottoms of the lipsticks meet (as shown here).

Step Six:

To make this mirror-like reflection look more realistic, go to the Layers palette and lower the Opacity of this flipped layer to 20% (as shown here).

Step Seven:

In the Layers palette, drag your flipped reflection layer below your original lipstick layer. Then, go under the Filter menu, under Blur, and choose Motion Blur. When the dialog appears, enter 90° for Angle and 20 pixels for Distance, and click OK to apply a bit of motion blur to the reflection. This helps put the focus on the real lipstick and not on the reflection.

Step Eight:

Now we're going to create a shadow for the lipstick. In the Layers palette, click on the original lipstick layer to make it the active layer, then hold the Command key (PC: Control key) and click on the Create a New Layer icon to create a new blank layer beneath your lipstick layer. Then, press the letter "d" to set your Foreground color to black, and press the letter "b" to switch to the Brush tool. Click on the icon next to the word "Brush" in the Options Bar to bring up the Brush Picker and choose a small, soft-edged brush. Trace along the bottom edge of the lipstick to paint in a drop shadow (as shown). Then, lower the Opacity of this layer to 45% in the Layers palette to soften the intensity of the shadow.

Continued

Step Nine:

Now that the reflection effect is complete, it's time to use the Type tool to add some text to finish off the project. The headline and subhead shown here are set in the font Helvetica Light, with the horizontal scaling set to 130% in the Character palette.

Step Ten:

Now you can add some type below the lipstick using the same typeface. The subheads are set in all caps.

Step Eleven:

The final step is to add the name of the fictitious company. In this case, the word "SALON" uses the same font; I just went to the Character palette and lowered the horizontal scaling back to 100%. The "22" and the slogan underneath it are set in Helvetica Bold. The word "NEW" in the circle above the lipstick is set in Helvetica Light. To create the circle, press Shift-M until you get the Elliptical Marquee tool. Then go to Edit>Stroke and choose a 1-pixel, red stroke in the dialog.

Colorizing Black-and-White Photos

There are half a dozen different ways to colorize a black-and-white image in Photoshop, but this is one of my favorites because it gives you some flexibility to change, adjust, and even delete colorizations. In this step-by-step tutorial, I have you create individual layers, but if you're more advanced, you can substitute Hue/Saturation adjustment layers instead. It's your call.

Step One:

Open the black-and-white photo you want to colorize. Make sure that it's in RGB mode and not grayscale by going to the Image menu, under Mode, and choosing RGB Color. Create a new layer by clicking on the Create a New Layer icon at the bottom of the Layers palette.

Step Two:

Press the letter "L" to switch to the Lasso tool and draw a selection around the woman's hair (as shown below). Once you get your selection in place, her right ear will also be selected, so you'll have to hold the Option key (PC: Alt key) and draw a selection around her ear (which actually removes her ear from your hair selection). Click on the Foreground color swatch, and choose the color you'd like for her hair (I chose R=117, G=93, B=79). You could also open a color photo of someone who already has the hair color you'd like to use and make that your Foreground color by pressing the letter "i" to switch to the Eyedropper tool and then clicking on that hair color to sample it. Once you've got your Foreground color in place, press Option-Delete (PC: Alt-Backspace) to fill your selection with that color (as shown far right). Press Command-D (PC: Control-D) to deselect.

Step Three:
To get the solid brown color to blend in with the photo (instead of covering it), just go to the Layers palette and change the layer blend mode from Normal to Color (as shown here). Now you'll be able to see the detail from the photo in your Background layer.

Step Four:
After you change the layer blend mode to Color, if the hair color still looks too intense, you can tone it down by going to the Layers palette and lowering the Opacity setting for this layer to between 60% and 70% (as shown here).

Continued

Step Five:

Create another new blank layer, then get the Lasso tool again, but this time select the flesh tone areas by either using the Shift key to add more to your selection (such as her ear) or using the Option (PC: Alt) key to deselect parts you don't want. You can choose a pinkish flesh tone color, but this is where it really pays to open a color photo and use the Eyedropper tool to sample a person's real skin tone. Once you've got that color, press Option-Delete (PC: Alt-Backspace) to fill your selection with your flesh tone hue (as shown here). Press Command-D (PC: Control-D) to deselect.

Step Six:

Once again, change the blend mode of this layer to Color, so the skin tone blends in (as shown here). If you need to lower the Opacity a bit, feel free. Also, if you missed anything with your selection, just press the letter "b" to switch to the Brush tool, click on the icon next to the word "Brush" to bring up the Brush Picker, choose a small, soft-edged brush, and paint over the missed area. Because you're on a separate layer that's set to the Color blend mode and your Foreground color is already set to the flesh tone, you can simply paint to add in the color.

Step Seven:

In the Layers palette, add another layer and change the layer blend mode to Color. This time use the Lasso tool to put a selection around her lips (you may have to press the letter "z" to switch to the Zoom tool and click on her lips a few times to zoom in a bit so you can make a fairly accurate selection). Change the Foreground color to a red lip color and press Option-Delete (PC: Alt-Backspace) to fill with a red shade. Press Command-D (PC: Control-D) to deselect. Next, go to the Layers palette and add another new layer for the whites of her eyes and teeth.

Step Eight:

Press the letter "d" then "x" to set white as your Foreground color. Select her teeth and the whites of her eyes with the Lasso tool (remember to hold the Shift key to add to your selection). Then, fill your selections with white. In this instance (when using white), if you change the layer blend mode to Color, it makes her eyes and teeth look gray, so instead, change the blend mode to Soft Light, and they'll look white. Again, if they look "too white" lower the Opacity of this layer. You can also add another Color blend mode layer and use the Brush tool to paint a color over the drapes (I used R=166, G=153, B=144), and on a separate Color blend mode layer, paint in green and orange for the accents on the drapes.

Continued

Step Nine:

Here's the final colorization. Now, we'll take the photo and use it on a postcard announcing a high-school reunion. But before we do that, we need to flatten the image, so go to the Layers palette's flyout menu and choose Flatten Image.

Step Ten:

Create a new document (File>New) that's approximately 7.75x5.625" set at 72 ppi in RGB mode. Go back to your colorized photo, press the letter "v" to switch to the Move tool, then click-and-drag this photo onto your new blank document and position it as shown here. If you need to resize your colorized image, press Command-T (PC: Control-T) to bring up the Free Transform command. Hold the Shift key and drag one of the corner points of the bounding box inward to shrink the image. Press Return (PC: Enter) to lock in the transformation.

Step Eleven:

Now you're going to add a fabric pattern behind the photo using the Pattern Overlay layer style. You can't apply layer styles to the Background layer, so hold the Command key (PC: Control key) and click on the Create a New Layer icon at the bottom of the Layers palette, and a new layer will be created directly below the photo layer (pretty slick, eh?). Press "d" to set the Foreground color to black, then press Option-Delete (PC: Alt-Backspace) to fill this new layer with black (as shown).

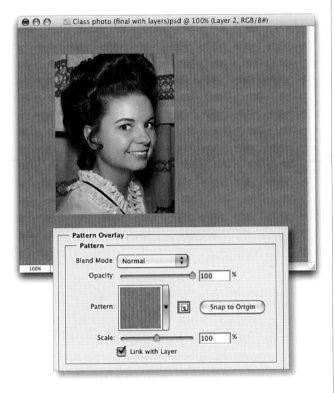

Step Twelve:
Choose Pattern Overlay from the Add a Layer Style pop-up menu at the bottom of the Layers palette. When the dialog appears, click on the icon next to the word "Pattern" (as shown) to open the Pattern Picker. When it opens, choose the Woven pattern, which is the third pattern in the default set. Click OK to put a blue linen pattern over your black background (as shown here).

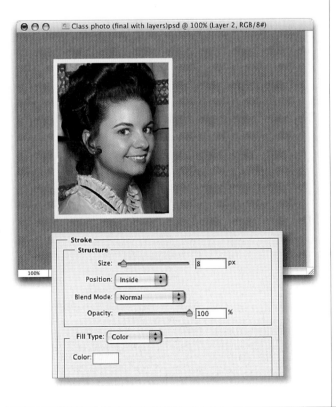

Step Thirteen:
Now click on the photo layer in the Layers palette to make it active and choose Stroke from the Add a Layer Style pop-up menu. Increase the Size of the Stroke to 8 pixels, change the Position pop-up menu to Inside (so the stroke doesn't have rounded corners), and then click on the red Color swatch and choose a very light yellowish color in the Color Picker so the Polaroid-like border looks a bit faded. Don't click OK yet. Instead, click directly on the words "Drop Shadow" from the list of Styles on the left-hand side of the dialog. Lower the Opacity to 67%, the Distance to 3, the Size to 4, and click OK to add a slight shadow behind the photo (as shown in Step Fourteen).

Continued

Step Fourteen:

Create another new layer (on this layer you'll create a piece of Scotch® tape). Press Shift-L until you get the Polygonal Lasso tool. Click to the left of the photo near the top-left corner. Then click above the photo to draw a diagonal line for one side of the tape. Hold the Option key (PC: Alt key) and click-and-hold the mouse button to temporarily switch to the regular Lasso tool. Now draw the top end of the tape. The reason we switch to the regular Lasso tool is so the end of the tape doesn't look perfectly straight, like the sides. Then, release the Option key (PC: Alt key) and the mouse button to return to the Polygonal Lasso tool and click on a point to draw the right diagonal side of the tape. Hold the Option key (PC: Alt key) and the mouse button again to draw the bottom end of the tape. Fill the tape selection with a light yellow, then change the layer blend mode to Soft Light to blend it in.

Step Fifteen:

To make your tape look a little more shiny (like real tape), go under the Filter menu, under Artistic, and choose Plastic Wrap. Use the default settings (shown here) and click OK. The effect won't be real dramatic (because you're already in Soft Light mode) but it does help to make the tape look a bit shinier. Press Command-D (PC: Control-D) to deselect.

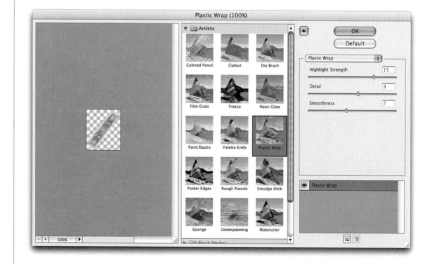

Step Sixteen:

Okay, now you've got a finished piece of tape on a layer, but you need three more pieces (one for each corner). Duplicate your tape layer by pressing Command-J (PC: Control-J), then use the Move tool to drag it to another corner of the photo. Press Command-T (PC: Control-T) to bring up the Free Transform command, then move your cursor outside the bounding box (as shown), and click-and-drag upward to rotate the tape around. You can also grab one of the corner points and drag inward to shrink it a bit, just so it looks a little different.

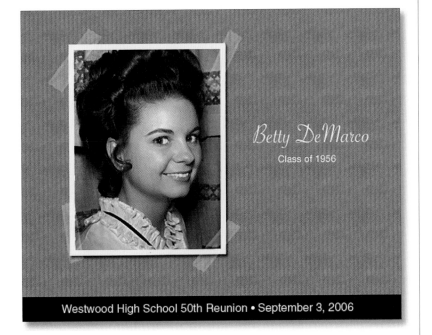

Step Seventeen:

For the other two corners, you can either duplicate your original tape layer two more times, and move and rotate each layer into position, or you could create two new layers and draw some new pieces of tape manually. It's up to you. To finish the project, add some text with the Type tool. The woman's name is set in the font Savoye LET, and the text underneath is set in Helvetica. You can also extend the bottom of your image area (to accommodate extra text) by going under the Image menu and choosing Canvas Size. Turn on the Relative checkbox, enter .5 inches for Height, and choose Black in the Canvas Extension Color pop-up menu. Click OK to add a half-inch of black under your image (as shown here). The white text in the black box is also in Helvetica.

Burning in Portraits

This burned-in edge effect adds an amazing amount of warmth to your portraits, and it's used by professionals everywhere on everything from magazine covers to print ads to the Web. In fact, once you've learned this simple technique, you'll use it again and again in combination with other projects in this book. (By the way—once you apply this technique, turn the layer with the effect on/off a couple of times and you'll see what a huge difference it makes.)

Step One:

Open the portrait that you want to "burn in."

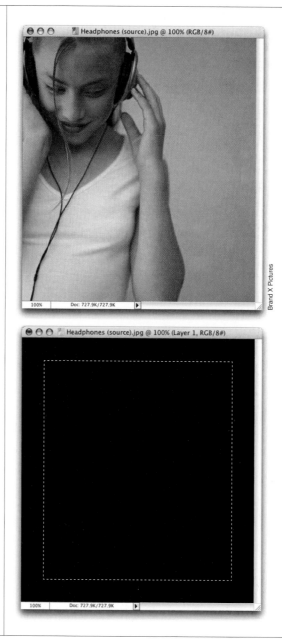

Step Two:

Create a new blank layer by clicking on the Create a New Layer icon at the bottom of the Layers palette. Press "d" to set your Foreground color to black, then fill this new layer with black by pressing Option-Delete (PC: Alt-Backspace). Press the letter "m" to switch to the Rectangular Marquee tool and draw a rectangular selection just inside the edges of your image (as shown here).

Step Three:

To soften the edges of your selection, go under the Select menu and choose Feather. When the Feather Selection dialog appears, enter 40 pixels (for high-res, 300-ppi images, try 150 pixels), then click OK.

Step Four:

Press Delete (PC: Backspace) to knock out a soft-edged hole in this black layer, revealing the photo on the layer beneath (as shown here). The only problem is the edges are too dark, but you'll fix that in the next step.

Step Five:

Press Command-D (PC: Control-D) to deselect. Then, go to the Layers palette and lower the Opacity of the black layer to around 60% to complete the burned-in effect (as shown here). Now, let's take a look at how this effect can be used on magazine covers: First, go under the Image menu and choose Canvas Size. Turn on the Relative checkbox, then under Height enter 2 inches. In the Anchor grid, click the bottom-center square, and in the Canvas Extension Color pop-up menu choose Black, then click OK to add 2 inches of black canvas above your photo.

Continued

Step Six:

To finish the cover, just add some text. From top to bottom, the "Special Issue" type is set in the font Helvetica Regular with the horizontal scaling set to 150% in the Character palette. The "portable audio" nameplate is set in CG Phenix American, as is the word "review," and the magazine topics are all set in the font Impact. The subheads beneath each topic are set in Futura Condensed Medium.

Almost Famous
classic effects you've seen a million times

PHOTOSHOP
CLASSIC
EFFECTS

CHAPTER

9

SIDE TWO
SK-355-A
STEREO

PRODUCED BY BIG ELECTRIC CAT RECORDING STUDIOS • MFG. BY KW MEDIA GROUP, INC.

Chapter NINE

ALMOST FAMOUS
CLASSIC EFFECTS YOU'VE SEEN A MILLION TIMES

This may well be the quintessential classic effects chapter because you're going to learn how to create some of the most famous techniques of all time. The most classic of classics. Now, before we go any further, I should come clean. You haven't seen these effects "a million times." It's really more like 360,000 times. So why did I exaggerate? That's not exaggeration. That's marketing. That's right, it's strictly marketing hype designed to pull you in and make you feel good about the chapter you're about to embark upon. Now, why is feeling good about the effects in a particular chapter so important? My therapist tells me it's so you can become one with your inner pixel. That really got me to thinking...I need to find a new therapist.

Backscreened Blocks

One of the most popular effects in wide use today is backscreening—creating areas of your image that are either lightened or darkened so that text placed on your photo is readable. In our project here, we're taking a photo that will be used for the cover of a cookbook and adding two backscreened areas so we can easily read the text that will be placed on the photo.

Step One:
Open the photo that you want to use as the background of your effect.

Step Two:
Create a new layer by clicking on the Create a New Layer icon at the bottom of the Layers palette. Press the letter "m" to switch to the Rectangular Marquee tool and draw a large rectangular selection that's just inside the borders of your entire image area (as shown here).

Step Three:
Now you're going to add a stroke around your selection. Press the letter "d" to set your Foreground color to black, then go under the Edit menu and choose Stroke. When the dialog appears, enter 1 pixel for Width and choose Center for Location. Click OK to put a thin, black stroke around your selection. Don't deselect quite yet.

Step Four:
We want to create another stroke just inside our current selection, so go under the Select menu, under Modify, and choose Contract. When the dialog appears, enter 5 pixels and click OK (as shown here). This shrinks your selection by 5 pixels.

Step Five:
Go back to the Edit menu, choose Stroke, apply a 1-pixel stroke to this smaller selection, and click OK. Deselect by pressing Command-D (PC: Control-D). In the Layers palette, click on the Create a New Layer icon to create a new blank layer, then take the Rectangular Marquee tool and make a rectangular selection inside the top third of your "double border".

Continued

Step Six:

Press the letter "i" to Switch to the Eyedropper tool and click once on one of the salad leaves to make that your Foreground color. Now you can fill the selection with this green leaf color by pressing Option-Delete (PC: Alt-Backspace). Deselect by pressing Command-D (PC: Control-D).

Step Seven:

Now you'll screen back this green block layer so you can see the background photo below it. Go to the Layers palette and lower the Opacity of the green block layer to 28% so you can see the background image. Now this area is set up so you can put type on it.

Step Eight:

Click on the Create a New Layer icon in the Layers palette, switch back to the Rectangular Marquee tool, and make a smaller rectangular selection at the bottom of your double-border area. Press the letter "d" and then "x" to set your Foreground color to white, and fill this selection with white by pressing Option-Delete (PC: Alt-Backspace). Go to the Layers palette and lower the Opacity of this layer to 60%, making another back-screened area where you can place type. Press Command-D (PC: Control-D) to deselect. In the Layers palette, drag the double-stroke layer (Layer 1) above the green and white block layers to make sure that the blocks are not covering your strokes (as shown here).

Step Nine:

To complete the project, you can add some type using the Type tool and the Character palette to turn this into the cover of a cookbook. The book title is set in Futura Light; the word "Cookbook" is set in Futura Medium; the author's name is set in Trajan Pro (which comes with Photoshop CS); and the tag line under her name is set in both Trajan Pro and Minion Italic.

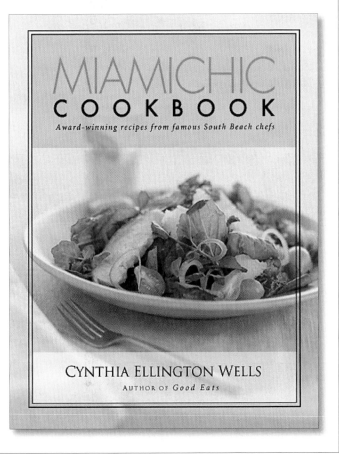

Realistically Adding a Sign or Logo to an Existing Photo

This is a trick we've been using for years to make a graphic that we've slapped onto another image really look like it's there. We do this by copying the surface of an element onto its own layer, then later we blend it in on top of our graphic. In this case, the dirt and metal panels on the side of a semi-trailer will help us make it look like our sign is under the dirt, not added on top.

Step One:

For this project we're going to create a vinyl sign for a semi-trailer, so start by creating a new document (File>New) that's 12.125x2.625" set at 72 ppi in RGB mode (as shown here).

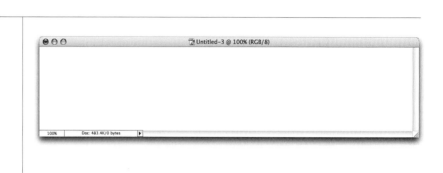

Step Two:

Open the object you want to appear on your trailer graphic (in this example, a hoagie) and select it. In this case, you can click on the white background behind the hoagie using the Magic Wand tool from the Toolbox. Go under the Select menu and choose Inverse. Press the letter "v" to switch to the Move tool, and then click-and-drag the hoagie to your other document. Resize the hoagie by pressing Command-T (PC: Control-T), hold the Shift key, grab a corner point, and drag inward (as shown here) until it fits comfortably within your image area. Then press Return (PC: Enter) to lock in your resize.

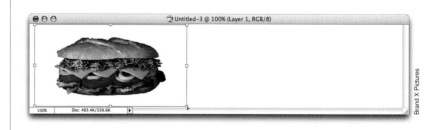

Brand X Pictures

Step Three:

Press "d" to set your Foreground color to black. Now you can press the letter "t" to switch to the Type tool and add the headline "Premium Meats & Cheeses" using a tall, thin typeface (the one shown here is Helvetica Ultra Compressed).

Step Four:
To finish off the trailer graphic, just use the Type tool to add the name of the company and its slogan. The name is set in the font Times, and the slogan is in Times Italic.

Step Five:
Now open the photo you want to add your graphic to (in this case, the side of a semi-trailer).

Step Six:
Press Shift-L until you have the Polygonal Lasso tool. Click on each corner of the white side of the trailer (then once more on the first corner you clicked on) to put a selection around it. (Because the Polygonal Lasso tool draws straight-line selections, making this selection should be pretty easy.) This step is particularly important because the side of the truck has detail (mostly dirt and vertical lines) that we'll need to use later to make the logo look like it's really on the truck.

Continued

Step Seven:

Press Command-J (PC: Control-J) to put your selected area up on its own layer. Hide it from view (for now anyway) by clicking on the Eye icon in the column beside it in the Layers palette (Layer 1). Click on the Background layer in the Layers palette to make it active. Then, Command-click (PC: Control-click) on your hidden layer's thumbnail (Layer 1), and even though it's hidden, it will put a selection around the side of the trailer.

Step Eight:

Go back to your hoagie document. In the Layers palette, click the Create a New Layer icon to create a new layer, and drag this new layer to the top of the stack of layers. Hold the Option key (PC: Alt key) and choose Merge Visible from the palette's fly-out menu. This puts a flattened version of your document on this one layer. Go under the Select menu and choose All, then press Command-C (PC: Control-C) to copy this image.

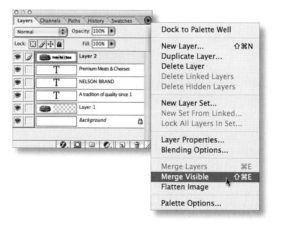

Step Nine:

Back in the semi-trailer document, go under the Edit menu and choose Paste Into to paste the graphic into your selection. Press Command-T (PC: Control-T) to bring up the Free Transform command. Hold the Shift key, grab a corner point (if you can't see the corner points of the bounding box, press Command-Zero [PC: Control-Zero] to zoom out), and drag inward to scale the graphic down so it fits on your trailer. Then, release the Shift key, move your cursor outside the bounding box to the right, and click-and-drag downward to slightly rotate the graphic to match the angle of the truck (as shown here).

Step Ten:
When you press Return (PC: Enter), your graphic will appear on the truck, but now you can see the problem—it looks "stuck on in Photoshop." It's too bright, too clean, too obvious. A dead giveaway. Well, remember that layer we hid earlier, the one with the dirt and lines? Now it's time to use that to help us make it look like the graphic is really on the truck.

Step Eleven:
Go to the Layers palette and make your hidden layer active and visible again by clicking on its name. Change the blend mode of this layer from Normal (which covers everything) to Multiply (which hides the white on that layer, and just leaves the dirt and lines visible). Then lower the Opacity of this layer to 75% to make it blend in with the sign.

Step Twelve:
See how much more realistic the graphic looks with the original dirt and metal panels on top of it? Ahh, that's better. Now, one last thing: To keep the graphic from looking too bright, go to the Layers palette and click on the graphic layer to make it active. Then lower the Opacity of this layer to around 80%, which makes the graphic less bright, and helps to make the entire effect look even more realistic (as shown here).

Creating Starry Skies

This effect has been around for quite a while, but I've seen it used most recently in print ads for the Wendy's® Old Fashioned Hamburgers chain. I use this same technique to add stars to the skies behind dusk shots of fine homes or buildings. Of course, we take the whole effect a step further by building a sign and then putting it on a roadside billboard.

Step One:

In this project, we're going to build a small roadside sign, so create a new document (File>New) that's 10x4.875" at 72 ppi in RGB mode. You're going to add some text on the right side of your image area, so you'll need to add a guide to help you separate the photo from the text. Make your rulers visible by pressing Command-R (PC: Control-R), then click on the left ruler and drag out a vertical guide to the 7" mark (as shown).

Step Two:

Open the photo of the mountains overlooking the city. Press the letter "L" to switch to the Lasso tool and draw a selection along the tops of the mountains, around the entire city, and foreground mountains (as shown here).

Step Three:

Press the letter "v" to switch to the Move tool and drag-and-drop your selected area onto your original document. Position the mountains at the bottom of the document and to the left of your guide (as shown).

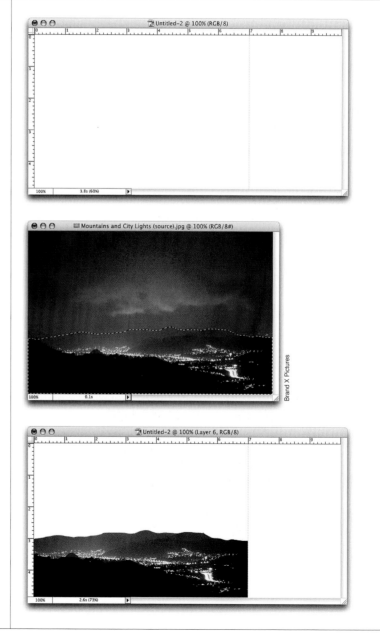

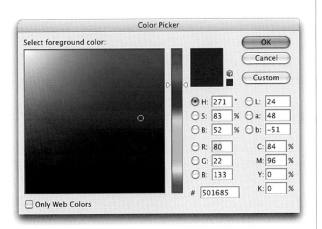

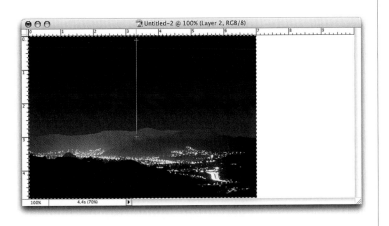

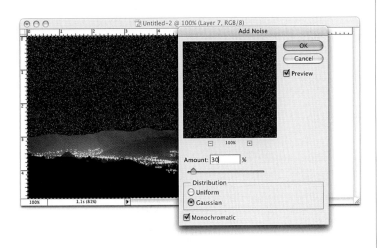

Step Four:
Press the letter "d" then "x" to set your Background color to black, then click on the Foreground color swatch at the bottom of the Toolbox to bring up the Color Picker. Choose a dark purple color (as shown) and click OK. Go to the Layers palette and click on the Background layer to make it active because this is where you'll add your nighttime background for the stars.

Step Five:
Press the letter "m" to switch to the Rectangular Marquee tool and draw a rectangular selection around your mountain scene and the white space above it. Then press the letter "g" to switch to the Gradient tool, and press Return (PC: Enter) to bring up the Gradient Picker. Make sure the first gradient in the Picker is selected (it's the Foreground to Background gradient) and that you've selected the Linear Gradient icon in the Options Bar. Then take the Gradient tool, click at the top of the mountains, and drag to the top of the document to add a gradient that blends from dark purple to black. Don't deselect yet.

Step Six:
Go to the Layers palette and click on the Create a New Layer icon to create a new blank layer above the Background layer. Press "d" to set your Foreground color to black, then fill this new layer with black by pressing Option-Delete (PC: Alt-Backspace). Go under the Filter menu, under Noise, and choose Add Noise. Set the Amount to around 30%, the Distribution to Gaussian, and turn on the Monochromatic checkbox (or your noise will appear as red, green, and blue dots). Click OK to apply noise to your black layer.

Continued

Step Seven:

Go under the Filter menu, under Blur, and choose Gaussian Blur. When the dialog appears, enter a Radius setting of 0.5 pixels (as shown here) to add just a tiny bit of blur to the noise and click OK.

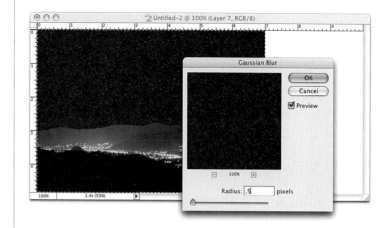

Step Eight:

Go under the Image menu, under Adjustments, and choose Threshold. When the Threshold dialog appears, grab the slider under the histogram and drag to the left (as shown), and as you do, you'll see stars appear on your black layer. The farther to the left you drag, the more stars will appear. Click OK when it looks good to you.

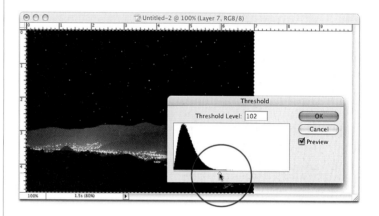

Step Nine:

Go back under the Filter menu, under Blur, and choose Gaussian Blur. You're going to add another 0.5 pixel blur to soften the stars again. This also helps vary the size of the stars. Click OK to apply this small blur. Now you can deselect by pressing Command-D (PC: Control-D).

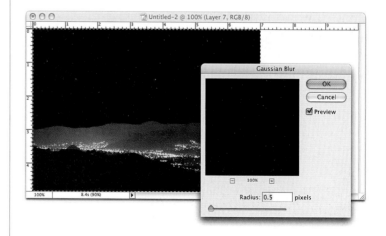

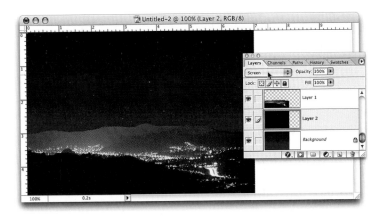

Step Ten:
Go to the Layers palette and change the layer blend mode of this black layer from Normal to Screen to make the stars appear over your purple to black gradient sky (as shown here).

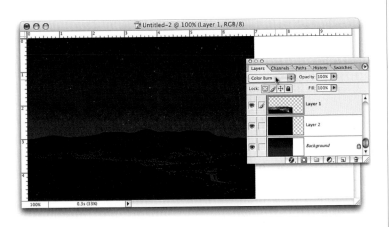

Step Eleven:
To make the photo blend in with the sky, go to the Layers palette, click on the photo layer, and then change its layer blend mode to Color Burn (as shown here). This creates a silhouetted effect, but it also lets some of the lights of the city pick up that purple color from the gradient on the layer below it.

Step Twelve:
Now open a photo of a hamburger, press the letter "v" to switch to the Move tool, and drag-and-drop the burger onto your stars document. Press Command-T (PC: Control-T) to bring up the Free Transform command. Hold the Shift key, grab a corner point (if you can't see the corner points of the bounding box, press Command-Zero [PC: Control-Zero] to zoom out), and drag inward to scale the burger down in size so it fits in the image area. Then release the Shift key, move your cursor outside the Free Transform bounding box to the right, and click-and-drag upward to rotate the burger (as shown here). Press Return (PC: Enter) to lock in your transformation.

Continued

Step Thirteen:

Press the letter "w" to switch to the Magic Wand tool and click it once in the white around the burger to select all of that white area. If the Wand doesn't select all of the white area around the burger, deselect (Command-D; PC: Control-D), set the Tolerance higher in the Options Bar, and try again.

Step Fourteen:

Press Delete (PC: Backspace) to remove that white area. Press Command-D (PC: Control-D) to deselect. Now you'll add a white glow around the burger. Choose Outer Glow from the Add a Layer Style pop-up menu at the bottom of the Layers palette. When the dialog appears, click on the beige color swatch and change the glow color to white in the Color Picker. Increase the Spread to 16, the Size to 21 (as shown), and click OK to add a soft glow around your burger.

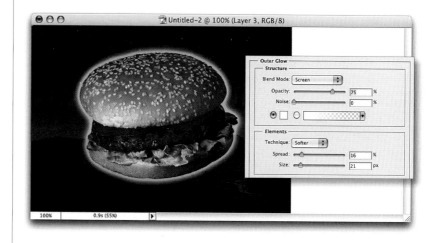

Step Fifteen:

Go to the Layers palette and click on the Create a New Layer icon to add a new blank layer. Press the letter "m" to switch to the Rectangular Marquee tool and draw a selection around the white area on the right side of your guide. Click on the Foreground color swatch in the Toolbox and choose a bright red in the Color Picker. Fill the selection with red by pressing Option-Delete (PC: Alt-Backspace). Deselect by pressing Command-D (PC: Control-D), and remove your guide by going under the View menu and choosing Clear Guides. Press "d" then "x" to switch your Foreground color to white, and now add your text with the Type tool. The type here is set in the font Impact, but any tall, thick typeface will do.

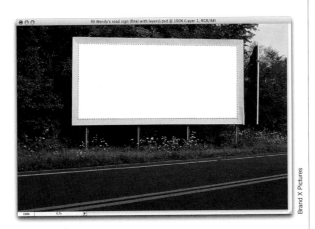

Step Sixteen:
Now you'll place your image into a road-side sign. Open a roadside sign photo, then press Shift-L until you have the Polygonal Lasso tool. Click on each corner of the white area of the sign (and once more on the first point that you clicked) to put a selection around the white area of the sign (as shown here). Then, go back to your starry sky burger image and from the Layers palette's flyout menu choose Flatten Image. Now press Command-A (PC: Control-A) to select the entire photo, then press Command-C (PC: Control-C) to copy the sign into memory.

Step Seventeen:
Switch back to the road sign image (your selection should still be in place) and go under the Edit menu and choose Paste Into to paste your image into your selected area. Press Command-T (PC: Control-T) to bring up the Free Transform command. Hold the Command key (PC: Control key), grab a corner point of the bounding box, and drag it to the corresponding corner on the sign.

Step Eighteen:
Keep holding the Command key (PC: Control key) and repeat this for the other three corners. Doing this aligns your graphic to the angle of the sign. Lastly, go to the Layers palette and lower the Opacity of your sign layer to around 85% to help it blend in better and not look so "pasted in." The final image is shown here.

Adding a Lens Flare

This is a nice way to add some visual interest to an image (not that a shuttle orbiting the Earth really needs more visual interest). The sad part about this technique is that photographers go out of their way to avoid lens flare, and here we're about to show you how to add it. It just ain't flare. ;-)

Step One:
Open the photo you want to apply a lens flare effect to, making sure it's set to RGB mode by choosing Image>Mode>RGB Color. In this example, we're going to apply it to a photo of the space shuttle orbiting the Earth, but this technique also works well with other night images or images that are dark. The photo has to be dark enough for the lens flare effect to be seen.

Step Two:
Go to the bottom of the Layers palette and click on the Create a New Layer icon to create a new layer. Press "d" to set your Foreground color to black, then fill this layer with black by pressing Option-Delete (PC: Alt-Backspace).

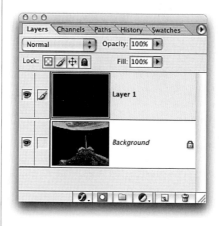

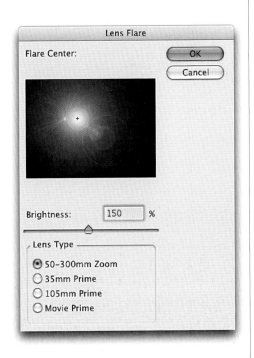

Step Three:
Go under the Filter menu, under Render, and choose Lens Flare. When the dialog appears, increase the Brightness to 150%, and choose 50-300mm Zoom for Lens Type. We're going to want the lens flare to appear as if it's peaking out from behind the Earth and we'll position it using the Move tool in a later step, but we don't want to have to move the lens flare too much once we've applied it. So while you're still in the Lens Flare dialog, click on the little crosshair in the preview area and drag the center of the lens flare to approximately where you want it located in the final image.

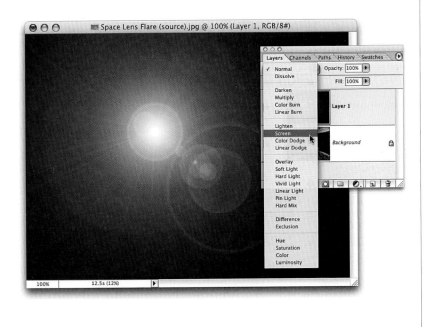

Step Four:
When you click OK it applies the lens flare to your black layer; however, the black layer completely covers the shuttle photo on the Background layer. So you'll need to go to the Layers palette and change the layer blend mode from Normal to Screen (as shown here).

Continued

Step Five:

When you change the blend mode, the lens flare will then blend in with your shuttle image (as shown here). Press the letter "v" to switch to the Move tool and move the center of the flare until it's half on the Earth and half out in space (as shown here).

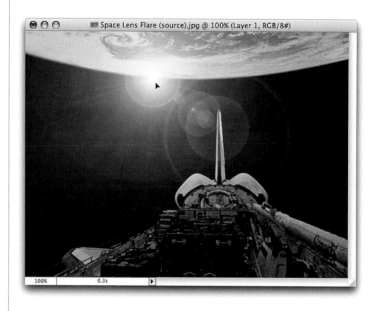

Step Six:

You want the flare to appear as though it's peeking out from behind the Earth, rather than just floating on top of it, so press the letter "e" to switch to the Eraser tool (or if you're comfortable with layer masks, use a layer mask). In the Options Bar make sure that the Mode pop-up menu is set to Brush, then click on the icon next to the word "Brush" to bring up the Brush Picker, and choose a soft-edged brush. Then erase over the Earth (as shown here), and as you do, it will erase the part of the flare that extends onto the Earth. That's it—you've completed your lens flare effect, but now you'll finish it up by using the image in a poster.

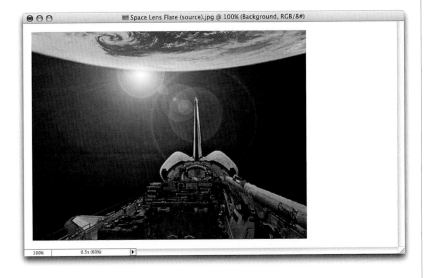

Step Seven:

Go under the Image menu and choose Canvas Size. Turn on the Relative checkbox, enter .5 inches for both Height and Width, choose White in the Canvas Extension Color pop-up menu, and click OK to add a half-inch of white canvas around your image. Then go to Image>Canvas Size again, but this time for Width enter 2.5 inches, and in the Anchor grid, click the left-center square, so the white space will be added to the right side of the photo (as shown here). Click OK.

Step Eight:

Now that you have some white space to the right of your photo, you may as well add some type, eh? The type at the top is set in Helvetica Light, and the center's name is set in Helvetica Black. The operating hours are set in Helvetica Regular.

Motion Blur Effect

Here's another classic effect that you see quite often—adding a sense of motion. However, the real trick isn't adding the motion; the real trick is removing the blur effect from where you don't want it. In this simple tutorial, we're going to use the Eraser tool on a duplicate layer; but if you're more advanced, you can use a layer mask instead.

Step One:
Open the photo that you want to apply a motion blur effect to.

Step Two:
Duplicate the Background layer by pressing Command-J (PC: Control-J).

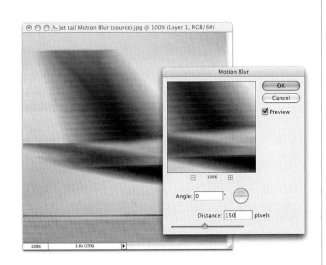

Step Three:
Go under the Filter menu, under Blur, and choose Motion Blur. When the dialog appears (shown here), enter 0° for the Angle so the blur is horizontal. For Distance enter 150 pixels (you can use your own discretion here—the higher the number, the more blur) and click OK.

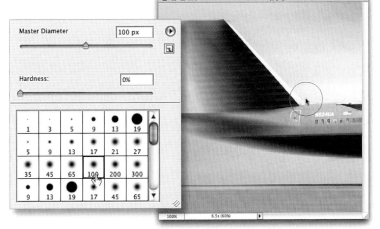

Step Four:
Press the letter "e" to switch to the Eraser tool. In the Options Bar, make sure the Mode pop-up menu is set to Brush, then click on the icon next to the word "Brush" to bring up the Brush Picker and choose the 100-pixel, soft-edged brush. Begin painting over the plane (as shown here) to erase the parts of the motion blur that you don't want. As we paint (erase) we need a way to avoid painting over the back edge of the tail and the bottom rear of the plane, where we want to maintain the blur.

Step Five:
Because we used such a large amount of blur, you might not be able to see the edges of the plane's tail (and if you can't see the edges, you won't know where you shouldn't paint). So go to the Layers palette and lower the Opacity of this blurred layer until you can clearly see the back edge of the tail on the Background layer below it.

Continued

Step Six:

If you get to areas where the 100-pixel brush is too large, just press the Left Bracket key ([) on your keyboard to shrink the size of the Eraser brush. Raise the Opacity back to 100% in the Layers palette. This completes the motion blur effect, and the blur appears only where you want it—at the end of the tail and the bottom rear of the plane. Now, for our project we're going to take this image and use it in the photo of a billboard.

Step Seven:

Create a new document (File>New) that's 11.222 inches wide by 3.333 inches high, with a resolution of 72 ppi (as shown here). This should give us the proper aspect ratio that we need to fit our final image into the billboard.

Step Eight:

Go back to the jet photo, and choose Flatten Image from the Layers palette's flyout menu. Press the letter "v" to switch to the Move tool, and click-and-drag the jet photo into your new blank document. Press Command-T (PC: Control-T) to bring up the Free Transform command. You probably won't be able to reach (or perhaps even see) the Free Transform handles, so press Command-Zero (PC: Control-Zero) and your image area will resize so you can see all four handles. Hold the Shift key, grab a corner point, and drag inward to scale it down to fit (as shown here). Click-and-drag inside the bounding box to position the image as needed. Press Return (PC: Enter) to lock in your transformation.

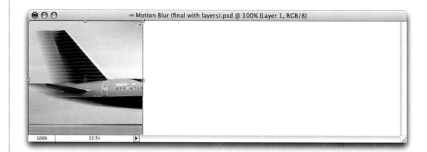

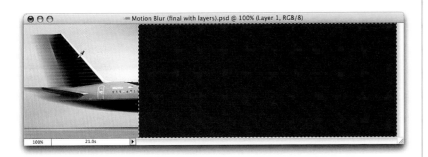

Step Nine:
Click on the Create a New Layer icon at the bottom of the Layers palette. Press the letter "m" to switch to the Rectangular Marquee tool and draw a selection around the white image area. Press the letter "i" to switch to the Eyedropper tool, and click on the light blue color on the airplane tail to make that your Foreground color, then press Option-Delete (PC: Alt-Backspace) to fill your selection with this blue (as shown). Press Command-D (PC: Control-D) to deselect.

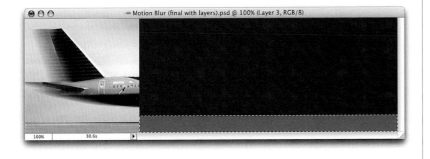

Step Ten:
Click the Create a New Layer icon, switch back to the Rectangular Marquee tool, and drag out a thin rectangular selection at the bottom of your blue area (as shown). Then, get the Eyedropper tool again and click on the jet's red stripe to make that your Foreground color. Press Option-Delete (PC: Alt-Backspace) to fill your selection with red (as shown here). Press Command-D (PC: Control-D) to deselect.

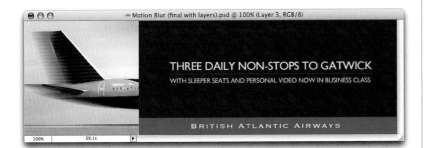

Step Eleven:
To complete the art for the billboard, just use the Type tool and the Character palette to add some white type. The headline and subhead are set in the font Gil Sans Regular and the name of the fictitious airline is set in Copperplate Gothic. Now go to the Layers palette and choose Flatten Image from the palette's flyout menu. Press Command-A (PC: Control-A) to select the entire photo, then press Command-C (PC: Control-C) to copy your flattened image into memory.

Continued

Step Twelve:

Open the billboard photo, then press Shift-L until you switch to the Polygonal Lasso tool (the Lasso that draws straight lines). Click once on the bottom-left corner of the white area of the billboard, then click on the top-left corner, and a straight selection is drawn between the two. Continue clockwise until the full billboard is selected (as shown here).

Step Thirteen:

Go under the Edit menu and choose Paste Into to paste the copied billboard into your selection (as shown here). The image will be too big for the billboard area, so press Command-T (PC: Control-T) to bring up the Free Transform command (so you can scale it down). You won't be able to see the Free Transform handles, so press Command-Zero (PC: Control-Zero) and you'll be able to reach the handles to scale it down (making sure you hold the Shift key as you scale). You can click inside the bounding box and drag the image into position on the billboard.

Step Fourteen:
Once you scale the image down to fit within the billboard and you have it in position, press Return (PC: Enter) to lock in your transformation and complete the project.

Adding Elegance with Transparent Type

This is a simple effect for adding elegance to a layout, but because the effect is so simple, it needs a dramatic presentation, so in this technique, we're building an ad for a kitchen and bath design firm. By doing this, we get to learn a few more handy techniques along the way.

Step One:
Create a new document (File>New) in RGB mode, but make sure the document is larger than the photo you'll be using in this effect. Next, open the photo, press the letter "v" to switch to the Move tool, and click-and-drag the image onto this blank document, positioning it near the top (as shown here).

Step Two:
In this step you're going to add a thick black stroke around the photo, so choose Stroke from the Add a Layer Style pop-up menu at the bottom of the Layers palette. When the Layer Style dialog appears, change the Position pop-up menu to Inside, which will keep the corners of the stroke from being rounded. Now increase the Size setting until the stroke is fairly thick (I used a Size setting of 9 pixels for this low-res, 72-ppi image—for high-res, 300-ppi images use a higher setting). Then click the Color swatch to select a color (I simply used black).

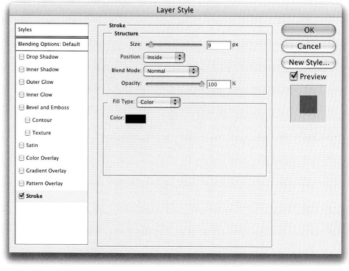

Step Three:
Click OK and a stroke is applied around the photo (as shown here).

Step Four:
Press the letter "t" to switch to the Type tool and create the type that you want to appear over the photo (the font shown here is Trajan Pro, which we selected from the Character palette under the Window menu).

Continued

Step Five:

Press Command-T (PC: Control-T) to bring up the Free Transform command. Hold the Shift key, move outside the bounding box, and click-and-drag upward to rotate the type until it's vertical (as shown here). Then click-and-drag inside the bounding box to move the type into position. When the type is vertical and in position, press Return (PC: Enter) to lock in your transformation.

Step Six:

Change your Foreground color to white by pressing "x", then fill your type with white by pressing Option-Delete (PC: Alt-Backspace).

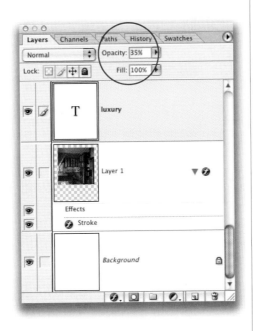

Step Seven:

In the Layers palette, lower the Opacity setting of your Type layer until it's fairly transparent. These previous two steps are what this effect is really about—placing large white type over your photo, and then lowering the opacity to get that elegant look.

Step Eight:

Open another photo and drag it into the main ad with the Move tool. Scale the photo down in size by pressing Command-T (PC: Control-T) for the Free Transform command. Hold the Shift key, grab a corner point, and drag inward to shrink the photo (as shown here). Press Return (PC: Enter) when you've finished sizing your image.

Continued

Step Nine:

Now we're going to add some body copy text. Set your Foreground color back to black by pressing "d". Get the Type tool and click-and-drag with it to make a text block (the text you create will now be contained within this box). Now enter some text (we just made up some copy, using the font Minion). Then go under the Window menu and choose Paragraph to bring up the Paragraph palette. Click on the last icon on the top row to make the text block justified.

Step Ten:

To complete the ad we'll just drop in the company logo. In this case, create a new layer by clicking on the Create a New Layer icon in the Layers palette. Grab the Elliptical Marquee tool and make a horizontal oval. Then click the Foreground color swatch to change it to orange and fill the oval selection with orange by pressing Option-Delete (PC: Alt-Backspace). Then, with the orange layer still selected, copy this layer by dragging-and-dropping it onto the Create a New Layer icon; change the Foreground color to white; and fill the oval selection with white. Switch to the Move tool, and drag this white copy down and to the right, so only the top-left corner of the orange oval is still visible behind it. Press Command-D (PC: Control-D) to deselect. Lastly, we added the name of the fictitious company with the Type tool inside the white oval (as shown), using the font Minion, which completes the effect.

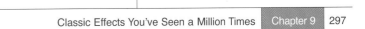

Chapter TEN

CUT TO THE CHASE
THIS ISN'T REALLY A CHAPTER

Okay, because this isn't really a chapter, I don't have to use a movie, song, or TV show as the chapter title. This final section was designed to help you when you're on a deadline and you need to "cut to the chase" and just do the classic effect you need, without having to go through the entire project (like the rest of the book). So, this is really like a bonus chapter, but I don't want to call it a chapter for two reasons: (1) It's just shortcuts for re-creating the effects that have already appeared earlier in  the book, and (2) if you make me call it a chapter, then I have to come up with a song, movie, or TV title. (Hey, actually the chapter title is a song by Rush, but don't tell my editors that. I have them fooled into thinking this is a nine-chapter book.) But coming up with a more obviously themed title would've been pretty easy. How about Bryan Adams' "Cuts Like a Knife"? Not bad. Or the 1994 movie *The Chase*? This is just way too easy—I knew I should've made this a chapter.

Backscreening Objects to Make Backgrounds

Step One:

Create a new document (File>New), and fill the background with a color (in this case, black) by setting your Foreground color and pressing Option-Delete (PC: Alt-Backspace). Open the image you want to use as a background, select just the object in that image, and drag-and-drop it onto the black background using the Move tool.

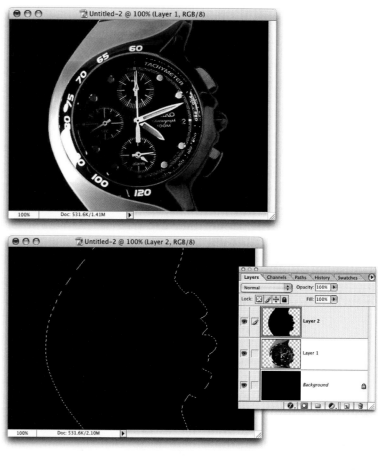

Step Two:

Go to the Layers palette, and Command-click (PC: Control-click) on the layer's thumbnail to put a selection around just the object on that layer. Create a new layer, then fill this selection with black by pressing Option-Delete (PC: Alt-Backspace) as shown here. Deselect by pressing Command-D (PC: Control-D).

Step Three:

In the Layers palette, lower the Opacity of this black layer that's covering your photo to around 70% and that image will appear screened back into the background. I dragged-and-dropped the same photo again, but I made it smaller using the Free Transform command (Mac: Command-T; PC: Control-T), so you can see the difference between the small foreground photo and the large backscreened version.

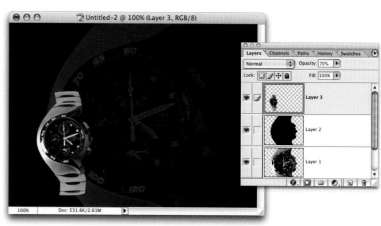

Moving a Background Object in Front of Type

Step One:
Open your photo, then get the Type tool and create your type.

Step Two:
Using either the regular Lasso tool or the Magnetic Lasso tool, draw a selection around the part of the photo you want to appear in front of the text (as shown here, where the top of the man's head is selected). Click on the Background layer in the Layers palette to make it active.

Step Three:
Press Command-J (PC: Control-J) to put that selected area of his head up on its own separate layer. Then in the Layers palette, drag this layer above your Type layer (as shown) to complete the effect.

Putting One Image Inside Another

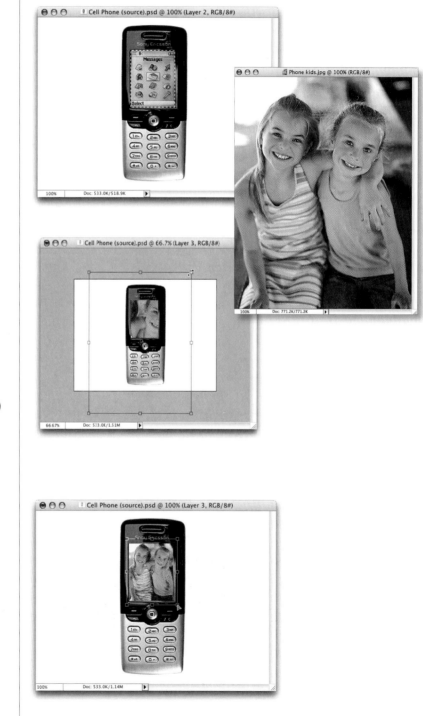

Step One:
Open the photo that has an area where you want to insert a different photo (in this case, we want to put a photo in the screen of a cell phone). With the Rectangular Marquee tool, draw a selection around the cell phone window (as shown). Open the photo you want to appear in the cell phone. Press Command-A (PC: Control-A) to select the entire photo, then press Command-C (PC: Control-C) to copy that photo into memory.

Step Two:
Go back to the phone document (your selection will still be in place), then go under the Edit menu and choose Paste Into to paste the photo into your rectangular selection. Press Command-T (PC: Control-T) to bring up the Free Transform command so you can scale it down to fit within your phone's screen. Press Command-Zero (PC: Control-Zero) and the window will resize so you can reach all the Free Transform handles (as shown here).

Step Three:
Grab a corner point, hold the Shift key, and drag inward to scale your photo down to size so it fits within the phone's screen. When it looks good to you, press Return (PC: Enter) to lock in your transformation. Choose Inner Shadow from the Add a Layer Style pop-up menu in the Layers palette, and lower the Distance and Size settings to 1. This completes the technique.

Blending from a Photo into a Solid Color

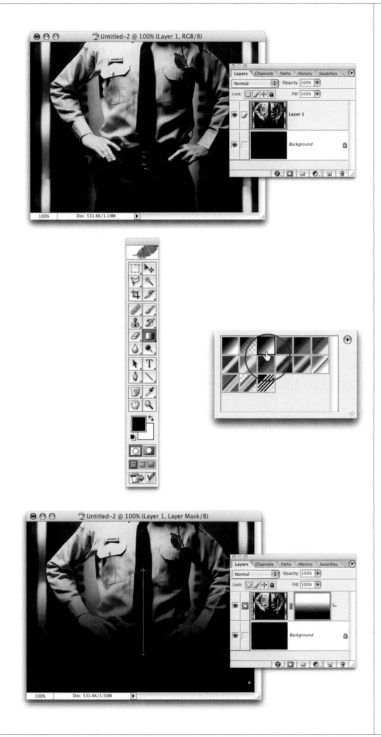

Step One:
Create a new document (File>New), and press Option-Delete (PC: Alt-Backspace) to fill the background with the solid color you'd like to blend into (in this case, black). Then open your photo, get the Move tool, and drag-and-drop the photo onto your black background (as shown here).

Step Two:
Get the Gradient tool, then press Return (PC: Enter) to bring up the Gradient Picker. Choose the Black to White gradient in the Picker (it's the third gradient in the default set of gradients, as shown here).

Step Three:
Go to the Layers palette and click the Add a Layer Mask icon. Click the Gradient tool on your photo where you want the blend to be the solid color, then drag the tool upward, stopping at the point where you want the blend to begin. When you release the mouse button, the photo will blend from that point down to the solid color you chose in Step One.

Two-Color Glow Effect

Step One:
Create a new document (File>New), and fill the background with a solid color (in this case, orange) by setting your Foreground color and pressing Option-Delete (PC: Alt-Backspace). Open the object you want to apply a two-color glow to, put a selection around the object, get the Move tool, and drag it onto your orange background.

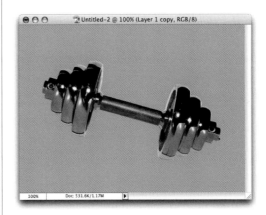

Step Two:
Choose Outer Glow from the Add a Layer Style pop-up menu at the bottom of the Layers palette. Click on the beige color swatch to bring up the Color Picker, then change the glow color to white. Set the Blend Mode pop-up menu to Normal, increase the Spread to 7, the Size to 16, and click OK to apply a white glow around your object.

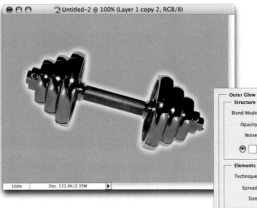
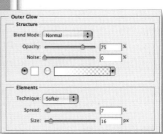

Step Three:
Duplicate your object layer by pressing Command-J (PC: Control-J), then go to the Layers palette and drag this layer below your original layer. On this duplicate layer, double-click on the words "Outer Glow." In the dialog, change the glow color to a bright yellow, increase the Size to 24, and click OK. This yellow outer glow will extend behind the white glow, creating the double-glow effect.

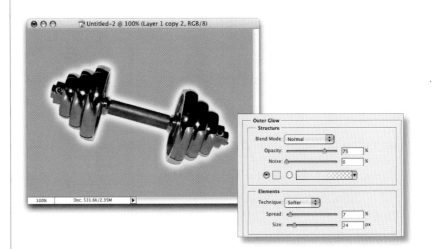

Fade-Away Reflection

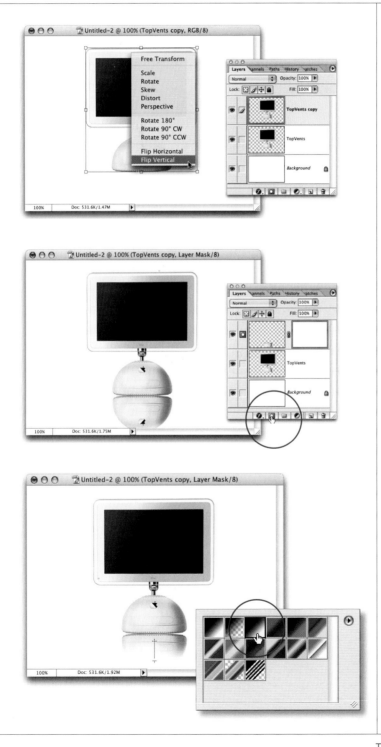

Step One:
Create a new document (File>New). Then open the object that you want to apply a fade-away reflection to. Put a selection around this object, get the Move tool, and drag the object onto your blank document. Duplicate your object layer by pressing Command-J (PC: Control-J), then press Command-T (PC: Control-T) to bring up Free Transform. Control-click (PC: Right-click) within the Free Transform bounding box, and choose Flip Vertical from the contextual menu.

Step Two:
Press Return (PC: Enter) to lock in your vertical flip. Get the Move tool and drag this flipped object straight down, until the two bases meet. Next, go to the Layers palette and click on the Add a Layer Mask icon. Now you're ready to create the reflection, so get the Gradient tool.

Step Three:
Press Return (PC: Enter) and the Gradient Picker will appear at the current location of your cursor. Choose the Black to White gradient, then take the Gradient tool, click at the point where you want your reflection to be completely transparent, and drag upward until you reach the top of the flipped object. This will create the fade-away effect because the area where you first clicked will become transparent, and the area where you stopped will be solid, with a smooth blend in between.

Cast Shadow Effect

Step One:
Open the document that has an object you want to add a cast shadow effect to (in this case, it's a steering wheel). Select just your object and press Shift-Command-J (PC: Shift-Control-J) to put the object on a new layer. Duplicate the object layer by pressing Command-J (PC: Control-J). This duplicate layer will become the cast shadow in the next steps.

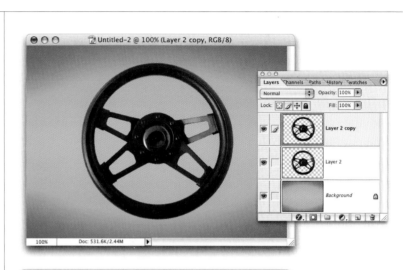

Step Two:
Make black your Foreground color, and press Shift-Option-Delete (PC: Shift-Alt-Backspace) to fill the object on your duplicate layer with black. Then press Command-T (PC: Control-T) to bring up Free Transform. Now hold the Command key (PC: Control key), grab the top-center point, and drag down and to the left to skew the shadow (as if you're laying it down) as shown here. Press Return (PC: Enter) to lock in your skew.

Step Three:
Go to the Layers palette and lower the Opacity of this layer to 50% (or less if you like), then go under the Filter Menu, under Blur, and choose Gaussian Blur. When the dialog appears, enter 3 pixels (for high-res, 300-ppi images enter 12 pixels) and click OK. Then drag the shadow layer below the object layer in the Layers palette.

Post-it® Notes Effect

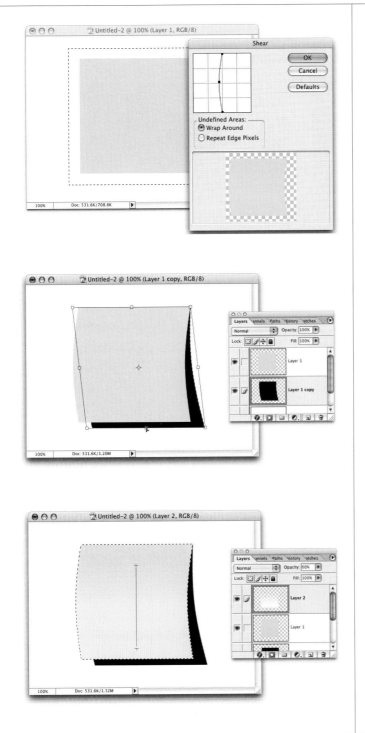

Step One:

Open a new document and create a new blank layer. Get the Rectangular Marquee tool, hold the Shift key, and make a square selection. Set yellow as your Foreground color, then fill this selection with yellow by pressing Option-Delete (PC: Alt-Backspace). Make another square selection that's larger than your yellow square, then go under the Filter menu, under Distort, and choose Shear. Click once in the center of the grid and drag to the left to bend the note. Click OK and deselect.

Step Two:

Press Command-J (PC: Control-J) to duplicate your yellow note layer. Set black as your Foreground color, then press Shift-Option-Delete (PC: Shift-Alt-Backspace) to fill this duplicate with black. In the Layers palette, drag this black layer below your yellow layer. Press Command-T (PC: Control-T) to bring up Free Transform. Hold the Command key (PC: Control key), and drag the top-center point to the left to skew it, then drag the bottom-center point to the right until it looks like the shadow here. Then, add a 3-pixel Gaussian Blur (Filter>Blur>Gaussian Blur), and lower the Opacity to 65%.

Step Three:

In the Layers palette, add another new layer, then Command-click (PC: Control-click) on the yellow note layer to select it. Set your Foreground color to white, get the Gradient tool, and choose the Foreground to Transparent gradient in the Gradient Picker. Drag the Gradient tool from the bottom of your note to the top (as shown here). Lastly, lower the Opacity of this layer to around 60%.

Quick Polaroid® Effect

Step One:
Open the photo you want to apply the Polaroid® effect to. Press Command-A (PC: Control-A) to select the entire photo, then press Shift-Command-J (PC: Shift-Control-J) to cut the image from the background and put it on a separate layer. Now go under the Image menu and choose Canvas Size. Check the Relative checkbox, then for Width and Height enter 2 inches, and click OK to add 2 inches of white space around your photo.

Step Two:
Choose Stroke from the Add a Layer Style pop-up menu at the bottom of the Layers palette. When the dialog appears, click on the red Color swatch and choose a very, very light gray color as your stroke. Set your Position to Inside, so the stroke has pointy corners, then increase the Size to 15 or more to make your border. Don't click OK yet.

Step Three:
In the Styles list on the left side of the dialog, click directly on the words "Drop Shadow." In the dialog, increase the Size setting to around 13, which softens the shadow and makes it a bit larger. Click OK to apply both the stroke and drop shadow effects to complete the technique.

Soft Spotlight Effect

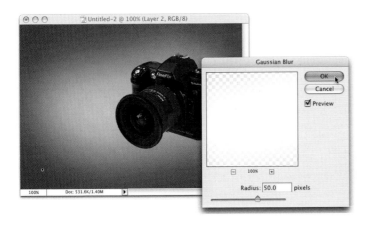

Step One:
Create a new document (File>New), choose a Foreground color, and press Option-Delete (PC: Alt-Backspace) to fill the background with that color. Open the object you want to appear on the background, put a selection around the object, and drag it onto your background document with the Move tool.

Step Two:
In the Layers palette, Command-click (PC: Control-click) on the Create a New Layer icon to create a new blank layer beneath your object layer. Get the Lasso tool and draw a selection around the object where you want your soft spotlight to appear. Press "d" then "x" to set your Foreground color to white, then press Option-Delete (PC: Alt-Backspace) to fill the selection with white. Now press Command-D (PC: Control-D) to deselect.

Step Three:
Go under the Filter menu, under Blur, and choose Gaussian Blur. Enter 50 pixels (try 170 pixels for high-res, 300-ppi images) and click OK to soften the white area enough that it looks like a soft spotlight. Then in the Layers palette, lower the Opacity of this layer to around 75% so it's not so intense and looks more realistic.

Creating a Reflection in Sunglasses

Step One:
Open a photo in which the subject is wearing sunglasses. Make a selection inside one lens using any selection tool (here I used the Lasso tool). Open the photo you want to appear as a reflection in the sunglasses and press Command-A (PC: Control-A) to select the entire photo, then press Command-C (PC: Control-C) to copy that selection.

Step Two:
Go back to your sunglasses document, and under the Edit menu, choose Paste Into. Press Command-T (PC: Control-T), hold the Shift key, and drag a corner point inward to scale the photo so it fits within the lens. Press Return (PC: Enter). Then choose Inner Shadow from the Add a Layer Style pop-up menu at the bottom of the Layers palette. For Distance choose 1, for Size choose 3, change the Angle to 120°, and click OK to add a shadow inside the image to make it look like it's in the lens.

Step Three:
In the Layers palette, lower the Opacity of this layer to around 50% and change the blend mode to Screen so you can see a little detail and some of the light source through the lens. (*Note*: If both lenses are showing in your sunglasses image, apply the same technique to the other lens.)

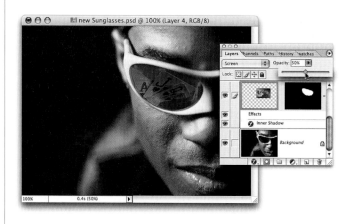

Brushed Metal Effect

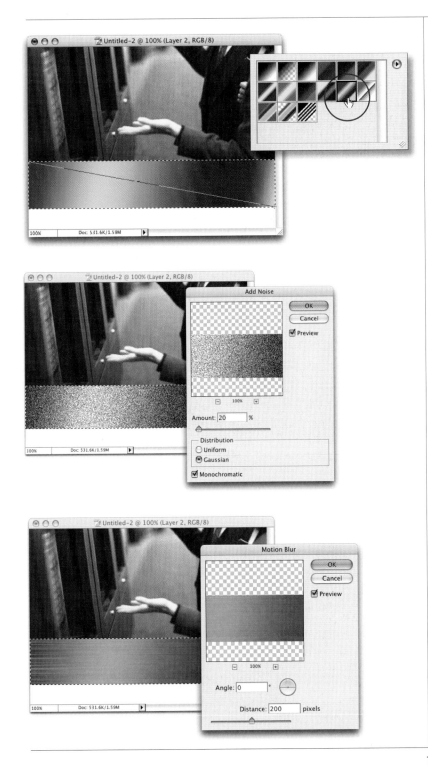

Step One:
Open the document that you want to apply a brushed metal effect to. Create a new layer, then get the Rectangular Marquee tool and draw a selection where you want your brushed metal to appear. Next, get the Gradient tool, then press Return (PC: Enter) to bring up the Gradient Picker. Choose the Copper gradient from the default set of gradients, then drag the Gradient tool diagonally through your selection (as shown here). (*Note:* This technique works best over a solid white or black background.)

Step Two:
You'll need to remove the copper color from your gradient, so go under the Image menu, under Adjustments, and choose Desaturate. Then, go under the Filter menu, under Noise, and choose Add Noise. When the dialog appears, for Amount enter 20%, for Distribution choose Gaussian, turn on the Monochromatic checkbox, then click OK to apply noise over your gradient.

Step Three:
Lastly, go under the Filter menu again, under Blur, and choose Motion Blur. When the dialog appears, set the Angle to 0°, set the Distance to 200 pixels, and click OK. This creates the brushed metal look. *Note:* If the metal seems too dark, press Command-L (PC: Control-L) to bring up Levels, then grab the bottom-left Output Levels slider and drag to the right to lighten the selected metal. Then press Command-D (PC: Control-D) to deselect.

Tinting a Photo

Step One:
Open the photo you want to tint.

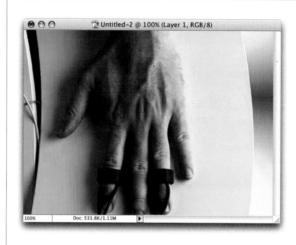

Step Two:
At the bottom of the Layers palette, choose Hue/Saturation from the Create New Adjustment Layer pop-up menu (as shown here).

Step Three:
When the Hue/Saturation dialog appears, turn on the Colorize checkbox, then move the Hue slider until you see the color you want for your tint. To make the color more intense, drag the Saturation slider to the right. To darken the image, drag the Lightness slider to the left, or to lighten the image drag it to the right. When the tint looks good to you, click OK to apply the tint effect to your image (as shown here).

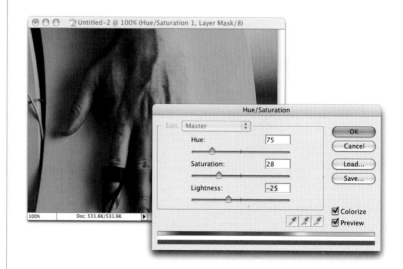

Adding a Pattern

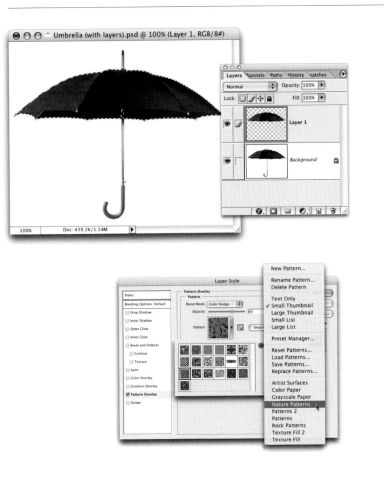

Step One:
Open your document with an image you want to apply a pattern to. Get the Magic Wand tool and make a selection of the area (here I'm selecting the umbrella's fabric). You may have to click once, hold the Shift key, and click a few more times to get the entire area selected. Once it's selected, press Command-J (PC: Control-J) to copy the fabric up onto its own separate layer. Now choose Pattern Overlay from the Add a Layer Style pop-up menu at the bottom of the Layers palette.

Step Two:
Click on the Pattern thumbnail to bring up the Pattern Picker. Click on the Picker's flyout menu and choose Nature Patterns. When the dialog appears, click the Append button to add these nature patterns to your Pattern Picker.

Step Three:
Select the Blue Daisies pattern and change the Blend Mode pop-up menu in the dialog to Color Dodge (which brightens the flowers) to blend the flower pattern in with the fabric. Then lower the Opacity in the dialog to 65% to keep the flowers from being too intense. Click OK to apply your pattern.

Creating a Tinted Noise Effect

Step One:
Open the photo that you want to apply noise to (in this case, a jet). Press Command-A (PC: Control-A) to Select All, then press Command-Shift-J (PC: Control-Shift-J) to cut the image from the background and copy it onto its own layer.

Step Two:
Go under the Image menu, under Adjustments, and choose Desaturate. This removes all the color from the photo. Then go under the Filter menu, under Noise, and choose Add Noise. When the Add Noise dialog appears, set the Amount to 7, for Distribution choose Gaussian, and make sure you check the Monochromatic checkbox (so the noise you create doesn't have little red, green, and blue dots). Click OK.

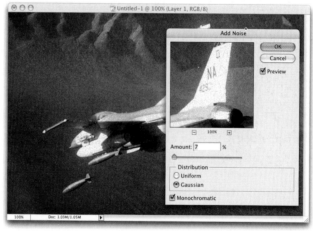

Step Three:
Choose Hue/Saturation from the Create New Adjustment Layer pop-up menu at the bottom of the Layers palette. When the dialog appears, click on the Colorize checkbox, then drag the Hue slider to 200 to put a blue tint over your noisy photo. Then click OK to complete the very popular noisy tinted image technique.

Adding a High-Tech Transparent Grid

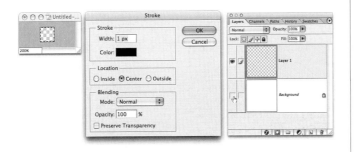

Step One:
Create a new document (File>New) that's .25x.25". Create a new blank layer, then in the Layers palette hide the Background layer from view by clicking on its Eye icon. Press Command-A (PC: Control-A) to put a selection around the document, then go under the Edit menu and choose Stroke. Enter 1 pixel for Width, choose black for Color, and choose Center for Location. Click OK.

Step Two:
Go under the Edit menu and choose Define Pattern. When the dialog appears, give your pattern a name and click OK. Now open the photo you want to apply your grid to. Add a new layer, then go to the Edit menu and choose Fill. In the Fill dialog, choose Pattern from the Use pop-up menu. Then, click on the Custom Pattern icon to bring up the Pattern Picker. Click on the last pattern (that's the one you just named), and click OK.

Step Three:
This fills your layer with a black grid. Press Command-I (PC: Control-I) to invert your grid, making it white. In the Layers palette, lower the Opacity of your grid to around 15%, and then add a layer mask to your white grid layer. Get the Gradient tool, press Return (PC: Enter), and choose the Foreground to Transparent gradient. Click on your photo where you want the grid to be fully transparent, then drag upward and release the mouse button at the point where you want the grid to be fully visible, making the grid fade into your photo.

Clipping into a Shape

Step One:
Create a new document, then click the Create a New Layer icon at the bottom of the Layers palette. Set black as your Foreground color, then get the Rounded Rectangle tool (it's one of the Shape tools). Go up to the Options Bar and click on the third icon from the left so the tool will create pixels, rather than a path or a shape layer. In the Options Bar, set the Radius (the roundness of the corners) to 10 pixels. Now use the tool to drag out a rounded rectangle in the shape of a credit card.

Step Two:
Open the first photo you want to "clip" into your credit card shape, get the Move tool, and drag-and-drop the image onto your credit card shape, positioning it where you want it to appear.

Step Three:
Press Command-G (PC: Control-G), which is the shortcut for Create Clipping Mask, and the photo will fit neatly inside the shape. Once it's clipped inside, if you need to reposition the image, just use the Move tool to position it where you want it, and it will stay within the boundaries of the shape.

Sepia Tone Effect

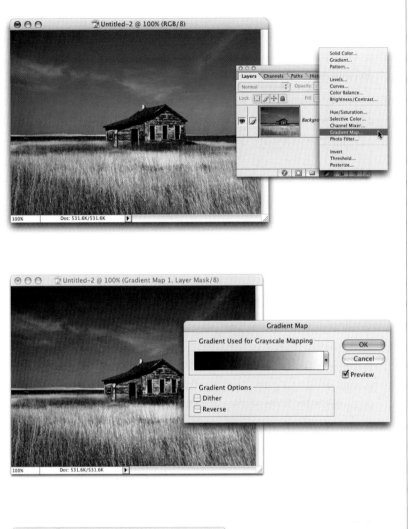

Step One:
Open your image. You'll want to convert your photo into a black-and-white image with added contrast, so choose Gradient Map from the Create New Adjustment Layer pop-up menu at the bottom of the Layers palette.

Step Two:
When the Gradient Map dialog appears, click on the down-facing arrow next to the gradient thumbnail to bring up the Gradient Picker, and select the Black to White gradient. Click OK so the gradient is mapped over your photo, giving it a very "contrasty" black-and-white effect.

Step Three:
Choose Solid Color from the Create New Adjustment Layer pop-up menu at the bottom of the Layers palette. When the Color Picker appears, click on the Custom button to bring up the Custom Colors dialog. Choose the color you want, then change the layer blend mode from Normal to Color in the Layers palette to apply the sepia tone effect to your photo.

Carved into Metal

Step One:

Open the image with the metal object. Set your Foreground to white, get the Type tool, and create the type you want carved into metal. Get the Move tool, then press Command-T (PC: Control-T) to bring up Free Transform. Rotate the text so it matches the angle of the object, then press Return (PC: Enter). Choose Inner Shadow from the Add a Layer Style pop-up menu at the bottom of the Layers palette. Increase the Opacity to 100% and decrease the Distance to 3, then click OK.

Step Two:

In the Layers palette, lower the Fill (not the Opacity) to 0%, so the white fill is hidden, but the inner shadow remains. In the Layers palette, Command-click (PC: Control-click) on your Type layer to put a selection around your type.

Step Three:

In the Layers palette, click on the object's layer and press Command-L (PC: Control-L) to bring up Levels. Drag the bottom-right Output Levels slider a little to the left to darken the area inside the letters. Click OK, but don't deselect yet. In the Layers palette, click on the Type layer, then click the Create a New Layer icon. Go to Edit>Stroke and choose 1 pixel for Width, white for Color, Center for Location, and click OK. Then, lower the Opacity to 50% and press Command-D (PC: Control-D) to deselect.

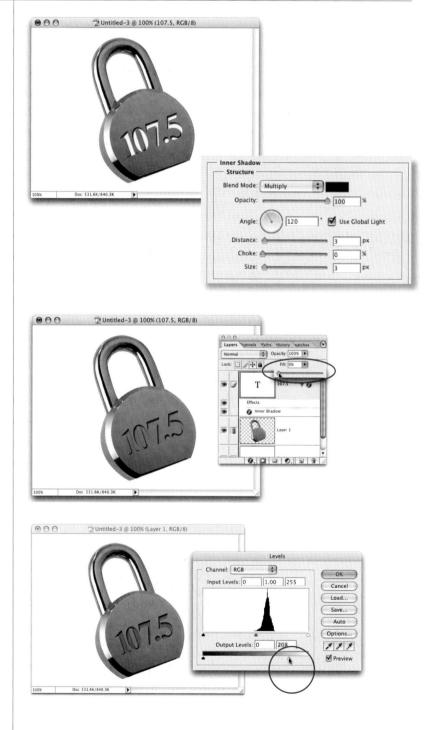

Vignette Edge Effect

Step One:
Open the photo that you want to apply a vignette soft-edged effect to. Get the Rectangular Marquee tool and draw a rectangular selection just inside the borders of your image.

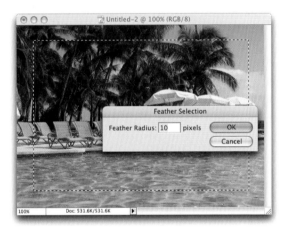

Step Two:
Set your Background color to white, then go under the Select menu and choose Feather. In the dialog, for Feather Radius enter 10 pixels (the higher the number, the softer your border will be), then click OK. You'll see the borders of your selection are now rounded, indicating that a feather has been applied. To select the area bordering your image, go under the Select menu and choose Inverse.

Step Three:
Now all you have to do is press Delete (PC: Backspace) to erase the edges and reveal the soft-edged border. Press Command-D (PC: Control-D) to deselect so you can see the final effect.

Ripped Edge Effect

Step One:

Open the photo you want revealed when you apply a ripped edge effect to an image above it. Then, open the image you want to rip, and drag it on top of your original photo with the Move tool. Get the Lasso tool and draw a somewhat jaggy selection where you want the rip (in this case, it's around the center of the image), then press Delete (PC: Backspace) to knock a hole out of this top layer, revealing the layer below.

Step Two:

To add some depth, choose Outer Glow from the Add a Layer Style pop-up menu at the bottom of the Layers palette. Set the Blend Mode to Normal, change the Size to 16, click on the beige color swatch, and change the glow color to black in the Color Picker. Click OK to apply a black glow inside your ripped area. Get the Lasso tool again, and draw another selection just outside the ripped area. Don't exactly trace the original rip, but loosely follow along the edge.

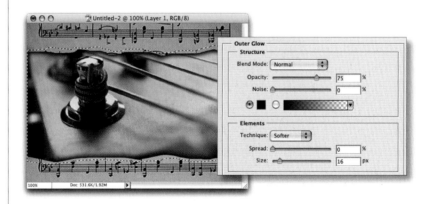

Step Three:

To make this slightly larger selection look like the paper behind the rip, press Command-L (PC: Control-L) to bring up Levels, then drag the bottom-left Output Levels slider almost all the way to the right. This lightens the selected area, adding more depth and interest to your ripped effect.

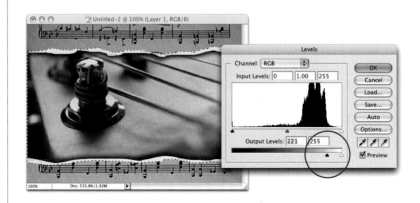

Adding Glints

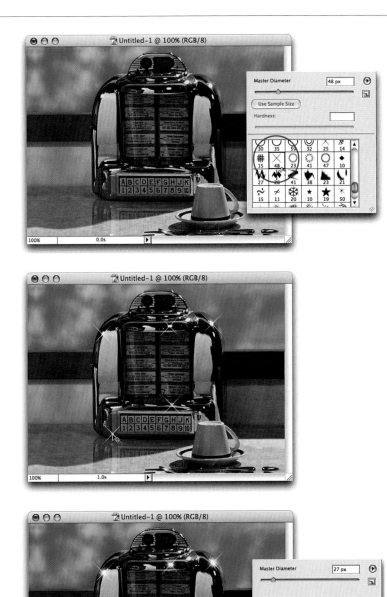

Step One:
Open the image that you want to add glints to. Get the Brush tool, then bring up the Brush Picker in the Options Bar. In the Picker's flyout menu, choose Assorted Brushes to load this set of brushes. When the dialog appears, click the Append button and these brushes will be added to your default set of brushes in the Picker. Scroll down the Picker until you see the 48-pixel brush that looks like an "X", and click on it to select it.

Step Two:
Create a new blank layer and press "d" then "x" to set your Foreground color to white. Take the Brush tool and click once directly over the areas where you want to add a glint. Don't paint—just click and an "X" glint will be added.

Step Three:
Once your glints are in place, go up to the Brush Picker again, scroll back toward the top, and choose the 27-pixel soft round brush. Click once with this brush in the center of each glint to enhance the effect.

Changing the Color of an Object

Step One:
Open the photo that has an object whose color you want to change. Press Command-J (PC: Control-J) to duplicate the Background layer.

Step Two:
Go under the Image menu, under Adjustments, and choose Hue/Saturation. When the dialog appears, click on the Colorize checkbox and move the Hue slider to the color that you want for your object (in this case, I want the guitar to be blue). To make the color more intense, drag the Saturation slider to the right. When you click OK, the color is added to the entire layer.

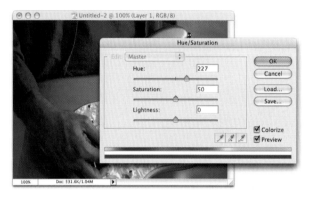

Step Three:
Hold the Option key (PC: Alt key) and click on the Add a Layer Mask icon at the bottom of the Layers palette. This hides the blue tint by adding a black mask over the blue layer. Set your Foreground color to white, get the Brush tool, choose a soft-edged brush in the Brush Picker found in the Options Bar, and start painting over the object to apply your new color. If you later decide to change the color of the object, click on the colorized layer's thumbnail (to the left of the layer mask thumbnail) in the Layers palette, return to Image>Adjustments>Hue/Saturation, turn on the Colorize checkbox, and adjust the Hue slider in the dialog.

TV Scan Lines Effect

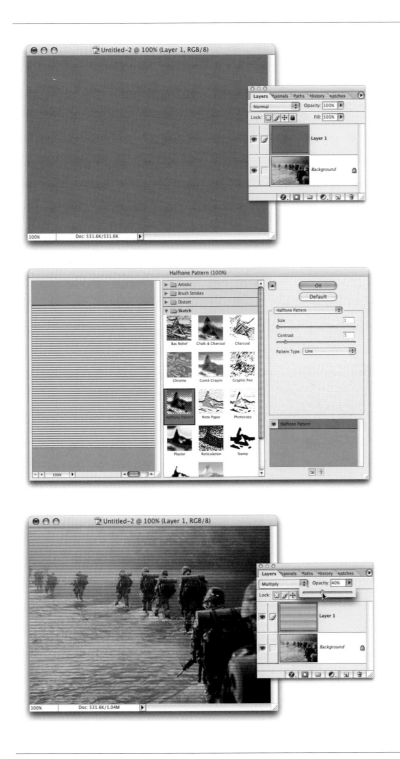

Step One:
Open the photo you want to apply a scan lines effect to. Click on the Create a New Layer icon at the bottom of the Layers palette. Set your Foreground color to a medium gray, and fill this new layer with gray by pressing Option-Delete (PC: Alt-Backspace).

Step Two:
Press "d" to set your Foreground color to black and your Background color to white. Then, go under the Filter menu, under Sketch, and choose Halftone Pattern. When the dialog appears, set the Size to 1, Contrast to 5, then in the Pattern Type pop-up menu choose Line.

Step Three:
Click OK in the dialog to apply a series of lines to your gray layer. To get this pattern to blend in with the photo on the Background layer, go to the Layers palette and change the layer blend mode to Multiply, then lower the Opacity of this layer so the scan lines effect isn't too intense (in this case, I set the Opacity to 40%).

Zoom Blur Effect

Step One:
Open the photo you want to apply the zoom blur effect to.

Step Two:
Go under the Filter menu, under Blur, and choose Radial Blur. Set the Amount to 100; for Blur Method choose Zoom; and set the Quality to Good.

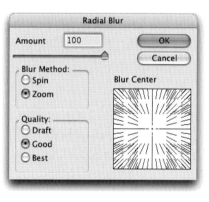

Step Three:
When you click OK, the zoom blur will be applied to the entire image.

Filter Edge Effect

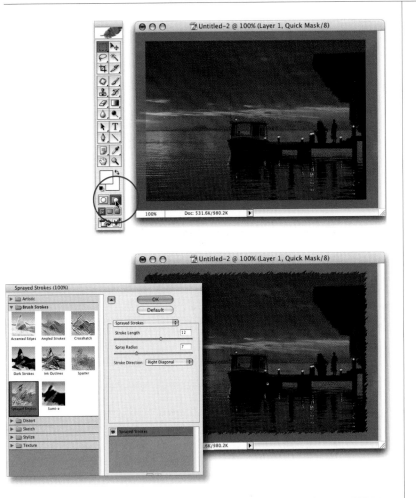

Step One:
Open the photo you want to apply a filter edge effect to. Get the Rectangular Marquee tool and draw a selection just inside the borders of the image. Click on the Quick Mask icon near the bottom of the Toolbox (or just press the letter "q") to enter Quick Mask mode. Now your selection border is hidden, and the area outside your selection appears in red.

Step Two:
Go under the Filter menu, under Brush Strokes, and choose Sprayed Strokes. Set the Stroke Length to 12, the Stray Radius to 7, and Stroke Direction to Right Diagonal. At the bottom-right side of the dialog, click on the New Effect Layer icon (to the left of the Trash icon). In the list of filters on the left, click on the Sketch folder, and click on the Torn Edges filter. Set the Image Balance to 25, Smoothness to 11, and Contrast to 18, then click OK to apply both of these filters to the edge area.

Step Three:
Press "q" to return to Standard mode, and you'll see your selection border reappear. Now choose Select>Inverse, so the outside area of your photo is selected. Press "d" to set your Background color to white, and press Delete (PC: Backspace) to delete the area around your photo, leaving you with the edge effect shown here. Now deselect by pressing Command-D (PC: Control-D) to see your final effect.

Painted Edge Effect

Step One:

Open the photo you want to apply the painted edge to. Press Command-A (PC: Control-A) to select the entire photo, then press Shift-Command-J (PC: Shift-Control-J) to cut the image from the background and put it on a separate layer. Under the Image menu, choose Canvas Size. Check the Relative checkbox, then enter 2 inches for both Width and Height, and click OK.

Step Two:

Command-click (PC: Control-click) on your photo layer in the Layers palette to put a selection around your photo. Then go to the Paths palette, and from the palette's flyout menu choose Make Work Path and click OK. Next, get the Brush tool, open the Brush Picker in the Options Bar, scroll to the bottom of the default set of brushes, and click on the 100-pixel Rough Round Bristle brush.

Step Three:

In the Layers palette, create a new layer, then go back to the Paths palette, and from the palette's flyout menu choose Stroke Path. When the dialog appears, turn on the Simulate Pressure checkbox, and for Tool choose Brush. Click OK, and the path around your photo will be stroked with your 100-pixel brush. Press Command-J (PC: Control-J) to duplicate the layer, making the stroke darker. Finally, drag your image layer to the top of the layers stack so the inside edge of the stroke will be smooth.

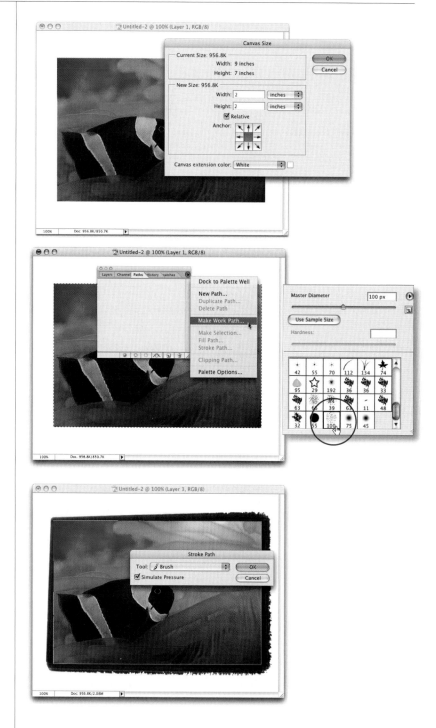

Fitting Your Image into Their Sign

Step One:
Open the photo that has an area where you want to insert your own image (in this case, I'm going to insert my sign over the original sign in this photo). Get the Polygonal Lasso tool and draw a selection around the interior of the sign.

Step Two:
Open the photo that you want to place inside the sign (in this case, a poster with a photo of a door). Press Command-A (PC: Control-A) to select the entire photo, then press Command-C (PC: Control-C) to copy it into memory. Then go back to the sign document and under the Edit menu choose Paste Into. This pastes the photo inside the selection, but you're going to have some adjusting to do because the sign is at an angle, and your poster is straight. To do this, press Command-T (PC: Control-T) to bring up the Free Transform command.

Step Three:
Hold the Command key (PC: Control key), grab the top-left control point of the bounding box and drag it until it meets the top-left corner of the sign in the photo. Release the mouse button, grab the top-right corner point and drag it until it touches the top-right corner of the original sign. Do the same for the two bottom points. This gives the pasted-in poster the same perspective as the sign. Return (PC: Enter) to lock in your transformation.

Digital Pixel Effect

Step One:

Open the photo you want to apply a digital pixel effect to. Press Command-J (PC: Control-J) to duplicate the Background layer.

Step Two:

Go under the Filter menu, under Pixelate, and choose Mosaic. In the dialog, set the Cell Size (in this case, it's set to 8), and click OK to apply a pixel effect to your entire layer. Now create a layer mask by clicking the Add a Layer Mask icon at the bottom of the Layers palette.

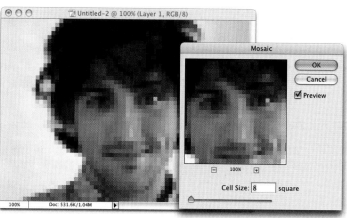

Step Three:

Get the Gradient tool, press Return (PC: Enter) to bring up the Gradient Picker, and choose the Black to White gradient. Click-and-drag the Gradient tool horizontally to blend the masked pixelated layer with the original layer underneath to complete the effect.

Creating the Stamp Effect

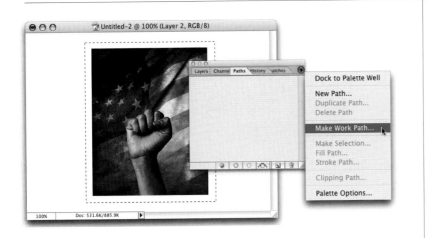

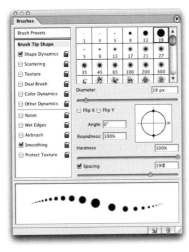

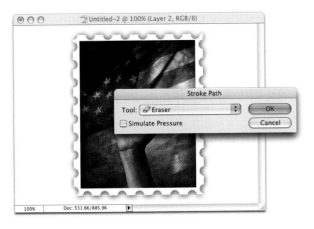

Step One:
Open the photo you want to apply the stamp effect to. Create a new document that's larger than your photo, get the Move tool, and drag your photo onto this blank document so it appears on its own layer. In the Layers palette, Command-click (PC: Control-click) the Create a New Layer icon. Get the Rectangular Marquee tool and draw a selection that's slightly larger than your photo, and fill this selection with white. Then choose Make Work Path from the Paths palette's flyout menu.

Step Two:
Choose Drop Shadow from the Layer Styles pop-up menu at the bottom of the Layers palette. Set the Angle to 71°, Distance to 3, Size to 16, and click OK to apply a soft shadow to your white box. Next, get the Eraser tool, then open the Brushes palette, click on the 19-pixel hard-edged brush, and click on "Brush Tip Shape" on the top-left of the dialog. Turn on the Spacing checkbox, and drag the slider to 190% so there are visible spaces in your stroke.

Step Three:
From the Paths palette's flyout menu choose Stroke Path. When the dialog appears, turn off Simulate Pressure, and for Tool choose Eraser. When you click OK, the eraser will instantly trace around the path on the edge of your white shadowed layer, knocking out little stamp-edge-like holes.

Curling Type Around an Object

Step One:

Open the photo that you want to curve type around. Get the Type tool and create your type. Go to the Layers palette and Control-click (PC: Right-click) on the Type layer's name, and from the contextual menu that appears, choose Rasterize Layer. Then get the Rectangular Marquee tool and draw a rectangular selection around your text.

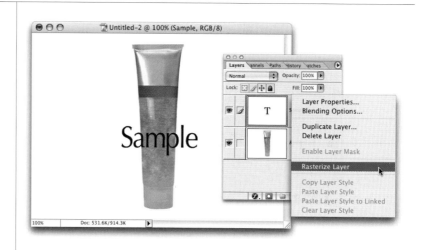

Step Two:

You're going to bend your type using the Shear filter, but since the filter only bends horizontally, you have to bend your type now, before you rotate it into position on the tube. Go under the Filter menu, under Distort, and choose Shear. When the Shear dialog appears, click once in the center of the grid and drag a little bit to the left, and you'll see your text bend in the preview area at the bottom of the dialog. Click OK, and then deselect by pressing Command-D (PC: Control-D).

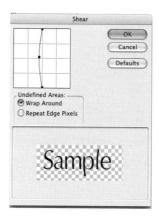

Step Three:

Now you can rotate your type into position. Press Command-T (PC: Control-T) to bring up Free Transform, then move your cursor outside the bounding box, click-and-drag upward to rotate the text, and position it on the hair gel tube. Press Return (PC: Enter) to lock in your rotation. You can see that the type now looks curved around the tube (in particular, look at the "l" and the "p"). You can then lower the Opacity of the Type layer for a more realistic look.

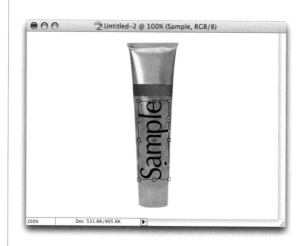

Blind Emboss Effect

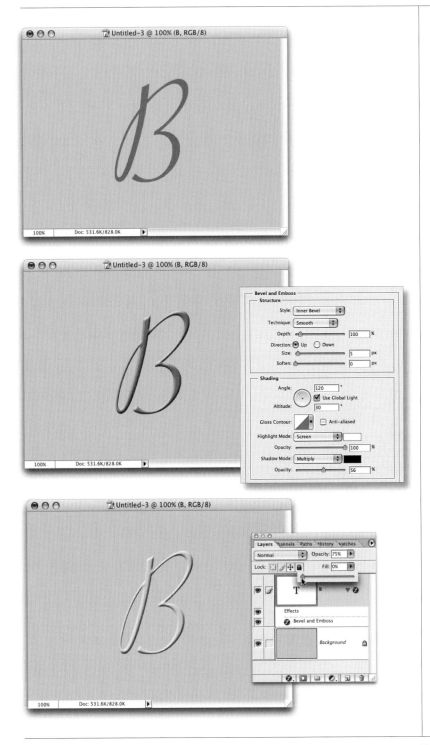

Step One:
Create a new document, set your Foreground color to a tan color, and fill your Background layer with this color by pressing Option-Delete (PC: Alt-Backspace). Then, set your Foreground color to a medium gray (the shade of gray isn't that critical, so any middle gray will do). Get the Type tool and create a large letter in a script font (in this case, a capital "B" set in the font Savoye).

Step Two:
Choose Bevel and Emboss from the Add a Layer Style pop-up menu at the bottom of the Layers palette. At the bottom of the dialog, drag the Highlight Opacity slider to 100%, and lower the Shadow Opacity slider to 50%. Then click OK to apply your bevel to your type.

Step Three:
Go to the Layers palette, and lower the Opacity of this layer to around 75%. Just below the Opacity setting you'll see a Fill field. Lower the Fill to 0%, and the gray fill inside your text will disappear, but the bevel and emboss effect will remain, giving you the look of a blind emboss.

Blending Fireworks into Nighttime Photos

Step One:
Open the night photo you want to add fireworks to, then open a fireworks photo and drag-and-drop that photo onto your night photo.

Step Two:
In the Layers palette, double-click on the fireworks layer's thumbnail image to bring up the Blending Options. At the bottom of the Blending Options dialog are four sliders. Hold Option (PC: Alt), then grab the top-left slider and drag to the right. Because you held the Option/Alt key, the slider will split into two, and as you drag to the right, the black background behind the fireworks disappears, blending the fireworks into your background photo. When it looks good, click OK.

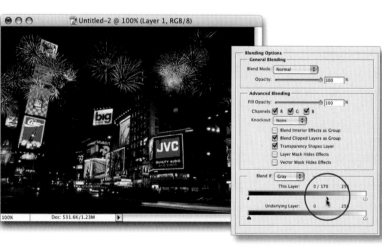

Step Three:
The fireworks appear in front of the buildings, rather than behind them. To fix that, go to the bottom of the Layers palette and click on the Add a Layer Mask icon. Then get the Brush tool, choose a hard-edged brush in the Brush Picker from the Options bar, set black as your Foreground color, and begin painting over the buildings. As you paint, the fireworks will appear to move behind the buildings (you're masking them away with your brush).

Instant Lightning Effect

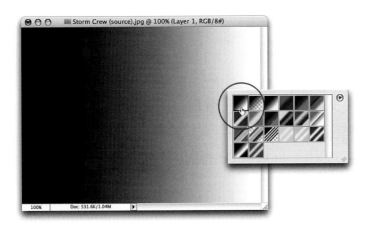

Step One:
Open the photo you want to apply a lightning effect to. Go to the Layers palette and add a new blank layer. Press "d" to set your Foreground/Background colors to their default. Get the Gradient tool from the Toolbox, press Return (PC: Enter) to bring up the Gradient Picker, and choose the Foreground to Background gradient. Then click-and-drag the Gradient tool from the left side of your image area all the way to the right.

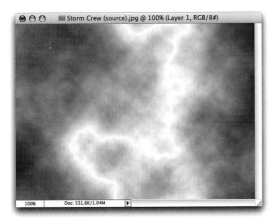

Step Two:
Go under the Filter menu, under Render, and choose Difference Clouds to apply a random cloud pattern over your gradient. Press Command-I (PC: Control-I) to invert your clouds. Reapply this step as needed until you get the lightning effect you desire.

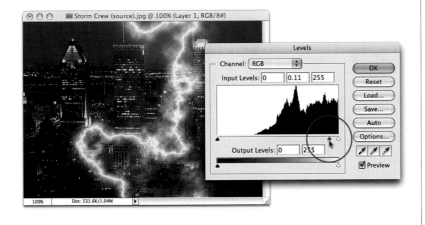

Step Three:
In the Layers palette, change the blend mode of your layer from Normal to Screen so the lightning will blend in with your photo. Press Command-L (PC: Control-L) to bring up Levels. Grab the center Input Levels slider (the midtones slider) and drag it almost all the way to the right to see the lightning effect appear within your photo.

Chrome Beveled Type

Step One:

Create a new document, and use the Type tool to enter your type (the font shown here is Savoye). In the Layers palette, Control-click (PC: Right-click) on the Type layer's name and choose Rasterize Layer from the contextual menu. Get the Gradient tool, and click on the Gradient thumbnail in the Options Bar to bring up the Gradient Editor. Create a gradient similar to the one you see here. Click the New button to save this gradient, then click OK. Turn on the Lock Transparent Pixels icon in the Layers palette, and click-and-drag on your type to apply the gradient.

Step Two:

Choose Stroke from the Add a Layer Style pop-up menu at the bottom of the Layers palette. Increase the Size to 7, then for Fill Type choose Gradient. Click on the Gradient thumbnail's down-facing arrow to bring up the Picker. Choose Metals from the flyout menu, click the Append button in the resulting dialog, then choose the Silver gradient. Don't click OK yet.

Step Three:

On the left of the dialog, choose Bevel and Emboss. For Style choose Stroke Emboss, increase the Depth to around 350%, lower the Size to 4, and turn on the Anti-aliased checkbox. Then, click on the down-facing arrow to the right of the Gloss Contour thumbnail to bring up the Contour Picker, choose Contours in the flyout menu, and click Append. Now choose the three-hill contour, then click OK to complete the effect.

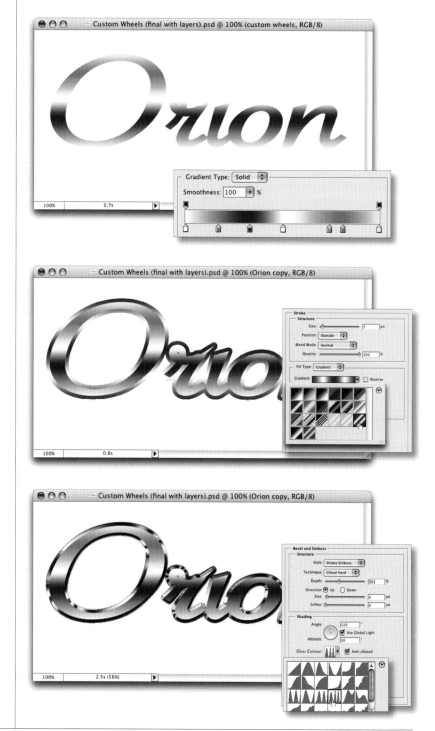

The Gel Look

Step One:

Create a new document, then get the Type tool and type in the number "5". Choose Color Overlay from the Add a Layer Style pop-up menu at the bottom of the Layers palette. When the dialog appears, click on the color swatch and choose a bright yellow in the Color Picker. Then, in the Styles list on the left side of the Layer Style dialog, click directly on the words "Inner Shadow." Increase the Distance to 7, set the Choke to 20%, and the Size to 10. Don't click OK yet.

Step Two:

From the Styles list, now choose Inner Glow. Click on the beige color swatch and choose black in the Color Picker, lower the Opacity to 50%, and change the Blend Mode pop-up menu to Multiply. Don't click OK quite yet. Instead, in the Styles list on the left side of the dialog, click directly on the words "Bevel and Emboss."

Step Three:

When the dialog appears, increase the Size to 7, set Soften at 1, and in the Shading section set the Angle to 90° and Altitude to 67°. Increase the Highlight Opacity to 100% and lower the Shadow Opacity to 0%, then turn on the Anti-aliased checkbox to give you the gel effect you see here.

Putting a Photo into Type

Step One:
Create a new document, then get the Type tool and type in the number "3" (I'm using the font Bullet from House Industries). Open the photo you want to appear within your type (in this case, I want the fire from the photo below to appear inside the "3").

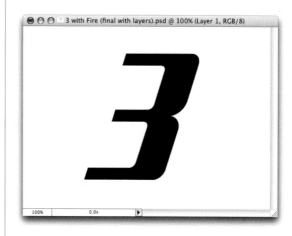

Step Two:
Get the Move tool and drag this photo over onto your number document. It will appear just above your number "3" layer in the Layers palette. Press Command-G (PC: Control-G), which is the shortcut for Create Clipping Mask, and basically everything outside your number "3" will be "clipped off" and your photo will appear within your type.

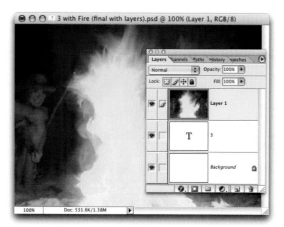

Step Three:
Now that the photo is inside your number, you can use the Move tool to reposition the photo within the type so it's right where you want it. To accent the edges, go to the Layers palette, make your Type layer active, and choose Stroke from the Add a Layer Style pop-up menu. Change the Color to black, and click OK to apply a black stroke around your type.

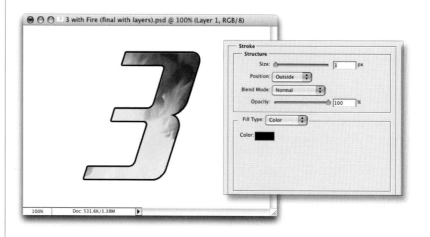

Multiple Inline/Outline Effect

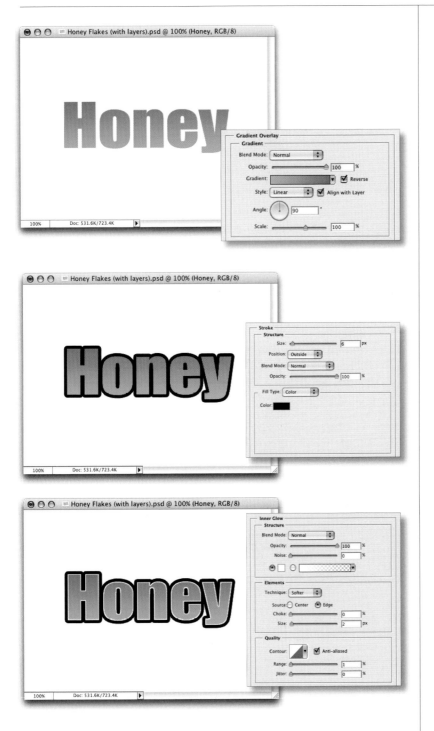

Step One:

Create a new document, get the Type tool, and create your type (the font shown here is Impact). This effect works with a solid color or gradient, so just for fun, we'll use a gradient here. Set your Foreground color to a dark green, your Background color to a light green, and then choose Gradient Overlay from the Add a Layer Style pop-up menu at the bottom of the Layers palette. Click the arrow to the right of the Gradient thumbnail to open the Gradient Picker, and choose the first gradient (Foreground to Background). Don't click OK yet.

Step Two:

In the Styles list on the left side of the Layer Style dialog, click directly on the word "Stroke." For Size choose 6, then change the Color from red to black to put a thick black stroke around your letters. Don't click OK—instead, in the Styles list click directly on the words "Inner Glow."

Step Three:

Click on the beige color swatch and change the glow color to white. Increase the Opacity to 100%, then lower the Size to 2. Lower the Range to 1, and turn on the Anti-aliased checkbox. Now when you click OK, the gradient, the black stroke on the outside, and the white stroke on the inside will all be applied to your type, giving you the multiple inline effect.

3D Type Effect

Step One:

Create a new document, set your Foreground color to a medium green, and then get the Type tool and enter your type (the type here is set using the font Impact). In the Layers palette, Control-click (PC: Right-click) on the Type layer's name and choose Rasterize Layer.

Step Two:

Press Command-T (PC: Control-T) to bring up Free Transform. Hold Shift-Option-Command (PC: Shift-Alt-Control) and drag the top-right corner point inward to create a perspective effect. Release the keys you were holding, then drag the top-center point straight down to make the type shorter. Press Return (PC: Enter) to lock in your transformation. Duplicate your Type layer by pressing Command-J (PC: Control-J). Press "d" to set your Foreground color to black, Command-click (PC: Control-click) the duplicate layer to select it, then fill it with black by pressing Option-Delete (PC: Alt-Backspace). Press Command-D (PC: Control-D) to deselect.

Step Three:

In the Layers palette, drag this black layer beneath your green Type layer. Get the Move tool, then hold down the Option (PC: Alt) key while pressing-and-holding the Down Arrow key on your keyboard for just a few seconds. This makes numerous copies of your black layer. In the Layers palette, hide your Background layer from view. In the palette's flyout menu, choose Merge Visible to combine all the Type layers into a single layer.

Perspective Type Shadow Effect

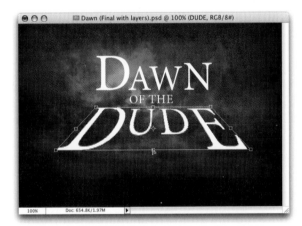

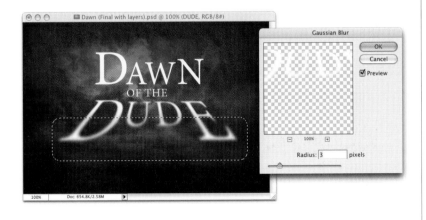

Step One:

Open your background image, set your Foreground color to white, get the Type tool, and enter three separate lines of type, each line on its own layer (the font shown here is Minion Pro). In the Layers palette, Control-click (PC: Right-click) on the "Dude" Type layer and choose Rasterize Layer.

Step Two:

Press Command-T (PC: Control-T) to bring up Free Transform, then hold Shift-Option-Command (PC: Shift-Alt-Control), and drag the bottom-right corner point outward. Release the keys and drag the center point straight down to exaggerate the effect. Press Return (PC: Enter) to lock in your transformation. Now, soften this perspective type by going under the Filter menu, under Blur, and choosing Gaussian Blur. Enter 1 pixel and click OK.

Step Three:

Get the Rectangular Marquee tool and draw a selection around the bottom half of the word "Dude". Soften the edge of this selection by going under the Select menu and choosing Feather. Enter 10 pixels and click OK. Now go back to Filter>Blur>Gaussian Blur and apply a 3-pixel blur to make the bottom of the letters appear more blurry, which enhances the perspective effect. Deselect by pressing Command-D (PC: Control-D) to complete the effect.

Distressed Type

Step One:

Create a new document. Create a new layer, get the Rectangular Marquee tool, and draw a square selection. Set your Foreground color to black, then fill your selection by pressing Option-Delete (PC: Alt-Backspace). Deselect by pressing Command-D (PC: Control-D). Set your Foreground color to white, then get the Type tool and type the word "JAM".

Step Two:

Press Command-J (PC: Control-J) to duplicate this Type layer. Drag the duplicate type to the bottom of the black box, and change the word to "FM". Press Command-T (PC: Control-T) to bring up Free Transform and stretch and compress the "FM" text. Add a new blank layer, make a rectangular selection in the center of your black block, fill it with white, then deselect. Set your Foreground color to black, then get the Type tool and enter "93.3". In the Layers palette, hide the Background layer from view, then choose Merge Visible from the palette's flyout menu.

Step Three:

Set white as your Foreground color. Get the Brush tool, and in the Brush Picker choose the 39-pixel Dry Brush. Click your brush over black areas of your image (don't paint strokes—just click), then move the cursor to another spot, click a few more times, and move again. Then, switch to the 100-pixel Rough Round Bristle brush in the Brush Picker (below the 39-pixel brush) and continue clicking. When you get to white letters, switch your Foreground color to black.

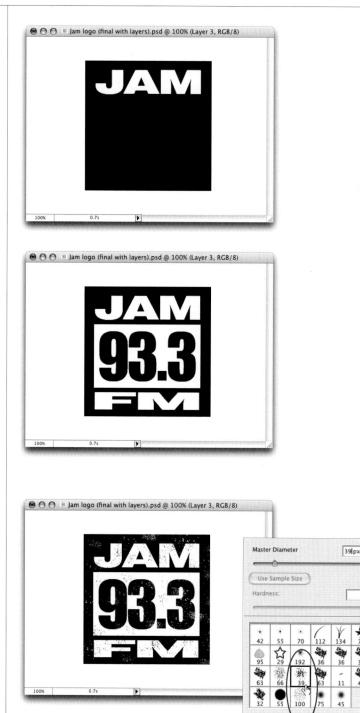

Chapter Opening—Airbrushed Chrome

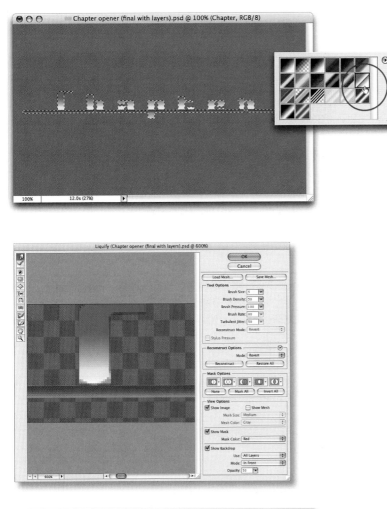

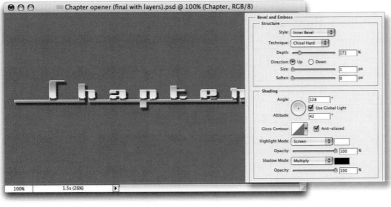

Step One:

Create a new document, fill it with a color, then enter your type with the Type tool. Control-click (PC: Right-click) on your Type layer's name and choose Rasterize Layer. With the Rectangular Marquee tool, add a thin selection under your type, fill it with any color, and deselect. Now Command-click (PC: Control-click) on your Type layer in the Layers palette. Get the Gradient tool, press Return (PC: Enter) to bring up the Gradient Picker, and choose the Chrome gradient. Drag the Gradient tool straight down through your text.

Step Two:

To smudge the brown and blue horizon in the letters, go to Filter>Liquify. Get the Magnify tool on the left and zoom in on a letter. Then get the Smudge tool (it's the top tool on the left), and choose a small brush size. Smudge upward at the edges of each letter, then smudge downward in the center of each letter. Repeat for each letter, then click OK.

Step Three:

Deselect, then choose Bevel and Emboss from the Add a Layer Style pop-up menu. Change the Technique to Chisel Hard, increase the Depth to 171%, and lower the Size to 1. Increase the Highlight and Shadow Opacity sliders to 100%, and turn on the Anti-aliased checkbox. From the Styles list on the left, choose Inner Shadow. Change the color to white, the Distance to 2, the Choke to 7%, and the Size to 2. Click on the Drop Shadow checkbox on the left, then click OK.

Quick Depth of Field

Step One:
Open the photo that you want to apply the effect to. Press Command-J (PC: Control-J) to duplicate the Background layer.

Step Two:
Go under the Filter menu, under Blur, and choose Gaussian Blur. When the dialog appears, increase the Radius to 4 pixels and click OK to put a blur over the entire image.

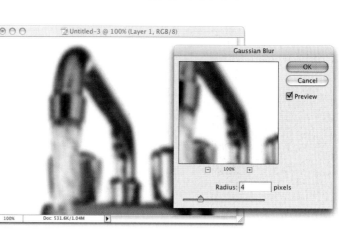

Step Three:
Get the Eraser tool and choose a large, soft-edged brush from the Brush Picker. Start erasing over the parts of the image that appear in the foreground (in this case, erase over the head of the faucet and the water). Erasing on this blurred layer reveals the original, un-blurred image on the Background layer.

Blending Two Images

Step One:
Open the first image you want to use in your two-image blend.

Step Two:
Open the second photo you want to use in your two-image blend. Get the Move tool and drag-and-drop this image on top of your first image. Click on the Add a Layer Mask icon at the bottom of the Layers palette, then press "x" until you've set your Foreground color to black.

Step Three:
Get the Brush tool, and choose a large (200-pixel), soft-edged brush from the Brush Picker in the Options Bar. Begin painting over your photo, and as you paint, the photo beneath it (the soccer players) will be revealed. Because you're using such a large, soft-edged brush, the blend is very smooth. If you make a mistake, just switch your Foreground color to white, paint over the mistake, then switch back to black and continue painting.

Layer Masking One Photo Inside Another

Step One:

Open a background photo, then open the photo that contains the object that you want to layer mask into the background photo. Select the object and drag-and-drop it into the background image. (In this case, we want to make it appear that the water is splashing around the cologne bottle, instead of looking like the cologne bottle is placed on top of the water.)

Step Two:

Click on the Add a Layer Mask icon at the bottom of the Layers palette. Lower the Opacity of this layer to 50% in the Layers palette so you can see the water drops through the bottle. Set your Foreground color to black, get the Brush tool, and choose a soft-edged brush from the Brush Picker in the Options Bar. Start painting over any water drops that appear over the bottle.

Step Three:

As you paint over the drops, they become visible in front of the bottle. You'll have to vary the size of your brush as you go to accommodate the size of the drops, so use the Right and Left Bracket keys on your keyboard to make your brush size larger or smaller. Once you've painted over most of the drops, raise the Opacity back to 100% in the Layers palette and the drops appear in front of the bottle. Also, you can change the blend mode in the Layers palette to Darken to help make the bottle look more transparent.

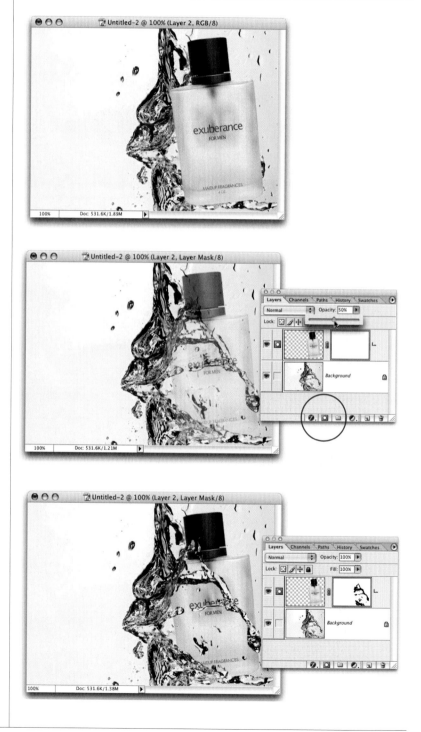

Creating Reflections

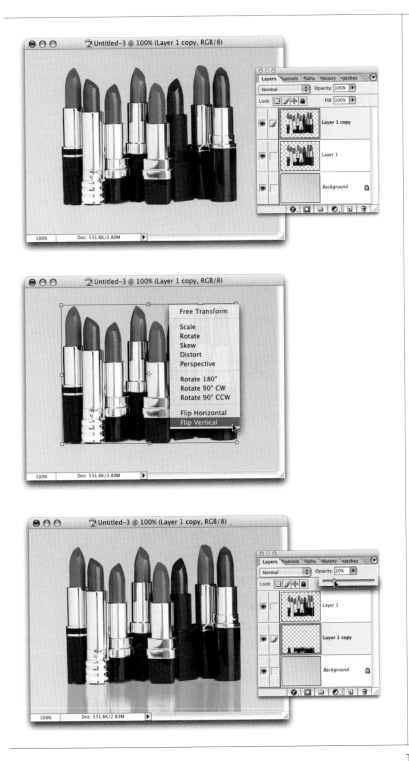

Step One:
Create a new document, then set the Foreground color to a medium gray and the Background to a light gray. Get the Gradient tool, press Return (PC: Enter) to bring up the Gradient Picker, and choose the Foreground to Background gradient. Click the Linear Gradient icon in the Options Bar, then drag the Gradient tool from the top of the document to the bottom. Now, open the photo you want to add a reflection to. Select just the object (in this case, a row of lipstick), get the Move tool, and drag-and-drop the image onto your background. Duplicate your lipstick layer by pressing Command-J (PC: Control-J).

Step Two:
Press Command-T (PC: Control-T) to bring up Free Transform. Control-click (PC: Right-click) within the bounding box and choose Flip Vertical, then press Return (PC: Enter). Get the Move tool, hold the Shift key, and drag straight down until the bottoms of the lipsticks touch each other, creating a mirror-like reflection.

Step Three:
In the Layers palette, lower the Opacity of this flipped layer to 20%, then drag this layer below your regular lipstick layer. Then, go under the Filter menu, under Blur, and choose Motion Blur. When the dialog appears, for Angle enter 90° and for Distance enter 20 pixels, and click OK to apply a slight motion blur to give you the final effect shown here.

Colorizing a Black-and-White Photo

Step One:
Open the black-and-white photo you want to colorize. Add a new layer by clicking on the Create a New Layer icon at the bottom of the Layers palette. Get the Lasso tool and select the first area you want to colorize (in this example, we're going to start by colorizing her hair, so put a selection around her hair).

Step Two:
Choose a brown color for her hair. Then, press Option-Delete (PC: Alt-Backspace) to fill your hair selection with brown. (*Note:* Rather than just blindly choosing a color, you're better off opening a color photo of someone who has the shade of brown hair you're looking for, then getting the Eyedropper tool and clicking on that person's hair to make that exact shade of brown your Foreground color.)

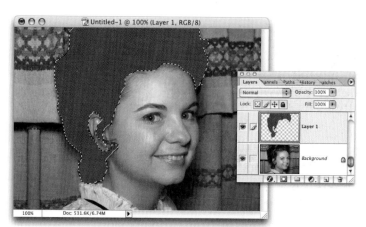

Step Three:
Go to the Layers palette and change the layer blend mode for this layer from Normal to Color. This blends the brown color into your image without covering the detail. Lower the Opacity of this layer until the hair shade looks more natural. That's the technique, so continue the process of adding a layer, selecting an area to be colorized (as shown here), fill that with color, then change the blend mode to Color and lower the Opacity until it looks natural.

Burned-In Edge Effect

Step One:
Open the photo you want to add the burned-in edges to. In the Layers palette, add a new layer by clicking on the Create a New Layer icon.

Step Two:
Press "d" to set your Foreground color to black, and fill your new layer with black by pressing Option-Delete (PC: Alt-Backspace). Get the Rectangular Marquee tool and draw a selection just inside the borders of the image. Next, go under the Select menu and choose Feather. When the dialog appears, enter around 40 to 50 pixels (enter 150 pixels for high-res, 300-ppi images), and click OK to soften the edges of your selection.

Step Three:
Press Delete (PC: Backspace) to knock a soft-edged hole out of your black layer, revealing the photo beneath, but now with a burned-in edge look. Press Command-D (PC: Control-D) to deselect. Lastly, go to the Layers palette and lower the Opacity setting of this layer to 50% to lighten the burned-in edges, giving you the final effect shown here.

Backscreened Blocks for Type

Step One:

Open the photo you want to put type over; and therefore you want to add backscreened blocks so your text is easily legible. Start by creating a new blank layer, then get the Rectangular Marquee tool and draw a selection around the area where you want your text to appear.

Step Two:

Set your Foreground color (in this example, I used a medium green), and fill your selection with this color by pressing Option-Delete (PC: Alt-Backspace). Then, go to the Layers palette and lower the Opacity for this block to around 28% so the block becomes see-through, yet there's still enough color there to easily support some text. Deselect by pressing Command-D (PC: Control-D).

Step Three:

To add a second backscreened block, go to the Layers palette and create another new layer. Get the Rectangular Marquee tool and draw a selection along the bottom. Press "d" then "x" to set your Foreground color to white, then fill your selection with white by pressing Option-Delete (PC: Alt-Backspace). Now, lower the Opacity of this layer to around 65% (white backscreens don't usually need their opacity lowered as much as colored backscreens). Deselect by pressing Command-D (PC: Control-D). Now add your type above the blocks.

Realistically Adding a Sign or Logo

Step One:
Open the photo you want to add your graphic to (in this case, the side of a semi-trailer). Get the Polygonal Lasso tool and put a selection around the white side of the trailer, with all the lines and dirt on it. Press Command-J (PC: Control-J) to put your selection on its own layer. Hide this layer from view by clicking on the Eye icon to its left in the Layers palette. Open your sign image, press Command-A (PC: Control-A) to select all, then press Command-C (PC: Control-C) to copy the sign.

Step Two:
In the semi-trailer image, Command-click (PC: Right-click) on your hidden layer to put a selection around the trailer. Go under the Edit menu and choose Paste Into to paste the graphic into your selection. Press Command-T (PC: Control-T) to bring up Free Transform, hold the Shift key, and scale the graphic down so it fits on your trailer. Then release the Shift key and slightly rotate the graphic to match the angle of the truck. Press Return (PC: Enter) to lock in your transformation.

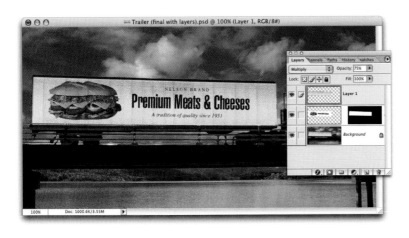

Step Three:
In the Layers palette, make your hidden layer visible again and drag it above your sign layer. Change the blend mode of this layer from Normal to Multiply so the dirt and lines from the side of the trailer appear on top of the sign, then lower the Opacity to around 75%.

Adding Stars to the Sky

Step One:
Open your nighttime photo, then click the Create a New Layer icon in the Layers palette. Press the letter "d" then "x" to set your Background color to black, then choose a dark purple for your Foreground. Get the Gradient tool, press Return (PC: Enter) to bring up the Gradient Picker, and choose the Foreground to Background gradient. Drag the Gradient tool from the bottom of the document to the top, then create a new layer and fill it with black. Go to Filter>Noise>Add Noise. Set the Amount to around 20%, the Distribution to Gaussian, and turn on the Monochromatic checkbox. Click OK.

Step Two:
Go to Filter>Blur>Gaussian Blur and enter a Radius setting of 0.5 pixels to blur the spots. Go to Image>Adjustments> Threshold and drag the slider to the left, and as you do, you'll see stars appear on your black layer. The farther to the left you drag, the more stars will appear. Click OK when it looks good to you.

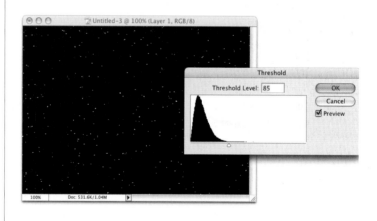

Step Three:
Press Command-F (PC: Control-F) to apply another 0.5-pixel Gaussian Blur to your stars (this helps vary the size of the stars). In the Layers palette, change the layer blend mode of this black layer to Screen to make the stars appear over your purple-to-black gradient sky.

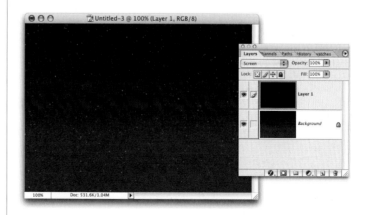

Lens Flare Effect

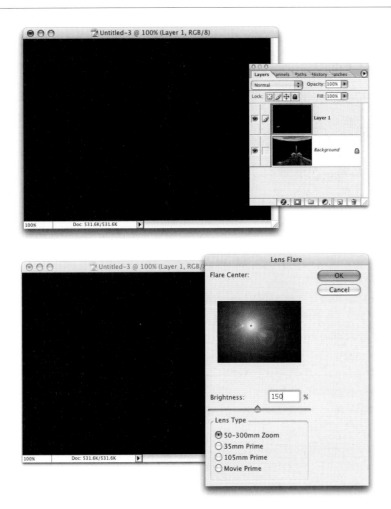

Step One:
Open the photo you want to apply the lens flare effect to (in this case, it's a shuttle orbiting the Earth). Go to the bottom of the Layers palette and add a new blank layer by clicking on the Create a New Layer icon. Press "d" to set your Foreground color to black, then fill this layer with black by pressing Option-Delete (PC: Alt-Backspace).

Step Two:
Go under the Filter menu, under Render, and choose Lens Flare. When the dialog appears, increase the Brightness to 150%, set the Lens Type to 50-300mm Zoom, and click OK to apply a lens flare to this blank layer.

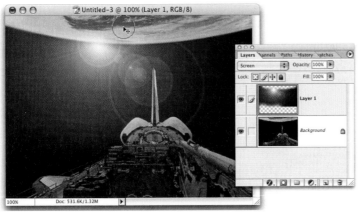

Step Three:
To get this lens flare to blend in with your photo, change the blend mode of this layer to Screen in the Layers palette. Then, get the Move tool and drag the center of the Flare until it extends half on the edge of the earth and half in space. Get the Eraser tool, choose a soft-edged brush, and paint over the Earth until only the part of the flare that extends out into space remains visible. If you can see a visible edge after moving the flare, take the Eraser tool and erase away the edges.

Motion Blur Effect

Step One:

Open the photo you want to apply the Motion Blur effect to. Duplicate your Background layer by pressing Command-J (PC: Control-J).

Step Two:

Go under the Filter menu, under Blur, and choose Motion Blur. When the dialog appears, set the Angle so the blur is going in the direction that you want it to appear (in this case, we want it to appear that the jet is moving horizontally down the runway, so set the Angle to 0°). Set the Distance to 150 pixels and click OK to apply the Motion Blur to this entire layer.

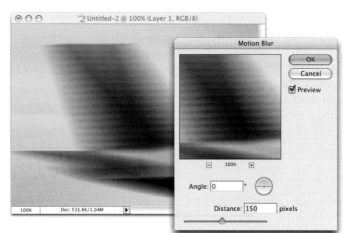

Step Three:

Get the Eraser tool, then choose a 65-pixel, soft-edged brush from the Brush Picker. Begin painting over the body and tail of the jet so the blur only appears on the back edge and bottom of the plane. It will make it easier to see where the un-blurred jet is if you lower the Opacity of this blurred layer to around 50% while you're painting. Once you're done erasing away the blurred areas where you want to maintain detail, raise the Opacity setting of your blurred layer back up to 100%, and you'll see the effect shown here.

Screened Type Effects

Step One:

Open the photo you want to add transparent type to. Get the Type tool and create your type (this effect works best on large-sized type).

Step Two:

Press "d" then "x" to set white as your Foreground color, then press Option-Delete (PC: Alt-Backspace) to make your type white. Then, in the Layers palette, lower the Opacity setting of this layer until the type looks transparent (as shown here, with the Opacity lowered to 35%).

Step Three:

An alternate method is to leave the Opacity set at 100%, and in the Layers palette change the blend mode of this layer to Soft Light. This not only adds transparency to your type but also picks up the colors from the photo beneath it.

COLOPHON

The book was produced by the author and the design team using all Macintosh computers, including a Power Mac G5 Dual 2-GHz, a Power Mac G5 1.8-GHz, a Power Mac G4 1.25-GHz, a Power Mac G4 733-MHz, and a Power Mac G4 500-MHz. We use Sony Artisan, LaCie Electron Blue 22, and Apple Studio Display monitors.

Page layout was done using Adobe InDesign 2.0. The headers for each technique are set in 20 point CronosMM700 Bold with the horizontal scaling set to 95%. Body copy is set using CronosMM408 Regular at 10 points on 13 leading, with the horizontal scaling set to 95%.

Screen captures were made with Snapz Pro X and were placed and sized within InDesign. The book was output at 150-line screen, and all in-house proofing was done using a Tektronix Phaser 7700 by Xerox.

ADDITIONAL PHOTOSHOP RESOURCES

Photoshop Down & Dirty Tricks
Scott is also author of the best-selling book *Photoshop CS Down & Dirty Tricks,* and the book's companion website has all the info on the book, which is available at bookstores around the country.

http://www.downanddirtytricks.com

The Photoshop CS Book for Digital Photographers
This book cuts through the bull and shows you step by step the exact techniques used by today's cutting-edge digital photographers, and it shows you which settings to use, when to use them, and why.

http://www.scottkelbybooks.com

ScottKelbyBooks.com
For information on Scott's other books, visit his book site. For background info on Scott, visit www.scottkelby.com.

http://www.scottkelbybooks.com

National Association of Photoshop Professionals (NAPP)
The industry trade association for Adobe® Photoshop® users and the world's leading resource for Photoshop training, education, and news. Scott is President of the NAPP, as well as the Editor-in-Chief of *Photoshop User* magazine, NAPP's official trade publication.

http://www.photoshopuser.com

KW Computer Training Videos
Scott Kelby is featured in a series of more than 20 Photoshop training videos and DVDs, each on a particular Photoshop topic, available from KW Computer Training. Visit the website or call 813-433-5000 for orders or more information.

http://www.photoshopvideos.com

Adobe Photoshop Seminar Tour
See Scott live at the Adobe Photoshop Seminar Tour, the nation's most popular Photoshop seminars. For upcoming tour dates and class schedules, visit the tour website.

http://www.photoshopseminars.com

PhotoshopWorld Conference & Expo
The convention for Adobe Photoshop users has now become the largest Photoshop-only event in the world. Scott Kelby is technical chair and education director for the event, as well as one of the instructors.

http://www.photoshopworld.com

PlanetPhotoshop.com
"The Ultimate Photoshop Site" features Photoshop news, tutorials, reviews, and articles posted daily. The site also contains the Web's most up-to-date resource on other Photoshop-related websites and information.

http://www.planetphotoshop.com

Photoshop Hall of Fame
Created to honor and recognize those individuals whose contributions to the art and business of Adobe Photoshop have had a major impact on the application or the Photoshop community.

http://www.photoshophalloffame.com

Kelby's Notes
Now you can get the answers to the top 100 most-asked Photoshop questions with Kelby's Notes, the plug-in from Scott Kelby. Simply go to the How Do I? menu while in Photoshop, find your question, and the answer appears in an easy-to-read dialog. Finally, help is just one click away.

http://www.kelbysnotes.com

Mac Design Magazine
Scott is Editor-in-Chief of *Mac Design Magazine,* "The Graphics Magazine for Macintosh Users." It's a tutorial-based print magazine with how-to columns on Photoshop, Illustrator, InDesign, Dreamweaver, Flash, Final Cut Pro, and more. It's also packed with tips, tricks, and shortcuts for your favorite graphics applications.

http://www.macdesignonline.com

Index

Express your creativity.

(Not your frustration with outdated technology.)

Adobe

Nothing brings the creative process to a screeching halt like a slow system or aging software. That's where CDW comes in. We understand that not all creative professionals think or work alike. That's why we offer the widest selection of products and technology to help you explore the outer reaches of your creativity-whether you work on a Mac or Windows. With unmatched customer service and the latest PC and Mac technology products in stock and ready to ship, we're sure to have what you're looking for.

For the right technology, call or visit CDW.com today.

CDW.com • 800.800.4CDW

Photography that has the power to make you ## STOP.